GLENCOE

The

AMERICAN VISION

MODERN TIMES

Reading Essentials and Note-Taking Guide

STUDENT WORKBOOK

Mc
Graw
Hill
Glencoe

New York, New York   Columbus, Ohio   Chicago, Illinois   Woodland Hills, California

To the Student

The *American Vision: Modern Times* **Reading Essentials and Note-Taking Guide** is designed to help you use recognized reading strategies to improve your reading-for-information skills. For each section of the student textbook, you are alerted to key content. Then, you are asked to draw from prior knowledge, organize your thoughts with a graphic organizer, and follow a process to read and understand the text. The **Reading Essentials and Note-Taking Guide** was prepared to help you get more from your textbook by reading with a purpose.

The McGraw-Hill Companies

 Glencoe

Send all inquiries to:
Glencoe/McGraw-Hill
8787 Orion Place
Columbus, OH 43240

ISBN: 978-0-07-878518-4
MHID: 0-07-878518-9

Printed in the United States of America.
2 3 4 5 6 7 8 9 10   024   10 09 08

Table of Contents

Chapter 24: A New Century Begins, 2001–Present

Converging Cultures

Big Idea

As you read pages 4–13 in your textbook, complete the outline using the major section headings.

Converging Cultures

I. The Earliest Americans
   A. _____
   B. _____

II. _____
   A. _____
   B. _____
   C. _____

III. _____
   A. _____
   B. _____
   C. _____

IV. _____
   A. _____
   B. _____
   C. _____
   D. _____

Notes   Read to Learn

The Earliest Americans *(page 4)*

Identifying the Main Idea

Place an X next to the sentence that best states the passage's main idea.

____ *Native American groups created complex societies suited to the area they lived in.*

____ *Native Americans learned to farm, which led to the first permanent settlements.*

No one knows when the first people came to America. Research suggests nomads might have arrived between 15,000 and 30,000 years ago. These Native Americans eventually learned how to plant and raise crops. This led to permanent villages and more complex societies. Civilizations emerged with knowledge of trade, government, arts and science, and often a written language.

The Olmec may have created the earliest civilization in the Americas. This took place between 1500 B.C. and 1200 B.C. in southern Mexico. The Maya and Aztec later founded civilizations in Central America. They built amazing temples and pyramids and set up trade networks. Around the time of the Olmec, other groups were developing their own cultures in North America's eastern woodlands. The Mississippian created Cahokia, one of the largest early American cities.

Native Americans hunted, fished, or farmed, depending on where they lived. The Cherokee were the largest group in the Southeast. The Apache and the Navajo came to the Southwest around the 1500s. They settled in farming villages but many remained nomadic hunters. On the Great Plains, the Sioux and other peoples followed buffalo herds and camped in tepees. By the 1500s, Native Americans had set up a variety of cultures, languages, and lifestyles. Each was suited to its own special environment.

 **Notes** | # Read to Learn

European Explorations *(page 6)*

Drawing Conclusions

Underline sentences in the passage that support this conclusion:

Europeans carried diseases Native Americans had never been exposed to.

After the Middle Ages, Europeans became interested in finding a sea route to Asia. Spain funded Christopher Columbus's expedition across the Atlantic. He thought he had reached Asia, but it was a new area of the world. Spain acquired rights to most new lands in the Americas. Spanish conquerors like Francisco Pizarro easily defeated the local peoples. Spanish explorers like Ponce de Leon claimed new areas.

Native Americans and Europeans introduced each other to new foods. They traded information about useful inventions and skills. But Europeans also brought with them deadly germs and diseases. Millions of Native Americans died in epidemics. Military conquests took their lands and ways of life.

Early French and English Settlement *(page 8)*

Comparing and Contrasting

Place an X by the statement in the passage that reveals how Separatists' reasons for coming to America differed from other groups.

France and England began exploring eastern North America soon after Columbus's voyage. The French founded Quebec, where they profited from the fur trade with Native Americans. After settling Louisiana, they imported enslaved Africans to work in the fields. The English founded Jamestown in Virginia. It was funded by a **joint-stock-company,** a private group that funded big projects to make a profit.

A group of Puritans called "Separatists" came to America for religious freedom. In 1620, a small band of Separatists sailed for America on the *Mayflower*. They came to be called **Pilgrims.** Later, other Puritans settling in Massachusetts set up a government with an elected assembly.

The Thirteen Colonies *(page 9)*

Problems and Solutions

Problem:

_____

_____

Solution:
Rhode Island and Providence Plantation were founded.

Puritan efforts to restrict religious beliefs in the Massachusetts Bay Colony led to the founding of new colonies. Free-thinking Puritans founded Rhode Island and Providence Plantation, a colony based on the separation of church and state. Life in New England centered on town life. Colonists practiced **subsistence farming,** or raising only enough food to feed their families. Some prospered in the fishing and the lumber industries.

In 1681, King Charles permitted William Penn, a Quaker, to found a new Middle Colony south of New York. In Pennsylvania, settlers would have religious freedom and a voice in government. Farmers in this area worked their fertile lands to produce a number of cash crops.

The Thirteen Colonies *(page 9 continued)*

Tobacco helped Virginia to thrive in the South. Another Southern Colony, Maryland, was **a proprietary colony.** A proprietary colony was one owned by an individual who could govern it any way he chose. Many English people came to work as **indentured servants** in the South. They signed contracts with colonists to work for four or more years in return for paid passage to America and free food and shelter.

Section Wrap-up

Answer these questions to check your understanding of the entire section.

1. What led to the first civilizations in America?

_____

_____

_____

2. How did Puritans influence colonial life in New England?

_____

_____

_____

Descriptive Writing

Write a diary entry in the voice of an early resident of Cahokia. Briefly describe your life, including your family, home, and the activities that occupy your daily life.

_____

_____

_____

_____

_____

_____

_____

_____

_____

_____

_____

_____

_____

A Diverse Society

Big Idea

As you read pages 16–21 in your textbook, complete the graphic organizer by identifying why immigrants settled in the colonies.

Group	Where They Settled	Reasons for Immigrating
Germans	1.	2.
Scots-Irish	3.	4.
Jews	5.	6.

Notes

Read to Learn

Growth of Colonial America (page 16)

Making Inferences

Make an inference based on the passage.

_____

_____

_____

_____

_____

_____

_____

_____

_____

_____

_____

The population in the American colonies grew rapidly in the 1700s. High birthrates and better housing and sanitation encouraged this growth. A rise in trade contributed to the growth of cities in the North. Merchants created systems of **triangular trade,** through which goods were exchanged among the colonies, England, Caribbean sugar planters, and Africa. Cities' growth brought changes to society. Distinct social classes developed. Wealthy trade merchants were at the top, and indentured servants and enslaved Africans were at the bottom.

Between 1700 and 1775, hundreds of thousands of white immigrants flowed into America. Most settled in the Middle Colonies. Many, such as the Germans, Scots-Irish, and Jews, came to escape problems in their own countries.

Colonial women did not have the same rights as men. Married women could not legally own property, for example. Single women and widows had more rights, and could own property and run businesses. Enslaved Africans faced the greatest hardships in the colonies. By about 1775, they numbered around 540,000—about 20 percent of the colonial population. Laws called **slave codes** prohibited Africans from owning property, testifying against whites in court, receiving an education, moving about freely, or meeting in large groups.

New Ideas (page 18)

Copyright © Glencoe/McGraw-Hill, a division of The McGraw-Hill Companies, Inc.

Analyzing Information

Which statement would the author most likely agree with? Circle it.

1. The ideas of the Enlightenment were important to the colonies' development.

2. The ideas of the Enlightenment remain a fundamental part of U.S. society.

Formulating Questions

Write a P by the question that is answered by the passage. Write an S by the question that needs further study.

1. _____ How was the Glorious Revolution important to the colonies?

2. _____ Where did Governor-General Andros go after being expelled by Boston colonists?

King Charles II wanted the colonies to create wealth for England. He asked Parliament to pass the Navigation Acts of 1660. They required all goods shipped to and from the colonies be carried on English ships. Three years later, Parliament passed another law restricting colonial imports and increasing the cost of goods in the colonies.

Merchants in the colonies began smuggling goods to Europe, the Caribbean, and Africa. In response, the new king, James II, created a royal province called the Dominion of New England. It included Plymouth, Massachusetts, Rhode Island, Connecticut, New Jersey, and New York. Sir Edmund Andros became the governor-general. He angered colonists by levying new taxes and enforcing the Navigation Acts.

King James also angered people in England by converting to Catholicism. The birth of his son led to protests against a Catholic heir. His Protestant daughter, Mary, and her husband, William of Orange, claimed the throne in a change of power called the Glorious Revolution. Before taking the throne, they had to accept the English Bill of Rights. Boston colonists expelled Governor-General Andros. William and Mary then granted Rhode Island and Connecticut their previous forms of government. They issued a new charter for Massachusetts. It included the right to assemble and freedom of worship.

Both the Glorious Revolution and the English Bill of Rights were important to the colonies. They suggested that revolution was justified when individual rights were violated. The English Bill of Rights helped shape American government.

During the 1600s and 1700s, an era known as the Age of Enlightenment was influencing people in Europe. Philosophers theorized that natural laws ruled both the physical world and human nature. They believed that anyone using reason could understand these laws. John Locke was an important Enlightenment writer. His ideas influenced American political leaders. In his *Two Treatises of Government,* he tried to discover the natural laws that would apply to politics and society. He reasoned that people should be free to choose their own government. In drafting the Declaration of Independence in 1776, Thomas Jefferson relied on Locke's ideas. Locke's beliefs—that all people have rights and that society can be improved—became core beliefs in America.

During the 1700s, religious revivals were sweeping the colonies. This surge of religious zeal was called the Great Awakening. It stressed an individual's personal relationship with God. Baptist churches in the South welcomed African Americans to their revivals and condemned slavery.

Section Wrap-up

Answer these questions to check your understanding of the entire section.

1. How did the population of the colonies change during the 1700s?

_____

_____

_____

_____

2. Why was the English Bill of Rights important to the American colonies?

_____

_____

_____

_____

Expository Writing

Suppose you are living in New England during the 1700s. List some events that have recently taken place in England. Explain why each event is important in England and in the colonies.

_____

_____

_____

_____

_____

_____

_____

_____

_____

_____

_____

_____

_____

The American Revolution

Big Idea

As you read pages 22–29 in your textbook, complete the graphic organizer to describe some causes that led the colonies to declare their independence.

Causes

1. _____
2. _____   **Declaration of Independence**
3. _____

 **Notes**   # Read to Learn

Growing Rebelliousness *(page 22)*

Predicting

Underline two statements in the passage that indicate Britain's tax on tea might stir up future trouble.

From 1754 to 1759, the French and British fought a war in the Ohio River valley. Britain won, but it needed money to pay its war debts. As a solution, British leaders adopted policies that outraged American colonists. The first was the Proclamation Act of 1763, which banned colonial expansion west of the Appalachian Mountains. This would prevent costly wars. Next, the British tightened customs controls. They had learned that colonists were smuggling goods without paying **customs duties**, or taxes on imports and exports. They passed the Sugar Act of 1764 to raise taxes on certain imports. The Quartering Act of 1765 forced colonists to share expenses for their defense by boarding British troops.

The Stamp Act of 1765 further enraged colonists. It was a direct tax on printed material—the first Britain had imposed. In October 1765, representatives from the colonies formed the Stamp Act Congress. They declared that Parliament had no right to tax them. The colonies boycotted all British goods, forcing Britain to repeal the Stamp Act in 1766.

Parliament passed the Townshend Acts in 1767, placing new customs duties on some imports. Colonists responded with great resistance. On March 5, 1770, British troops fired on a crowd of colonists, killing five. The event became known as the Boston Massacre. Tensions eased when Britain repealed most of the Townsend Acts—except for its tax on tea.

 **Notes** | **Read to Learn**

The Road to War (page 25)

(page 25)

Detecting Bias

Based on the passage, was Parliament partial to British interests in business and trade? Circle your answer.

Yes   **No**

Then underline a sentence in the passage to support it.

Problems with Britain resumed when 150 colonists captured and burned a British customs ship. The suspects were taken to England for trial. Colonists believed they were denied certain rights. Thomas Jefferson suggested they create **committees of correspondence**. These helped them communicate and coordinate strategy.

In May 1773, Parliament passed the Tea Act. Its terms favored a British tea company. In response, colonists blocked new deliveries of British tea in American harbors. In Boston, about 150 men dumped 342 chests of tea overboard into Boston Harbor. The raid was later named the Boston Tea Party. In the spring of 1774, Parliament passed the Coercive Acts to punish Massachusetts. The colonies sent representatives to the First Continental Congress in Philadelphia, where they planned their next step. The town of Concord created a special unit of **minutemen**. They were trained and ready to "stand at a minute's warning in case of alarm."

In April 1775, fighting broke out between minutemen, colonial militia, farmers, and British troops in Massachusetts. George Washington became general and commander in chief of a new Continental Army. Thomas Paine's pamphlet *Common Sense* urged colonists to declare independence. On July 4, 1776, the Continental Congress issued a Declaration of Independence. The American Revolution had begun.

War for Independence (page 28)

(page 28)

Determining Cause and Effect

List one cause for the effect listed below.

Cause:

_____

_____

Effect: The United States won the war.

Britain could not afford a long and costly war. Its troops quickly seized New York City in October 1776, and headed south. George Washington won two small victories before winter. In one, he led his men across the icy Delaware River to surprise British forces in New Jersey.

General Washington made the most of his small army. In October 1777, Americans surrounded a British force of 5,000 that had failed to link up with a larger unit. The Battle of Saratoga was a stunning victory.

American troops held the upper hand on the western frontier. In the South, the British captured Savannah, Georgia. Then a huge British force led by General Cornwallis forced the surrender of nearly 5,500 American troops at Charles Town, South Carolina. It was America's biggest defeat in the war. The tide turned again, however, in October 1780 at the Battle of Kings Mountain. Patriot forces drove the British out of most of the South.

War for Independence *(page 28 continued)*

The last major battle took place in the fall of 1781 at Yorktown, Virginia. Washington's army and the French navy trapped 8,000 British troops. Cornwallis surrendered. Parliament voted to end the war. In the Treaty of Paris, Britain recognized the United States of America as an independent nation. The Revolutionary War had ended.

Section Wrap-up

Answer these questions to check your understanding of the entire section.

1. How did the colonists respond to the Stamp Act of 1765?

_____

_____

2. How did the colonists prepare for war?

_____

_____

Persuasive Writing

In the space provided, write a letter to Parliament asking its members to reconsider their unfair policies toward the colonies. Be specific in your requests, referring to actions such as the Stamp Act, the Quartering Act, and the Tea Act.

_____

_____

_____

_____

_____

_____

_____

_____

_____

_____

The Constitution

Big Idea

As you read pages 34–41 in your textbook, complete the graphic organizer
by listing the supporters and goals of the Federalists and Anti-Federalists.

	Federalists	Anti-Federalists
Source of Support	1.	3.
Goals	2.	4.

Notes Read to Learn

The Young Nation (page 34)

Making Inferences

Make an inference based on the passage.

_____
_____
_____
_____
_____
_____
_____
_____
_____
_____
_____

In creating the United States of America, the new nation's leaders made a choice to replace royal rule with a republic. In a republic, citizens who vote have the power. They elect officials who are responsible to the citizens and who must govern according to laws or a constitution. Before the Revolutionary War ended, each state had drafted its own constitution. Those drawn up by Virginia and Massachusetts became models for other states to follow. Both constitutions established a separation of powers among the executive, legislative, and judicial branches of government.

In the 1780s, state constitutions showed that American society was changing. A focus on individual liberty led to greater separation of church and state. Voting rights also expanded. Many states allowed any white male taxpayer to vote, not just property owners. African Americans and women were still denied political rights but made some gains. Several Northern states took steps to end slavery.

America's leaders began work on a central government. The Articles of Confederation loosely unified the states. The Confederation Congress had limited powers. It could raise armies and declare war, but could not regulate trade or impose taxes. Without the power to tax, Congress could not raise money to pay its expenses. In 1787, as the country slipped into a severe recession, people saw the need for a stronger central government.

A New Constitution (page 37)

Formulating Questions

Place an X by the question that is answered in the passage.

1. ____ What is the purpose of having checks and balances in government?

2. ____ Why did delegates choose to not have a direct democracy?

In May 1787, states sent delegates to Philadelphia to create a new central government. The meeting was known as the Constitutional Convention. All delegates wanted a stronger national government that could levy taxes and make laws binding.

The delegates compromised on how states would be represented in Congress. Then they focused on how the new government would operate. They based the new government on the principle of **popular sovereignty**, or rule by the people. They devised a representative form of government, not a direct democracy. Elected officials would speak for the people. The new Constitution also set up a system called **federalism**, in which power is divided between the national and state governments.

The Constitution also provided for **separation of powers** by dividing power among three branches of government. These are the legislative, executive, and judicial branches. Each has different duties. The framers of the Constitution also created a system of **checks and balances**. This prevented any one of the branches from becoming too powerful. Each branch could limit the power of the other two. The president, for example, could **veto**, or reject, a law proposed by the legislative branch. The delegates knew the Constitution might need to be revised over time. They created a clear—but difficult—process for making changes.

Ratification (page 39)

Evaluating Information

Explain why it is important to know that people all over the country debated the issue of ratification.

_____

_____

_____

_____

_____

_____

To take effect, the new Constitution required **ratification**, or approval, of 9 of the 13 states. People debated the issue all over the country. They discussed it in state legislatures, meetings, newspapers, and conversations. The Constitution's supporters called themselves Federalists. Opponents were called Anti-Federalists. In Massachusetts, opponents believed the Constitution threatened states' independence. They thought it failed to protect Americans' rights. This led Federalists to promise to add a bill of rights when the Constitution was ratified. Massachusetts agreed to ratify it. The Bill of Rights was added in 1791.

Other states followed Massachusetts's lead and began to ratify the Constitution. Federalists soon had the minimum number of states needed to put the Constitution into effect. Virginia and New York, however, with about 30 percent of the nation's population, had not ratified it. Without them, many feared the Constitution would not work. With James Madison's promise to add a bill of rights, Virginia voted to approve. When New York learned the Constitution already had gone into effect, it also voted to ratify. No one knew if it would work, but many grew hopeful when George Washington became the nation's first president.

Section Wrap-up

Answer these questions to check your understanding of the entire section.

1. How was society changing in the new United States of the 1780s?

_____

_____

_____

2. Why were some states slow to approve the new Constitution?

_____

_____

_____

Suppose you are a student at the time the Constitution was being written and ratified. Write an account of the process to be included in your school's time capsule. Remember to include relevant events, people, places, and dates.

_____

_____

_____

_____

_____

_____

_____

_____

_____

_____

The New Republic

Big Idea

As you read pages 80–85 in your textbook, complete the graphic organizer by indicating the tasks completed by the first Congress under the Constitution.

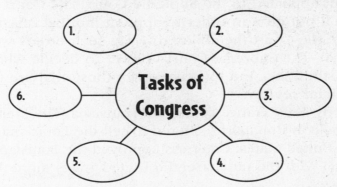

Notes   Read to Learn

The Early Years of the Republic *(page 80)*

Comparing and Contrasting

Compare the Federalists' and the Republicans' opinions on the national government.

Federalists:

_____

_____

_____

Republicans:

_____

_____

_____

In 1789 Congress began organizing the federal government. President George Washington chose his **cabinet**. These are people that would be in charge of departments and give him advice. Ten amendments to the Constitution, known as the **Bill of Rights**, were approved. They explained the rights of American citizens. To deal with the nation's struggling finances, Alexander Hamilton wanted to create a national bank. Some people thought that creating a bank was not one of the government's **enumerated powers**, or a power specifically mentioned in the Constitution. Hamilton argued that establishing a bank was an **implied power**, or a power not explicitly listed in the Constitution but necessary for the government to do its job. The national bank was created.

Arguments over the national bank led to the development of rival political parties. Hamilton and his supporters were called Federalists. They wanted a strong national government. Thomas Jefferson and his supporters were called Republicans. They favored states' rights over a strong national government. Under President John Adams, a Federalist, Congress passed the Alien and Sedition Acts in 1798. One law made it a crime to say anything bad against the government. Many people thought the laws went against people's freedoms. After a close election, Thomas Jefferson became president in 1800.

Notes | Read to Learn

Republicans in Power (page 82)

Making Inferences

Make an inference about the Louisiana Purchase based on the passage.

_____

_____

_____

_____

Analyzing Information

Complete the sentence.

That "The Star-Spangled Banner" became the national anthem shows that

_____

_____

_____

_____

President Jefferson's priority was to limit the powers of the federal government. He also wanted to reduce the Federalists' control of the judicial branch. President Adams had appointed many Federalist judges. Jefferson asked Congress to undo these appointments. One person who did not get his appointment appealed to the Supreme Court. The Court ruled that it could not give an order to appoint him because the law that gave the Court the ability to write such orders was unconstitutional. The Supreme Court's power to decide whether laws are constitutional and to strike down those that are not is called **judicial review**.

By 1800 France controlled Louisiana. The French leader, Napoleon Bonaparte, offered to sell the Louisiana Territory to the United States. Congress approved the Louisiana Purchase in 1803. With the purchase, the United States more than doubled in size.

Republican James Madison became president in 1809. He soon faced a foreign relations crisis. The British frequently took American ships and kidnapped American sailors to serve in the British navy. After attempting to end the crisis with embargos against Britain, President Madison and Congress declared war. One goal of the War of 1812 was conquering Canada. Battles took place on Lake Erie and Lake Champlain. The British attacked Washington, D.C. A fight in Baltimore harbor that Americans won was the inspiration for Francis Scott Key to write "The Star-Spangled Banner." The poem later became the national anthem. The Treaty of Ghent was signed in 1814 and ended the war. The American victory created a new spirit of patriotism. The Federalists, who had been against the war, lost their influence.

Section Wrap-up

Answer these questions to check your understanding of the entire section.

1. What were the two political parties during the late 1700s and how did they differ?

_____

_____

_____

2. What caused the War of 1812?

_____

_____

_____

Persuasive Writing

In the space provided, write a newspaper editorial from the viewpoint of a U.S. citizen in the late 1700s who supports the addition of a Bill of Rights to the Constitution.

_____

_____

_____

_____

_____

_____

_____

_____

_____

_____

_____

_____

_____

The Growth of a Nation

Big Idea

As you read pages 86–93 in your textbook, complete the graphic organizer by listing actions that strengthened the federal government after the War of 1812.

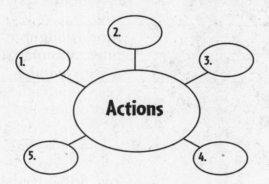

 ## Notes | ## Read to Learn

Growth of American Nationalism (page 86)

Determining Cause and Effect

Write the effect.

Cause: Congress passed the Tariff of 1816.

Effect:

_____

_____

_____

After the War of 1812, the United States began an "Era of Good Feelings." This was a time of increased nationalism. With the end of the Federalist Party, the Republicans grew stronger. In 1816, Republican James Monroe became president. Monroe worked to strengthen the American financial system. Republicans saw a need for a national bank to regulate currency and control state banks. The Second Bank of the United States was created in 1816. Republicans also wanted to protect American manufacturers from foreign competition. Congress passed the Tariff of 1816. This was a **protective tariff** to protect American manufacturers by taxing imports to drive up their prices. It was unlike earlier **revenue tariffs.** These had given money to the federal government.

The Supreme Court also supported federal power and boosted nationalism. In one case, the Court supported the government's creation of a national bank. In another case, the Court ruled that control of commerce between states was a federal right.

Nationalism affected the way the United States dealt with other nations. The U.S. government pressured Spain to give all of Florida to the United States in 1819. Russia's claim of the Pacific Coast also worried the government. President Monroe issued the Monroe Doctrine in 1823. It declared the American continents closed to future colonization.

A Growing Nation (page 90)

Identifying the Main Idea

Write the main idea of the first paragraph.

_____

_____

_____

Drawing Conclusions

Underline two sentences in the passage that support the following conclusion.

Slave labor was important to the economy of the South.

Transportation improvements in the early 1800s helped connect a rapidly growing nation. Congress approved funding for the National Road in 1806. Rivers were a cheap and efficient way to move goods. The invention of the steamboat made it easy to transport heavy cargo upstream. Railroads also helped settle the West and expand trade throughout the nation.

The Industrial Revolution brought about large-scale manufacturing in the United States. Manufacturers had factories with complex machines—often with standardized components—and large, organized workforces. Manufacturers sold their goods nationally or abroad instead of just locally. Industrialization quickly took hold in the Northeast. An influx of immigrants to America between 1815 and 1860 included many people who settled in cities and provided cheap labor. Working conditions were hard and pay was low. Some factory workers started **labor unions,** or groups of workers who band together to press for better working conditions and benefits.

Despite industrialization, the nation's economy depended on agriculture. Farming was most important in the South, which had less industry than the North. Cotton was the South's most important crop. With Eli Whitney's invention of the cotton gin in 1793, cotton production soared. Agriculture brought prosperity to the South, but it also increased the demand for slave labor. By 1850 there were 3.2 million enslaved people living in the South. They had few rights. They were forbidden to own property or to leave a slaveholder's land without permission. Many enslaved people resisted slavery. Some ran away or staged uprisings. Although slavery had been outlawed in the North, free African Americans were not always treated well there. Still, they were able to form churches and organizations, hold jobs, and earn money.

Section Wrap-up

Answer these questions to check your understanding of the entire section.

1. What steps did President Monroe and Congress take to improve the nation's economy?

_____

_____

_____

2. Why were transportation improvements important to the development of the United States in the early 1800s?

_____

_____

_____

Write a paragraph for a history textbook that tells how nationalism in the early 1800s contributed to the growth and prosperity of the United States.

_____

_____

_____

_____

_____

_____

_____

_____

_____

_____

_____

Growing Division and Reform

Big Idea

As you read pages 94–103 in your textbook, complete the graphic organizer by listing some of the divisive political issues of the 1820s.

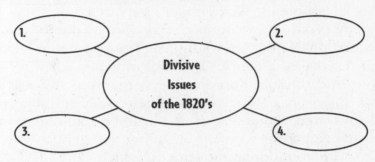

Divisive Issues of the 1820's

1.
2.
3.
4.

 **Notes**   **Read to Learn**

The Resurgence of Sectionalism *(page 94)*

Problems and Solutions

Write the solution.

Problem: South Carolina threatened to secede from the Union.

Solution:

_____

_____

_____

_____

In 1819 Missouri applied for statehood. Whether slavery would be legal in the new state was a controversial issue. The Senate admitted Missouri as a slave state and prohibited slavery in the Louisiana Territory north of Missouri's southern border. This was called the Missouri Compromise.

Many people gained voting rights in the early 1800s. Andrew Jackson became president in 1828. To make the government open to ordinary people, Jackson used the **spoils system**. This was the practice of giving people government jobs based on party loyalty and support. Jackson faced a crisis when Congress passed new tariff laws. These taxed imported foreign goods. South Carolina, which imported many goods, threatened to **secede**, or withdraw, from the Union. South Carolina voted to nullify the law. In answer, Congress passed a bill to lower the tariffs.

People who opposed President Jackson formed a new political party, the Whigs. They wanted to expand the federal government. Despite opposition to Jackson, Democrat Martin van Buren became president. Shortly after, an economic crisis hit the nation. Van Buren was criticized, and Whig William Henry Harrison won the 1840 presidential election. He died shortly after becoming president, and Vice President John Tyler, a former Democrat, took over.

The Reform Spirit *(page 100)*

Identifying the Main Idea

Write the main idea of the passage.

_____

_____

_____

_____

Detecting Bias

Put an X by the statement with which an abolitionist in the 1800s would most likely agree.

____ *African Americans have the right to freedom and the pursuit of happiness.*

____ *The economy of the South will not suffer from the loss of slave labor.*

During the mid-1800s, many people worked to reform, or improve, American society. Religious leaders organized to strengthen Americans' commitment to religion. This was called the Second Great Awakening. Church membership grew. Religious leaders taught that individuals could improve themselves and the world. In response to this, groups known as **benevolent societies** formed throughout the nation. These groups focused on spreading the word of God and fixing social problems. Women were very active in these groups. Many groups saw the use of alcohol as one of the greatest social problems. They supported **temperance**, or moderation in the use of alcohol. Other reformers worked to improve prisons and schools. Some women organized to seek greater rights for themselves. Some created better educational opportunities for women. Others, such as Elizabeth Cady Stanton, proposed equal rights for women, including the right to vote.

The abolitionist movement, which called for an immediate end to slavery, was the most controversial reform movement of the time. In the early 1800s, an antislavery group worked to resettle African Americans in Africa. However, many African Americans had made the United States their home. They did not want to return to Africa. Later antislavery groups worked for the immediate **emancipation**, or freeing, of enslaved people. Free African Americans, such as Frederick Douglass and Sojourner Truth, promoted abolition by publishing newspapers and giving speeches. Many people in both the North and the South were against abolition. Some Northerners thought abolition would lead to a war between the North and the South. Others thought abolition would destroy the South's economy. Most Southerners defended slavery. They believed it was crucial to the Southern economy and way of life. In response to a violent slave rebellion in 1831, the South demanded that abolitionist material stop being produced. Despite this, abolitionists continued their work.

Section Wrap-up

Answer these questions to check your understanding of the entire section.

1. What was the spoils system and why did President Jackson use it?

_____

_____

_____

2. What social issues did reform movements of the 1800s tackle?

_____

_____

_____

In the space provided, write a journal entry describing your experiences at a reform group meeting in the 1800s. Use sensory images to describe what you see, hear, and feel.

_____

_____

_____

_____

_____

_____

_____

_____

_____

_____

_____

_____

Manifest Destiny and Crisis

Big Idea

As you read pages 104–113 in your textbook, record main ideas about the United States's westward expansion and its results using the major headings in this section.

Manifest Destiny and Crisis

I. Manifest Destiny
A. _____
B. _____
C. _____

II. _____
A. _____
B. _____
C. _____
D. _____

III. _____
A. _____
B. _____
C. _____

Notes | Read to Learn

Manifest Destiny (page 104)

Distinguishing Fact from Opinion

Reread the passage. Underline one opinion many Americans held about westward expansion. Circle one fact about Americans' westward expansion.

In the mid-1800s many people moved west to farm, enter the fur trade, or trade with nations across the Pacific. Most Americans believed in Manifest Destiny. This was the idea that the nation was meant to spread to the Pacific. They traveled across the country on the Oregon Trail, the California Trail, the Santa Fe Trail, and other routes. Plains Indians did not like travelers moving across their land. The federal government negotiated with the Indians to ensure peace and create specific boundaries for Indian land.

Texas was a region of Mexico, but some Americans lived there. Americans Stephen Austin and Sam Houston disagreed with Mexico's policies. They led a fight against Mexico to create their own government. In 1845 Texas became a state. Soon after, the United States also received land from Britain that became the states of Oregon, Washington, and Idaho. Texas's entry into the Union angered Mexico. The United States and Mexico also disputed Texas's southwestern border. This led to war with Mexico. Even before war began, settlers in California fought against the Mexican presence there to become independent. The United States claimed California for itself. The United States won the war against Mexico and received land that is now California, Nevada, Utah, Arizona, New Mexico, Colorado, and Wyoming.

 **Notes** | **Read to Learn**

Slavery and Western Expansion *(page 107)*

Problems and Solutions

Write the problem.

Problem:

_____

_____

_____

Solution: One Congressman suggested a policy of popular sovereignty.

The debate about the westward expansion of slavery continued. When California applied for statehood, Congress tried to find a compromise between opposing viewpoints on slavery. One Congressman suggested that the people of each new territory should be allowed to decide for themselves if they wanted to permit slavery. This idea was called **popular sovereignty**. In 1848 gold was discovered in California. Many people moved to California to make their fortunes. California wanted to enter the union as a free state. At the time, the Union had an equal number of free and slave states. Southerners did not want slaveholding states to become a minority in the Senate. Some Southern politicians threatened **secession**, or taking their states out of the Union. Congress passed the Compromise of 1850. This made California a free state and did not place any restrictions on slavery in the rest of the land given to the United States by Mexico. The Compromise also included the Fugitive Slave Act, which made it easier for slaveholders to reclaim alleged runaways. Many people opposed this law in the North, where the Underground Railroad helped enslaved people run away.

As the country expanded, many people wanted a transcontinental railroad, but they argued over where the railroad would start in the East. A route from the north would run through lands west of Missouri and Iowa. A proposed bill organized these lands into a new territory called Nebraska. Southern Senators wanted Congress to allow slavery in the new territory. Congress passed an act that divided the region into two territories: Nebraska, which would be free, and Kansas, which would allow slavery.

The Crisis Deepens *(page 111)*

Making Inferences

Compete the sentence.

John Brown's death increased Northern support for abolition because _____

_____

_____

_____

_____ .

The creation of Kansas and Nebraska angered many opponents of slavery. It undid part of the Missouri Compromise. It also reopened the territories to slavery. The controversy caused the reorganization of political parties and the creation of new parties. In 1856 the Supreme Court ruled in the *Dred Scott* case that the Missouri Compromise's ban on slavery in territory north of Missouri's southern border was unconstitutional. This decision increased the debate over whether Kansas would allow slavery. After several years of debate, Kansas became a free state. During the conflict, abolitionist John Brown seized a store of weapons in Harpers Ferry (today in West Virginia). He planned to arm the area's enslaved people and start a rebellion against slaveholders. Brown was captured and put to death. Brown's death increased Northern support for abolition.

Section Wrap-up

Answer these questions to check your understanding of the entire section.

1. How did the United States gain more territory in the 1800s?

_____

_____

_____

2. What was the Fugitive Slave Act?

_____

_____

_____

In the space provided, discuss why the question of whether slavery would be allowed in newly established territories was a divisive issue in the 1800s. Explain the two sides of the slavery debate at this time.

_____

_____

_____

_____

_____

_____

_____

_____

_____

_____

_____

_____

The Civil War Begins

Big Idea

As you read pages 122–129 in your textbook, complete the outline using major headings of the section.

The Civil War Begins

I. **The Union Dissolves**

    A. _____

    B. _____

    C. _____

II. _____

    A. _____

    B. _____

    C. _____

Notes

The Union Dissolves *(page 122)*

Identifying the Main Idea

Place an X by the sentence that best tells the passage's main idea.

____ *Americans were divided over the events leading up to the Civil War.*

____ *Abraham Lincoln won the election of 1860.*

Read to Learn

Abraham Lincoln won the election of 1860. Many Southerners saw Lincoln's election as a threat to their way of life. Southern states began voting to leave the Union. South Carolina, Mississippi, Florida, Alabama, Georgia, Louisiana, and Texas voted to secede. Delegates from these states met in 1861 to declare themselves a new nation. They called themselves the Confederate States of America. They chose Mississippi senator Jefferson Davis as their president. He wanted the rest of the Southern states to join the Confederacy.

The Civil War began with a battle at Fort Sumter in 1861. President Lincoln asked for 75,000 volunteers to serve in the military. Many people in the Upper South did not want to fight against fellow Southerners. Virginia, Arkansas, North Carolina, and Tennessee chose to leave the Union.

Lincoln did not want to lose the slaveholding border states. He imposed **martial law**—military rule—on Maryland to prevent it from seceding. Kentucky wanted to stay neutral. When Confederate troops occupied parts of Kentucky, the state declared war on the Confederacy. The Civil War divided Americans. It cost hundreds of thousands of lives.

 **Notes** | **Read to Learn**

The Opposing Sides *(page 126)*

Formulating Questions

Place a P next to the question answered in the passage. Place an S next to the question that requires further study.

1. _____ Was attrition a strategy used by the Union or the Confederacy?

2. _____ What was the most successful military strategy used in the Civil War?

Analyzing Information

Reread the passage. List four advantages the North had over the South.

1. _____

_____

2. _____

_____

3. _____

_____

4. _____

_____

General Winfield Scott asked Robert E. Lee to lead Union troops, but Lee's home state of Virginia had just voted to leave the Union. Lee resigned from the military to join the Confederacy. The South had many experienced military officers to lead its troops.

The North, however, had a bigger population and more factories. Industry gave the North an economic advantage over the South. Factories in the North could produce ammunition, and supplies would get to Union troops more easily. The North also had more railroad lines, too. The North could prevent the movement of troops and supplies to the Confederate states. The Union also had large amounts of cash in Northern banks. The Confederacy's financial situation was poor. Many Southern planters were in debt. Southern banks were small and did not have cash reserves.

President Lincoln wanted to preserve the Union at any cost. Republicans and Democrats in the North clashed on many issues. One major issue was whether or not the government should force people into military service through a draft.

Congress criticized President Lincoln's decision to suspend writs of **habeas corpus.** A writ of habeas corpus is a court order that says a government must charge an imprisoned person with a crime or set the person free. A person can be held in jail without a trial for as long as the government wants when writs of habeas corpus are suspended. President Lincoln wanted to be able to jail anyone who openly supported rebels or told others to resist the military draft.

The fighting between the states put Europe in a difficult situation. The Union did not want Europe getting involved. The Confederacy wanted military help from Europe. Britain and France decided to stay out of the war.

Modern military strategies were used in the Civil War. Troops used trenches and barricades to protect themselves. **Attrition**—the wearing down of one side by the other through exhaustion of soldiers and resources—was also used by both sides. The South believed they could use attrition to force the Union to spend all its resources. Then the Union might have to agree to discuss a solution. However, Jefferson Davis felt pressured to try for quick victory. Heavy losses in the South resulted. The Union thought they could divide the Confederacy in two by cutting off ports. Lincoln and other Union leaders realized that only a long war that destroyed the South's armies would succeed.

Section Wrap-up

Answer these questions to check your understanding of the entire section.

1. With which side did Kentucky align itself during the Civil War? Why?

_____

_____

_____

2. Why did President Lincoln suspend writs of habeas corpus?

_____

_____

_____

Descriptive Writing

Suppose you are a Southerner at the start of the Civil War. Write a journal entry in which you describe the early stages of the war and how you feel about it.

_____

_____

_____

_____

_____

_____

_____

_____

_____

_____

_____

_____

Fighting the Civil War

Big Idea

As you read pages 130–137 in your textbook, complete the graphic organizer by filling in the results of each battle listed.

Battle	Results
First Battle of Bull Run	1.
Battle of Shiloh	2.
Second Battle of Bull Run	3.
Antietam	4.

 **Notes** | **Read to Learn**

The Early Stages (page 130)

Making Inferences

Circle the paragraph that supports the following inference.

Lincoln believed cutting off the South's ability to trade for supplies was an effective military strategy.

The Confederates defeated the Union forces in the first Battle of Bull Run. It became clear the North would need a large, well-trained army to win the war. Both the Union and Confederacy had to draft soldiers.

To cut off Confederate trade with the world, President Lincoln sent Union ships to block southern ports. The South used **blockade runners**—small, fast vessels—to smuggle goods past the blockade. The South traded cotton with Europe for shoes, rifles, and other supplies.

Battles raged from west to east. The Union's navy captured New Orleans, the center of the cotton trade. Union general Ulysses S. Grant seized control of the Cumberland and Tennessee rivers. This cut Tennessee in two and gave the Union a river route into Confederate territory. The Union won the Battle of Shiloh, but the South forced the North to retreat in the second Battle of Bull Run. The Confederates were only 20 miles from Washington, D.C. They wanted to invade Maryland, thinking this would convince the North to accept the South's independence.

The Turning Point (page 134)

Predicting

Based on the passage, predict what postwar relations between the North and South will be like.

_____

_____

_____

_____

_____

_____

Synthesizing Information

Number the events below in the order in which they occurred.

____ *Sherman and his troops set fire to Atlanta.*

____ *Union forces defeat the Confederates at Gettysburg.*

____ *The railroad at Chattanooga is captured by Union forces.*

Three major Union victories in 1863 marked the turning point of the war. The first was at Vicksburg, which had been the last Confederate stronghold on the Mississippi River. Grant put the city under **siege,** or cut off its food supplies and bombarded it until its defenders gave up. The Confederate commander at Vicksburg surrendered.

Meanwhile, Lee had defeated Union forces in Virginia. He and his troops headed into Gettysburg, Pennsylvania to seize a supply of shoes. Instead, they met Union soldiers. The Confederates pushed the Union troops out of the city. Lee attacked the Union forces, but he could not defeat them. The South lost more lives than the North. Lee blamed himself. His forces were on the defensive for the rest of the war.

The third victory for the Union was near Chattanooga, Tennessee. The Union wanted to control a major railroad that ran south to Atlanta. Union forces succeeded in scattering the Confederate soldiers who blocked the way to the city.

Grant was determined to march south and attack Lee's forces until the South surrendered. He kept his forces on the move and gave Lee no time to recover. He attacked in several locations in Virginia, and then he put the town of Petersburg under siege in order to prevent the city of Richmond from receiving supplies.

William Tecumseh Sherman was in charge of Union operations in the west. Sherman marched into Georgia and captured Atlanta. Troops set fires to railroads, warehouses, mills, and factories. The fires spread and destroyed more than one-third of Atlanta. The capture of Atlanta inspired Northern support for the war and for Lincoln. He was elected president for another term. Lincoln thought his reelection was a **mandate**—or authorization—to end slavery permanently. The Thirteenth Amendment to the Constitution banned slavery in the United States.

Lee's troops surrendered to Grant at Appomattox Courthouse in 1865. Grant's terms of surrender were generous. The United States would not charge Confederate soldiers with treason, and the Confederate soldiers could take their horses home with them so they could plant crops and provide for their families. After the war, Lincoln gave a speech describing his plan to bring the Southern states back into the Union. Some of his ideas were unpopular, and his advisers were concerned. On April 14, 1865, John Wilkes Booth shot President Lincoln in the back of the head. The president died the next morning.

Section Wrap-up

Answer these questions to check your understanding of the entire section.

1. What was the original cause of the Civil War, and why did it change?

_____

_____

_____

2. Why were Grant's terms of surrender good for the North as well as the South?

_____

_____

_____

Informative Writing

In the space provided, write an encyclopedia entry about the events leading to the Union's ultimate victory.

_____

_____

_____

_____

_____

_____

_____

_____

_____

_____

_____

Reconstruction

Big Idea

As you read pages 140–149 in your textbook, complete the graphic organizer to explain how each piece of legislation listed affected African Americans.

Legislation	Effect
black codes	1.
Civil Rights Act of 1866	2.
Fourteenth Amendment	3.
Fifteenth Amendment	4.

 **Notes**

Read to Learn

Reconstruction Begins (page 140)

Determining Cause and Effect

Write the cause.

Cause:

_____

_____

_____

Effect: Congress established the Freedmen's Bureau.

President Lincoln set out his plan for reuniting the country in 1863. He offered **amnesty,** or pardon, to all Southerners who took an oath of loyalty to the United States. Some people did not like Lincoln's plan. Radical Republicans wanted to prevent Confederate leaders from returning to power after the war. Some moderate Republicans thought Lincoln was too easy on Southerners. These groups wrote the Wade-Davis Bill in 1864, requiring the majority of white men in a former Confederate state to take an oath of loyalty to the Union before establishing a new state government. Congress passed it, but Lincoln blocked it with a **pocket veto.**

Congress established the Freedmen's Bureau in 1865 to help feed and clothe war refugees in the South. The Bureau also helped formerly enslaved people find work. Lincoln was killed not long after the Freedmen's Bureau was established. Vice President Andrew Johnson pushed the reconstruction plan forward. Congress gathered for its next session in December of 1865, and Congressional Republicans were angry with new members of Congress. Southern voters had elected many Confederate leaders. The Southern state legislatures passed laws called **black codes.** These laws would keep African Americans in a condition similar to slavery. Congress passed the Civil Rights Act of 1866 to override the black codes.

Read to Learn

Republican Rule *(page 145)*

Making Generalizations

Underline two sentences in the passage that support the generalization below.

Many Southerners were against the Republicans and Reconstruction.

Many Northerners traveled to the South during Reconstruction. Southerners called these newcomers **carpetbaggers.** Their name came from the suitcases they carried, which were made of carpet fabric. Local residents saw them as intruders. Some white Southerners supported Reconstruction and worked with Republicans. Their fellow Southerners called these supporters **scalawags**—meaning weak, underfed, worthless animals. Some scalawags were owners of small farms. They did not want the wealthy to regain power. Others were business people who supported Republican economic plans.

African American men had gained the right to vote. They served as legislators and in local offices. Republican candidates were elected by poor Southern-born whites, African Americans, and Northern carpetbaggers. The Republican governments repealed the black codes. They established state hospitals and institutions for orphans. They rebuilt roads, railways, and bridges that were damaged during the Civil War.

Some Southerners did not like the reforms. They started secret societies to undermine Republican rule. The largest of these groups was the Ku Klux Klan, started in 1866. Congress passed laws in 1870 and 1871 to outlaw the activities of the Klan.

Reconstruction Ends *(page 147)*

Distinguishing Fact from Opinion

Read the fact. Write the opinion a plantation owner would likely have about sharecropping.

Fact: The end of Reconstruction forced many African Americans back to plantations owned by whites.

Opinion:

_____

_____

_____

The nation elected Ulysses S. Grant president in 1868. Although known as a commander of Union forces, Grant did not have much experience in politics. This lack of experience divided the Republican Party. It also began to undermine support for Reconstruction.

Democrats rose to power in the midterm elections of 1874. Many Northerners were becoming more concerned about the economy. By 1877 the nation was tired of the politics of Reconstruction. Even Republicans were ready to end Reconstruction.

The end of Reconstruction meant a return to the "Old South" for many African Americans. African Americans no longer hoped for their own land. Instead, many returned to plantations owned by whites. They worked for wages or became tenant farmers. Tenant farmers paid rent for the land they farmed. Most tenant farmers became **sharecroppers,** meaning they paid a share of their crops for rent. The cost of seed and supplies put many sharecroppers in debt. Sharecroppers became trapped on the land because they could not pay their debts. Failure to pay could lead to imprisonment or forced labor. Many African Americans were trapped in poverty.

Section Wrap-up

Answer these questions to check your understanding of the entire section.

1. How did some Southern whites attempt to block Reconstruction reform?

_____

_____

_____

2. What changes did the end of Reconstruction bring for African Americans?

_____

_____

_____

In the space provided, write a persuasive letter to Southerners against ending Reconstruction. In it, convince them of the benefits of Reconstruction for the South.

_____

_____

_____

_____

_____

_____

_____

_____

_____

_____

_____

_____

Miners and Ranchers

Big Idea

As you read pages 158–165 in your textbook, complete this graphic organizer by listing the locations of mining booms and the discoveries made there.

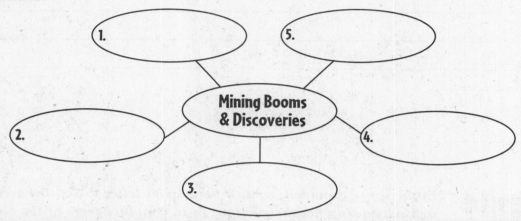

1.

5.

2.

Mining Booms & Discoveries

4.

3.

 **Notes**

Read to Learn

Growth of the Mining Industry *(page 158)*

Comparing and Contrasting

Describe each mining method.

Placer mining

_____

_____

Hydraulic mining

_____

_____

Quartz mining

_____

_____

Throughout the 1800s, people flooded the West hoping to strike it rich by mining minerals such as gold and silver. Almost overnight, tiny frontier towns were transformed into small cities. These "boomtowns" were often rowdy places with rampant crime and lawlessness. Self-appointed volunteers, called **vigilance committees,** were the only law enforcers. Many boomtowns went "bust" when the exhausted mines closed. Mining spurred development in western states such as Nevada, Colorado, Arizona, the Dakotas, and Montana. Railroads came to these areas, and farmers and ranchers followed. By 1889, North Dakota, South Dakota, and Montana were admitted as states. Arizona's population grew more slowly, but it applied for statehood by 1912.

Early miners had extracted ore by hand in a process called placer mining. Later, miners sprayed hills or mountains with high-pressure water in a process called **hydraulic mining.** Although effective, this process devastated the environment. After 1884, most mining companies shifted to quartz mining, a process in which miners are sent down deep shafts to extract minerals.

Read to Learn

Ranching and Cattle Drives (page 162)

Determining Cause and Effect

What two causes prompted ranchers to undertake long drives?

1. _____
_____
_____
_____

2. _____
_____
_____
_____

Cattle ranching prospered in the Great Plains during the 1800s partly thanks to the **open range,** a vast, federally owned grassland where ranchers could graze their herds for free. Americans had long believed it was impossible to raise cattle in the Plains. Water was scarce, and the prairie grasses were too tough for cattle from the East to eat. But the longhorn, a breed of cattle from Texas, had adapted to life on the Plains.

During the Civil War, eastern cattle were slaughtered as food for armies. After the war, beef prices shot up. By this time, railroad lines also had reached the Great Plains. These factors made it worthwhile for ranchers to drive the longhorns north to the railroad, where they could be shipped east. In 1866, on the first **long drive** to Sedalia, Missouri, many of the cattle perished. The survivors, however, sold for 10 times their Texas price. Many trails, such as the Chisholm Trail, soon opened up between Texas and towns in states such as Kansas and Montana.

"Range wars" eventually broke out among ranchers, newly settled farmers, and sheep herders in Wyoming, Montana, and other territories. The open range was soon fenced off. This, along with an oversupply of cattle and blizzards in 1886 and 1887, meant the end of the open range.

Settling the Hispanic Southwest (page 164)

Identifying the Main Idea

Write the main idea of the passage.

_____
_____
_____
_____
_____
_____
_____
_____

Spain, and then Mexico, ruled the region now called the American Southwest before it came under U.S. control in 1848. The region's Spanish-speaking residents became American citizens. They were assured they would retain their property rights. However, the new Southwest attracted settlers from the East. They often clashed with the Mexican Americans, whose claims of land ownership dated back to centuries-old, vague Spanish land grants. American courts usually refused to accept these grants as proof of ownership.

In California, Hispanic landowners who owned **haciendas—** or huge ranches—clashed with "Forty-Niners." Elsewhere, English-speaking ranchers claimed large tracts of land of Mexican origin so they could expand their ranches. In some cases, the Hispanic population fought back, sometimes with violent force. In New Mexico, Hispanics retained their majority in the population and in the state legislature. Throughout the late 1800s, the Southwest also attracted immigrants from Mexico. They often settled in urban neighborhoods called **barrios.**

Section Wrap-up

Answer these questions to check your understanding of the entire section.

1. How did the mining industry help some territories become U.S. states?

_____

_____

_____

2. Why did the open range disappear?

_____

_____

_____

Write a paragraph explaining your beliefs from either the point of view of a judge that does not see Spanish land grants as proof of ownership of land, or the point of view of a Mexican American who believes his land grant entitles him to the land.

_____

_____

_____

_____

_____

_____

_____

_____

_____

_____

_____

Farming the Plains

Big Idea

As you read pages 166–169 in your textbook, complete this graphic organizer by listing the ways the government encouraged settlement.

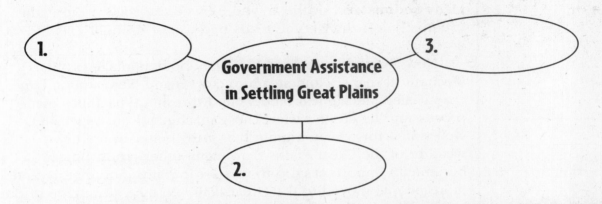

1.

3.

Government Assistance in Settling Great Plains

2.

Notes

Read to Learn

The Beginnings of Settlement (page 166)

Problems and Solutions

List some of the problems faced by early Great Plains settlers.

_____

_____

_____

_____

_____

_____

_____

_____

The Great Plains region receives little rain, and has few trees. In 1819 Major Stephen Long traveled through the region and declared it to be a desert not fit for settlement. In the late 1800s, several factors helped change the Plains' desert image. Railroad companies sold land along the rail lines that they built through the Plains. They sold the land at low prices, attracting settlers there. Pamphlets and posters spread the news across the United States and Europe that the Plains were a ticket to prosperity. A Nebraskan claimed that farming the Plains would increase rainfall there, a claim seemingly supported by above average rainfall in the 1870s.

The government passed the Homestead Act in 1862. One could file for a **homestead,** or a tract of open public land, for a $10 fee. A person could claim up to 160 acres of land and would own it after five years. The environment was harsh for Plains settlers. Summer temperatures soared above 100°F, and winters brought blizzards. Prairie fires were a danger, and sometimes grasshoppers destroyed crops.

Notes

Read to Learn

The Wheat Belt (page 168)

Determining Cause and Effect

What two factors caused many Plains farmers to take out loans on their property?

1. _____

_____

_____

2. _____

_____

_____

Formulating Questions

Write two questions you still have after reading the section.

1. _____

_____

_____

_____

2. _____

_____

_____

_____

_____

New farming methods and inventions helped to make farming on the Great Plains profitable. One method was called **dry farming.** It involved planting seeds deep in the ground where there was enough moisture for them to grow. By the 1860s, farmers were using steel plows, reapers, and threshing machines. The new machines made dry farming possible. However, dry prairie soil could blow away in a dry season. Many **sodbusters,** or those who plowed the soil on the Plains, eventually lost their homesteads because of drought or wind erosion.

New technology helped large landholders make profits. Mechanical reapers and steam tractors made harvesting a large crop easier. Mechanical binders and threshing machines made processing the crops easier. These machines were especially well suited for wheat, a grain that grew better in the dry weather of the Great Plains than many other crops. Wheat became an important crop to the Great Plains. Soon, more and more people moved to the Great Plains to take advantage of the inexpensive land and the new technology. The Wheat Belt eventually included much of the Dakotas and the western parts of Nebraska and Kansas.

The new technology allowed some farms to become very large. These **bonanza farms** brought huge profits to their owners. By the 1880s, the Wheat Belt helped to make the United States the world's leading exporter of wheat.

However, Plains farmers also faced difficulties. A long drought that began in the late 1880s destroyed many crops and turned the soil to dust. The nation began to face competition from other wheat-producing countries. By the 1890s, an oversupply of wheat caused prices to drop. To make it through bad times, some farmers took out loans based on the value of their property. If they did not meet their payments, they had to give the land to the bank. Many then worked as tenant farmers for the new owner.

On April 22, 1889, the government opened for settlement one of the last large territories. Within hours, over 10,000 people raced to stake claims. This was called the "Oklahoma Land Rush." In 1890 the Census Bureau reported that there was no true frontier left in America, although there was still much unoccupied land. Many people believed that this was the end of an era.

Section Wrap-up

Answer these questions to check your understanding of the entire section.

1. Why and how did people begin to settle the Plains?

   _____

   _____

   _____

2. What was the Wheat Belt and how did it get its name?

   _____

   _____

   _____

In the space provided write a paragraph about the advantages and disadvantages of participating in the Oklahoma Land Rush.

_____

_____

_____

_____

_____

_____

_____

_____

_____

_____

Native Americans

Big Idea

As you read pages 170–175 in your textbook, complete this time line by recording the battles between Native Americans and the United States government and the results of each.

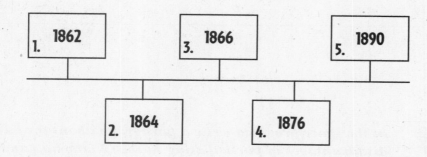

1. 1862
2. 1864
3. 1866
4. 1876
5. 1890

 **Notes** | **Read to Learn**

Struggles of the Plains Indians *(page 170)*

Making Inferences

Why did the Indian Peace Commission's plan fail?

_____

_____

_____

_____

_____

_____

_____

For centuries, many Native American groups lived on the Great Plains, most as **nomads** who roamed the land. As settlers moved onto the Great Plains, they clashed with the Native Americans. In 1862 in Minnesota, the Dakota Sioux faced starvation and lived in poverty after failing to receive **annuities,** or money promised to them by the U.S. government. They staged an uprising, waging war against both soldiers and settlers. The rebellion was suppressed.

From 1866 to 1868, the Lakota Sioux clashed with U.S. soldiers. This was called "Red Cloud's War." In one major battle known as Fetterman's Massacre, the Lakota wiped out an entire unit of the U.S. Army—about 80 soldiers. In 1864, in response to Native American raids and attacks, Colorado's territorial governor ordered their surrender at Fort Lyon. When several hundred Cheyenne came to negotiate a peace deal they were attacked by U.S. troops.

In 1867 Congress formed an Indian Peace Commission. It proposed creating two large reservations. However, this plan failed. Many Native Americans refused to move. Those who did move faced miserable conditions.

 **Notes**

Read to Learn

The Last Native American Wars *(page 173)*

Predicting

Before you read, make a prediction about the passage based on the heading.

_____

_____

_____

_____

_____

_____

_____

Detecting Bias

Complete the following sentence.

Based on the title of her book, I expect Helen Hunt Jackson to believe

_____

_____

_____

_____

_____ .

By the 1870s, many Native Americans left the reservations in disgust. They joined others who shunned reservations to hunt buffalo on the open plains. However, the buffalo were disappearing. Migrants crossing the plains (professional hunters and sport hunters) killed many buffalo. Railroad companies killed buffalo that were blocking rail lines.

In 1876 miners overran the Lakota Sioux reservation. Seeing that American settlers were violating the treaty, many Lakota left the reservation to hunt in Montana. In response, the government sent troops, including Lieutenant Colonel George A. Custer. On June 25, Custer and about 210 soldiers attacked a very large group of Lakota and Cheyenne warriors camped along the Little Bighorn River. The warriors killed them all. The army then stepped up its campaign against the Plains Indians. Some fled to Canada, while others were forced back on the reservation.

In 1877 the Nez Perce, led by Chief Joseph, refused to move to a smaller reservation in Idaho. When the army came to force them to move, they fled for more than 1,300 miles. However, Chief Joseph surrendered in October 1877. He and his followers were moved to Oklahoma.

Against government orders, some Lakota on a reservation continued to perform the Ghost Dance. This ritual celebrated, among other things, a hoped-for day when settlers would leave. Federal authorities blamed Chief Sitting Bull for this defiance and sent police to arrest him. He died in the ensuing gunfire. Some Ghost Dancers fled, but troops pursued them. On December 29, 1890, fighting broke out at Wounded Knee Creek. About 25 soldiers and 200 Lakota died.

Some Americans opposed the government's treatment of Native Americans. Helen Hunt Jackson, in her book *A Century of Dishonor,* described the government's injustices against Native Americans. Some people believed that Native Americans should **assimilate,** or be absorbed, into American culture as citizens and landowners. Congress in 1887 passed the Dawes Act. It gave each head of a household 160 acres of reservation land. Although some Native Americans succeeded as farmers or ranchers, many did not. Many found their **allotment** of land was too small to be profitable. Assimilation failed, and no good solution replaced it. The Plains Indians depended on the buffalo for food, clothing, fuel, and shelter. When the herds were wiped out, they could not continue their way of life, but few were willing to adopt the settlers' way of life.

Answer these questions to check your understanding of the entire section.

1. What conflicts arose between the Plains Indians and American settlers?

_____

_____

_____

2. What problems were caused by attempts to assimilate Native Americans?

_____

_____

_____

In the space provided write a newspaper account of one of the conflicts between Native Americans and U.S. soldiers.

_____

_____

_____

_____

_____

_____

_____

_____

_____

_____

The Rise of Industry

Big Idea

As you read pages 182–187 in your textbook, complete this graphic organizer by listing some of the causes of industrialization.

Causes

| 1. |
| 2. |
| 3. |
| 4. |

→ **United States Becomes an Industrial Nation**

Notes

Read to Learn

The United States Industrializes (page 182)

Determining Cause and Effect

List two causes of American population growth.

1. _____
_____
_____
_____

2. _____
_____
_____
_____

After the Civil War, many people left their farms to find work in factories. By the late 1800s, the United States had become the world's leading industrial nation. By 1914 the **gross national product (GNP)**—or the total value of all goods and services produced by a country—was eight times greater than in 1865.

One reason that industries expanded was an abundance of natural resources such as coal and timber. Many resources were located in the West. The transcontinental railroad brought settlers to the West and resources to the East. A new resource, petroleum, was also being developed. It was turned into kerosene used in lanterns and stoves. In 1859 Edwin Drake drilled the first oil well near Titusville, Pennsylvania. Oil fields were soon developed across the country. Oil production helped to expand the nation's economy.

America's growing population provided industries with both a larger workforce and more demand for the goods they produced. The population increase resulted from large families and increased immigration. Between 1870 and 1910, over 20 million immigrants came to the United States.

 **Notes**

Read to Learn

New Inventions (page 184)

Problems and Solutions

What problem did Gustavus Swift solve?

_____

_____

_____

_____

_____

Inventions also contributed to the growth of industries. In 1876 Alexander Graham Bell developed the telephone. It changed both business and personal communication. Thomas Alva Edison invented the phonograph and the lightbulb, among other devices. In 1882 an Edison company began to supply electric power to New York City. Electric power changed American society.

Technology affected other parts of American society. In 1877 Gustavus Swift shipped the first refrigerated load of fresh meat. Refrigeration kept food fresh longer. New machines helped the textile industry produce cloth faster. Standard sizes were used to make ready-made clothes. The clothing business moved from small shops to large factories. Similar changes took place in the shoe industry. Many products' prices dropped as the United States industrialized.

Free Enterprise (page 186)

Identifying the Main Idea

Write the main idea of the passage.

_____

_____

_____

_____

_____

_____

The free enterprise system also helped industry in the United States expand. In the late 1800s, many Americans embraced a **laissez-faire** policy. This means government should not interfere in the economy, except to protect property rights and maintain peace. They believed a free market, in which companies compete, leads to more wealth for everyone. This policy promotes keeping taxes low and limiting government debt. The chance to gain wealth attracted **entrepreneurs.** These are people who risk their capital in organizing and running businesses. Many New Englanders invested capital in building factories and railroads. Foreign investors also invested in American industries.

In many ways, the U.S. government was laissez-faire in the late 1800s. In other ways, it actively aided industry. Congress passed the Morrill Tariff. It nearly tripled tariffs. This made imported goods cost more than American goods. The government gave land grants to western railroads and sold land with mineral resources for less than its true value.

High tariffs ran counter to laissez-faire policies. Tariffs also caused foreign countries to raise tariffs against American goods. This hurt Americans trying to sell goods abroad, particularly farmers. Despite this effect, many business and government leaders thought tariffs helped new American industries compete with large European industries. By the early 1900s, many American industries were large and competitive. Business leaders then began to push for free trade.

Section Wrap-up

Answer these questions to check your understanding of the entire section.

1. What effects did the expanding population have on industry?

_____

_____

_____

2. How did Alexander Graham Bell and Thomas Alva Edison influence American society?

_____

_____

_____

In the space provided, write a brief letter to a U.S. representative during the late 1800s arguing for or against passing the Morrill Tariff.

_____

_____

_____

_____

_____

_____

_____

_____

_____

_____

_____

The Railroads

Big Idea

As you read pages 188–193 in your textbook, complete this graphic organizer by listing some of the effects of the nationwide rail network on the nation.

Effects

| Nationwide Rail Network | 1. _____ |
| 2. _____ |
| 3. _____ |
| 4. _____ |

Notes

Read to Learn

Linking the Nation (page 188)

Comparing and Contrasting

Compare and contrast workers hired to build the two railroads.

Union Pacific:

_____

_____

Central Pacific:

_____

_____

Both:

_____

In 1862 President Lincoln signed the Pacific Railway Act. It called for a transcontinental railroad to be built by the Union Pacific and Central Pacific railroad companies. Each company got land along the route of the tracks. The Union Pacific started in Omaha, Nebraska, in 1865. It employed as many as 10,000 workers at one time, including Civil War veterans, immigrants, and ex-convicts. Because of a labor shortage in California, the Central Pacific hired about 10,000 workers from China.

Before 1860 the United States had hundreds of small railroad lines. Then, large rail lines began to take over and combine them. To fix scheduling and safety problems, in 1883 the American Railway Association divided the country into four **time zones.** The large railroads benefited the nation in other ways. They could shift railcars from one section of the country to speed long-distance transportation. New technology let railroads put longer and heavier trains on their lines. More powerful locomotives made operations more efficient. Railroads also united people from many regions.

Robber Barons (page 192)

Evaluating Information

Complete the statements to evaluate the passage.

This passage included good information about

_____

_____

_____.

This passage should include more information about

_____

_____

_____.

Making Generalizations

Write a generalization about the Crédit Mobilier scandal.

_____

_____

_____

_____

_____

_____

_____

_____

_____

The federal government encouraged railroad building by giving railroad companies **land grants.** Railroads then sold the land to settlers and businesses to raise the money they needed to build the railroad. By the 1860s, the railroads received land larger in area than New England, New York, and Pennsylvania combined. Some railroad companies earned enough money from the land grants to cover much of the cost of building their lines.

Some railroad entrepreneurs in the late 1800s got their wealth by cheating investors, bribing government officials, and cheating on their contracts. Corrupt railroad owner Jay Gould was infamous for manipulating stock.

Bribery also occurred often. This was partly because government helped fund railroads. Railroad investors knew that they could make more money by getting government land grants than by operating a railroad. As a result, investors bribed politicians to vote for more grants.

Crédit Mobilier was a construction company started by several stockholders in the Union Pacific. The investors set up contracts with themselves. Crédit Mobilier greatly overcharged the Union Pacific for the work it did. Because investors owned both companies, the railroad agreed to pay. The investors had made several million dollars by the time the Union Pacific was completed. However, the railroad had used up its land grants and was almost bankrupt. To convince Congress to give the railroad more grants, one of the investors gave members of Congress shares in the Union Pacific at a price well below what these shares were worth. In the 1872 election campaign, a letter to a New York newspaper listed the members of Congress who had accepted the shares. A further investigation into the scandal showed that the vice president at the time had also accepted shares from the railroad.

Not all railroad entrepreneurs were robber barons, or people who loot an industry and give nothing back. James J. Hill built the Great Northern Railroad without federal land grants. It ran between Minnesota and Washington state. He planned the route to pass near towns in the region. To increase business, he promised low fares to settlers who homesteaded along the route. He transported American products that were in demand in China to Washington, where they were shipped to Asia. In this way the railroad made money by transporting goods both east and west. The Great Northern became the most successful transcontinental railroad and the only one that did not eventually go bankrupt.

Section Wrap-up

Answer these questions to check your understanding of the entire section.

1. How were some railroad owners corrupt?

   _____

   _____

   _____

2. How were railroads financed, and how did they grow?

   _____

   _____

   _____

In the space provided, write a brief essay explaining how James J. Hill was different from the robber barons of the time.

_____

_____

_____

_____

_____

_____

_____

_____

_____

_____

Big Business

Big Idea

As you read pages 194–199 in your textbook, complete this graphic organizer to show some steps large business owners took to weaken or eliminate competition.

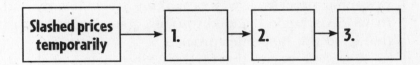

Slashed prices temporarily → 1. → 2. → 3.

 **Notes** | **Read to Learn**

The Rise of Big Business (page 194)

Predicting

Skim the passage. Predict what you will learn.

_____

_____

_____

_____

_____

_____

_____

_____

By 1900 big businesses dominated the economy. Big businesses became possible because of the **corporation,** an organization owned by many people but treated as one person by the law. Corporations sell shares of ownership called **stock.** By issuing stock, a corporation can raise money while spreading out the financial risk. Corporations use the money they receive from selling stock to invest in new technologies, hire workers, and buy machines. Corporations achieve **economies of scale,** in which they make goods cheaply by quickly making large quantities of them.

Businesses have two kinds of costs. A company pays fixed costs, such as taxes, whether or not it is operating. A company pays operating costs, such as wages and supplies, only when it is running. Before the Civil War, small companies usually had low fixed costs but high operating costs. If sales decreased, they usually shut down. Corporations had high fixed costs and low operating costs, so they could keep operating even during a recession. Corporations could cut prices to increase sales, rather than shutting down. Small businesses could not compete with big businesses, so many failed.

Notes | Read to Learn

Consolidating Industry *(page 196)*

Copyright © Glencoe/McGraw-Hill, a division of The McGraw-Hill Companies, Inc.

Identifying the Main Idea

Write the main idea of the passage.

_____

_____

_____

_____

_____

Comparing and Contrasting

Compare and contrast vertical integration with horizontal integration.

Vertical integration:

_____

_____

_____

Horizontal integration:

_____

_____

_____

Both:

_____

_____

_____

Many corporate leaders disliked competition. Lower prices helped consumers but hurt corporations' profits. Many corporations organized **pools,** or deals to keep prices at a certain level. The courts disapproved of pools and would not enforce them. Pools usually fell apart when one company lowered prices to take business away from another.

Andrew Carnegie was a poor immigrant who became a business leader. While working for a railroad, he realized he could make money by investing in companies that served the railroad industry. Carnegie met Henry Bessemer, inventor of the Bessemer process, a way of making steel cheaply and efficiently. In 1875 Carnegie decided to open a steel company in Pittsburgh that used the Bessemer process.

Carnegie began the **vertical integration** of the steel industry. A vertically integrated company owns all the businesses that it depends on to run. Carnegie's company bought mines, quarries, and ore fields. Business leaders also pushed for **horizontal integration,** or combining similar companies into a large corporation. When one company controls a market, it is a **monopoly.** People who opposed monopolies believed they could charge whatever price they wanted for their products. Other people thought monopolies had to keep prices low to keep competition down.

Many states made it illegal for one company to own stock in another. In 1882 the Standard Oil Company formed the first **trust** to get around these laws. A trust lets one person, the trustee, manage another's property. Instead of buying a company, Standard Oil had the stockholders give their stock to Standard Oil trustees. In exchange, the stockholders received shares in the trust. In this way, the trustees ran many companies as if they were one.

In 1889 New Jersey passed a law allowing corporations to own stock in other businesses. Many companies soon formed new businesses called holding companies. A **holding company** does not produce goods itself, but owns the stock of companies that do and runs them like one large corporation.

American industries were producing many different products, and retailers needed to attract consumers to buy them. Advertising changed as large illustrated ads replaced small print ads in newspapers. Department stores changed how people shopped. Each sold a variety of products in one large, elegant building. Chain stores, or groups of similar stores owned by one company, offered low prices rather than variety. To reach people who lived in rural areas, retailers issued mail-order catalogs.

Section Wrap-up

Answer these questions to check your understanding of the entire section.

1. How did large corporations come to dominate American business?

_____

_____

_____

2. How did the way retailers advertise goods to consumers change in the late 1800s?

_____

_____

_____

Descriptive Writing

In the space provided, write a description of how Andrew Carnegie's innovations transformed the steel industry.

_____

_____

_____

_____

_____

_____

_____

_____

_____

_____

_____

Unions

Big Idea

As you read pages 200–207 in your textbook, complete this time line by filling in the incidents of labor unrest discussed and the results of each incident.

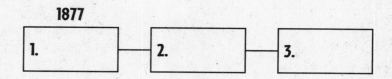

1877

| 1. | 2. | 3. |

 **Notes**　　　**Read to Learn**

Working in the United States *(page 200)*

Problems and Solutions

Explain how employers might respond to the problem.

Problem: Workers formed a union.

Solution:

_____

_____

_____

_____

_____

The difference in their standard of living caused workers to resent the wealthy. In the late 1800s **deflation,** a rise in the value of money, also hurt relations between workers and owners. Deflation caused companies to cut wages, so workers earned less money for the same work. Many workers then decided to organize unions. Industries had two kinds of workers. Craft workers had special skills and training. Common laborers had few skills and earned lower wages. In the 1830s, craft workers began to form **trade unions.** Employers opposed unions, especially **industrial unions,** which represented all craft workers and common laborers in the same industry.

Employers sometimes put those who tried to start a union or strike on a **blacklist,** a list of "troublemakers" no company would hire. Employers could use a **lockout**—when employers locked workers out of the property and refused to pay them—to break up unions that did form. If the union called a strike, employers hired replacement workers. Courts often fined labor leaders who led strikes.

Read to Learn

Struggling to Organize (page 203)

Making Inferences

Why did the Knights of Labor union lose members after the Haymarket Riot?

_____

_____

_____

_____

_____

_____

_____

_____

_____

In 1873, a recession forced many companies to cut wages. In 1877, one railroad cut wages again, and its workers went on strike. More than 80,000 railroad workers nationwide joined the protest. Some turned to violence, and President Hayes eventually ordered the army to open the railroads.

Founded in 1869, the Knights of Labor was the first nationwide industrial union. The Knights supported the eight-hour workday, equal pay for women, and the end of child labor. At first, the Knights preferred **arbitration,** in which a third party helps workers and employers reach agreements.

In 1886, about 3,000 protesters rallied at Chicago's Haymarket Square. When police arrived, someone threw a bomb that killed a police officer. Violence erupted, and about 100 people, including nearly 70 police officers, were injured in the Haymarket Riot. No one knew who threw the bomb, but eight men were convicted for it. One was a member of the Knights of Labor. The union lost members as a result.

Railroad workers formed the industrial American Railway Union (ARU) in 1893. The ARU unionized workers at the Pullman Palace Car Company in Illinois. The Pullman Company required workers to live in the town it built and to buy goods from its stores. When Pullman cut wages in 1893, workers could not afford their rent or the store's high prices. They began a strike. Other ARU members refused to pull Pullman cars. President Cleveland sent in troops, and a federal court issued an **injunction** ordering the strike to end. Both the strike and the union were ended.

New Unions Emerge (page 206)

Predicting

Make a prediction about women's working conditions in the 1800s.

_____

_____

_____

_____

_____

Trade unions were more successful in the late 1800s. In 1886, several of them organized the American Federation of Labor (AFL). The AFL had three goals: to get companies to recognize unions and agree to negotiations; to create **closed shops,** which hired only union members; and to promote an eight-hour workday. By 1900, the AFL was the largest union in the country, but most workers were not union members.

After the Civil War, more women began earning wages. About one-third of them worked as domestic servants. One-third were teachers, nurses, and sales clerks. The final third were industrial workers, mostly in clothing and food processing factories. Women were paid less than men and could not join most unions. In 1903, two women founded the Women's Trade Union League to address women's labor issues.

Section Wrap-up

Answer these questions to check your understanding of the entire section.

1. What were some barriers to labor union growth?

_____

_____

_____

2. What were some goals of labor unions?

_____

_____

_____

Informative Writing

In the space provided, write an encyclopedia entry about the growth of trade unions, including why they first formed and how the AFL originated.

_____

_____

_____

_____

_____

_____

_____

_____

_____

_____

_____

_____

Immigration

Big Idea

As you read pages 214–219 in your textbook, complete this graphic organizer by filling in the reasons people left their homelands to immigrate to the United States.

Reasons for Immigrating	
Push Factors	**Pull Factors**
1.	3.
2.	4.

 **Notes**

Read to Learn

Europeans Flood Into America (page 214)

Identifying the Main Idea

Write the main idea of this section.

_____

_____

_____

_____

_____

_____

_____

In the late 1800s, a major wave of immigration began. More than half of all immigrants were from eastern and southern Europe. They immigrated for a variety of reasons. Some came for jobs. Some came to avoid military service. Others, particularly Jews, fled religious persecution.

Most immigrants who came to the United States booked passage in **steerage.** This was the cheapest accommodations on a steamship. After about two weeks, they arrived at Ellis Island. This is a tiny island in New York harbor. Immigrants had to pass a medical exam. Most immigrants passed through Ellis Island in about a day.

Many immigrants settled in cities. There, they often lived in neighborhoods separated into ethnic groups, where they spoke their native languages, worshipped in familiar surroundings, and published ethnic newspapers. Immigrants who could learn English quickly and adapt to American culture generally adjusted well to life in the United States. So did those who had marketable skills or who settled among members of their own ethnic groups.

 **Notes** | **Read to Learn**

Asian Immigration (page 217)

Making Generalizations

Complete the sentence to make a generalization.

Many Asian immigrants came to the United States because _____ _____ _____ _____ _____ _____ .

Chinese immigrants came to the United States for many reasons. They often came to escape poverty and famine or to find jobs. An 1850 rebellion in China also caused many Chinese to move to the United States. In the 1860s, demand for workers on the transcontinental railroad further increased Chinese immigration. Chinese immigrants mainly settled in cities on the West Coast. They often worked as laborers or servants or in skilled trades. Others became merchants or opened businesses.

Japanese immigration to the United States increased greatly between 1900 and 1910. As Japan industrialized, economic problems caused many Japanese people to leave.

At first, Asian immigrants arrived at a two-story shed at the wharf in San Francisco. In 1910, California opened a barracks on Angel Island for Asian immigrants. Most immigrants were young men. They were often kept at Angel Island for months awaiting the results of immigration hearings. Some immigrants wrote poems on the barracks walls.

Nativism Resurges (page 218)

Comparing and Contrasting

Complete the sentences.

1. The two laws from 1882 were similar because _____ _____ _____ _____ _____

2. The two laws from 1882 were different because _____ _____ _____ _____

This new wave of immigration to the United States increased feelings of **nativism.** This is an extreme dislike for immigrants by native-born people. In the late 1800s, these feelings were mainly directed at Asians, Jews, and eastern Europeans.

Religious and ethnic prejudices and economic fears led to the desire to limit immigration. Some people feared the large number of Catholic immigrants from Europe. Labor unions argued that immigrants would work for low wages or accept jobs as strikebreakers. Some nativists formed anti-immigrant organizations. Members of the American Protective Association would not hire or vote for Catholic immigrants. The Workingman's Party of California worked to stop Chinese immigration.

Anti-immigrant feelings led Congress to pass new laws in 1882. One banned convicts, paupers, and the mentally disabled from immigrating. It also taxed new immigrants 50 cents. The other was the Chinese Exclusion Act. It barred Chinese immigration for ten years. It also prevented Chinese already in the country from becoming citizens. The Chinese in the country protested the law. They pointed out that laws did not ban European immigration. Yet Congress renewed the law and made it permanent in 1902. It was not repealed until 1943.

Section Wrap-up

Answer these questions to check your understanding of the entire section.

1. Describe the new wave of immigrants who came to the United States during the late 1800s.

_____

_____

_____

2. How did nativism affect immigration policies in the United States?

_____

_____

_____

In the space provided, write an editorial taking a position either for or against the immigration laws of 1882.

_____

_____

_____

_____

_____

_____

_____

_____

_____

_____

Urbanization

Big Idea

As you read pages 222–227 in your textbook, complete this graphic organizer by filling in some of the problems the nation's cities faced.

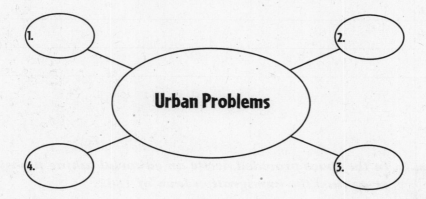

1.
2.

Urban Problems

4.
3.

 **Notes**

Read to Learn

Americans Migrate to the Cities (page 222)

Determining Cause and Effect

Explain the cause.

Cause: Cities offered

_____

_____

_____

_____

_____.

Effect: Many people migrated to cities.

The urban population of the United States had increased greatly by 1900. Most immigrants had neither the money to buy farms nor the education to get high paying jobs. They settled in the nation's growing cities and worked in factories. American farmers also moved to cities, looking for better paying jobs. Cities offered other benefits, such as running water and modern plumbing. They also had libraries, museums, and theaters.

As city populations grew, the land prices increased. Land was limited, so builders began to build up instead of out. Tall, steel frame buildings called **skyscrapers** began to appear. Chicago's Home Insurance Building, built in 1885, was the first of many such buildings.

To move people around cities, different kinds of transportation developed. At first, railroad cars pulled by horses were common. San Francisco and other cities began using cars pulled by underground cables. Other cities began using electric trolley cars. When congestion on streets became a problem, cities built elevated railroads or subway systems.

 **Notes** | # Read to Learn

Separation by Class *(page 224)*

Comparing and Contrasting

As you read, complete the sentences.

1. Many middle class families lived in

_____

2. Many working class families lived in

_____

Wealthy, middle class, and working class people lived in different parts of the cities. The wealthy lived in fashionable districts in cities' hearts. They built large, beautiful houses modeled after stylish European homes. For example, merchant Potter Palmer chose to model his Chicago home after a castle. In New York, Cornelius Vanderbilt's grandson's home included a two-story dining room, a gymnasium, and a solid marble bathroom.

The growing middle class included doctors, lawyers, engineers, teachers, and social workers. Many moved away from the central city to its suburbs. New commuter rail lines helped them travel back and forth to their jobs.

The working class generally lived in **tenements.** These were dark and crowded multifamily apartments. Many working families sent their children to work in factories or took in boarders to supplement their incomes.

Urban Problems *(page 226)*

Analyzing Information

Why did some city dwellers support political machines?

_____

_____

_____

_____

_____

_____

_____

_____

_____

People living in overcrowded city neighborhoods faced several problems, including crime, violence, fire, disease, and pollution. Both major and minor crimes increased as city populations grew.

Disease and pollution were even bigger threats. Improper disposal of sewage contaminated drinking water. This caused epidemics of diseases such as typhoid and cholera. Sources of pollution included horse manure on streets, chimney smoke, and soot and ash from coal or wood fires.

A new kind of political system took hold in cities. The **political machine** was an informal political group designed to gain and keep power. **Party bosses** provided people living in cities with jobs, food, housing, heat, and police protection. In exchange, they asked for votes. George Plunkett was one powerful New York City party boss.

Party bosses controlled the city's money. Machine politicians grew rich through fraud or **graft**—getting money by dishonest or questionable means. For example, a politician might find out where a park was being built. The politician would then buy the land and sell it to the city for a profit. Corrupt politicians often accepted bribes from contractors in exchange for city contracts.

One of the most famous political machines was Tammany Hall in New York City. William "Boss" Tweed was its corrupt leader. In some cities, the machines controlled all city services. Although corrupt, political machines provided necessary city services to the urban masses.

Answer these questions to check your understanding of the entire section.

1. What technological developments made the growth of cities possible?

_____

_____

_____

2. How did party bosses of the political machines grow wealthy?

_____

_____

_____

Suppose you are the child in a working class family, living in a large city around 1895. Describe some of the problems you face. Suggest possible solutions.

_____

_____

_____

_____

_____

_____

_____

_____

_____

_____

_____

The Gilded Age

Big Idea

As you read pages 230–239 in your textbook, complete this graphic organizer by filling in the main idea of each of the theories and movements listed.

Theory or Movement	Main Idea
Social Darwinism	1.
Laissez-Faire	2.
Gospel of Wealth	3.
Realism	4.

Notes

Read to Learn

Social Darwinism (page 230)

Synthesizing Information

Explain what Social Darwinists would think about regulating business.

_____

_____

_____

_____

_____

_____

The Gilded Age lasted from around 1870 to around 1900 and was named for a term from a novel by Mark Twain and Charles Warner. It was a time of new inventions, industrial growth, and growing cities. Something "gilded" is covered with gold only on the outside but made of cheap material on the inside. The writers meant that there was corruption, poverty, and crime beneath the Gilded Age's shiny surface.

New ideas took hold at this time. One of the strongest beliefs of the time was **individualism,** the idea that any person could succeed if he or she worked hard enough. Another powerful idea of the time was Herbert Spencer's **Social Darwinism.** Spencer applied Charles Darwin's ideas about evolution to human society. He claimed that human society evolved through competition and natural selection. The laissez-faire doctrine opposed government interference in business. Andrew Carnegie's Gospel of Wealth held that the wealthy should engage in **philanthropy** to help the society that made them rich.

Notes | Read to Learn

A Changing Culture (page 232)

Evaluating Information

Would The Adventures of Huckleberry Finn be a good book to read in history class? Circle your answer. List two reasons.

Yes   No

1. _____

2. _____

The nineteenth century was a time of great cultural change. Realism in art and literature became popular. This means artists and writers tried to portray the world more realistically. Thomas Eakins painted people doing everyday activities such as swimming. Realistic writers like Mark Twain tried to show the world as it was. His novel *The Adventures of Huckleberry Finn* presented realistic characters, dialect, and setting.

At this time, industrialization provided people with more money for recreation and entertainment. Saloons played a major role in the lives of workers and served as political centers. Families in the late 1800s enjoyed amusement parks. Many people enjoyed watching professional sports such as baseball and football. Some played tennis, golf, and basketball. Vaudeville and Scott Joplin's ragtime music also provided entertainment.

Politics in Washington (page 234)

Problems and Solutions

As you read, write the problem each act was intended to solve.

Pendleton Act:

_____

_____

Interstate Commerce Act:

_____

_____

Sherman Antitrust Act:

_____

_____

Under the spoils system, elected politicians had the power of patronage. This meant the winning party gave government jobs to those who had supported them. When Rutherford B. Hayes was elected President in 1877, he appointed reformers to his cabinet. His actions divided the Republican Party into two camps. The "Stalwarts" supported patronage. The "Halfbreeds," including Hayes, opposed patronage.

In 1880, Garfield, a Halfbreed, won the presidency. His vice president was a Stalwart. Garfield was assassinated by an unhappy job seeker. The assassin thought he could get a job at the White House if a Stalwart were President. Congress soon passed the Pendleton Act, which set up the civil service system. People applying for jobs had to pass an exam.

The Republicans and Democrats were very competitive in the late 1800s. In 1884, Democrat Grover Cleveland won the presidency. He faced many problems in office. Americans were upset about railroad rates and the power of big businesses such as Standard Oil. In 1887, Cleveland signed the Interstate Commerce Act, which limited railroad rates. Debate over tariff reduction was the major issue in the 1888 presidential election. Republican Benjamin Harrison won. In 1890, Congress passed the Sherman Antitrust Act to curb the power of trusts like Standard Oil. The law was ineffective.

The Rebirth of Reform *(page 236)*

Identifying the Main Idea

Complete the sentence.

The purpose of the new reform movements was _____ _____ _____ _____

The changes brought by industrialization led to debate over how to address society's problems. Henry George thought laissez-faire economics was making society worse, not better. Lester Frank Ward challenged Social Darwinism, too. He believed government regulation should replace wasteful competition. His ideas were called Reform Darwinism. A new style of writing called naturalism criticized industrial society. Its writers included Jack London and Stephen Crane. Jane Addams led the **settlement house** movement. It provided medial care, classes, and recreation programs for the poor. Increased public education furthered **Americanization,** in which immigrant children learned about American culture.

Section Wrap-up

Answer these questions to check your understanding of the entire section.

1. How did industrialism promote leisure time and new forms of entertainment?

   _____

   _____

2. Why was the Gilded Age a good description of this period in history?

   _____

   _____

Informative Writing

Suppose you just read a history book about the Gilded Age. Write a book review. Describe the main points of the book and how accurately the "author" described the period.

_____

_____

_____

_____

_____

_____

_____

Populism

Big Idea

As you read pages 242–247 in your textbook, complete this outline by using the major headings of the section.

Populism

I. **Unrest in Rural America**
   A. _____
   B. _____
   C. _____
   D. _____
   E. _____
II. _____
   A. _____
   B. _____
   C. _____
III. _____
   A. _____
   B. _____

 **Notes**

Read to Learn

Unrest in Rural America *(page 242)*

Determining Cause and Effect

As you read, complete the sentences.

Deflation hit farmers hard because

_____

_____

_____.

_____ *because they were too small to affect prices.*

Populism was a movement to increase farmers' political power and to pass laws in their interest. During the Civil War, the government issued **greenbacks,** paper money not backed gold or silver. This caused **inflation,** a decline in the value of money. Prices of goods rose. After the war, the government stopped printing greenbacks, paid off bonds, and stopped minting silver coins. As the economy grew, **deflation** occurred. The value of money increased and prices fell.

Deflation hurt farmers. Many had to borrow money for seeds and supplies. Falling prices meant farmers sold their crops for less. Many farmers joined the Grange. It organized **cooperatives** that worked for the benefit of their members. The Grange pressured state legislatures to regulate railroad rates. Cooperatives pooled crops and kept them off the market to force prices up. Many Grange cooperatives failed because they were too small to affect prices. Railroads and businessmen also refused to deal with them. In the 1880s, the Farmers' Alliance formed and organized larger cooperatives, which also failed.

The Rise of Populism (page 245)

Comparing and Contrasting

List characteristics of Farmers' Alliance members in the South and the West.

South: _____

_____

West: _____

_____

Both: _____

_____

_____

Farmers' Alliance members in the West formed the People's Party, or the Populists. They nominated candidates for Congress and state offices. Alliance leaders in the South did not want a third party. They wanted to produce a list of demands and vote for candidates that supported them. Part of their strategy was the subtreasury plan. It asked the government to set up warehouses to store crops and provide farmers with low interest loans. Southern Alliance leaders also called for free coinage of silver, an end to protective tariffs and national banks, more regulation of railroads, and direct election of senators. That year, the Populists in the West elected representatives. Alliance members in the South elected Democrats. Many Southern Democrats did not support the Alliance program once they took office.

In 1892, the People's Party held a national convention in Omaha, Nebraska. Its platform called for coinage of silver and a **graduated income tax.** This taxes higher earnings more heavily. The Democrats and Grover Cleveland won the election.

The Election of 1896 (page 246)

Making Inferences

Complete the inference.

Populists supported Bryan instead of nominating their own candidate because

_____

_____

_____

_____

_____

As the election of 1896 approached, leaders of the People's Party decided to make free coinage of silver an important issue. They held their convention after the Republican and Democratic conventions. The Republicans supported the gold standard, nominating William McKinley as their candidate. The Democratic Party nominated William Jennings Bryan, a strong supporter of free silver. The Populist Party decided to support Bryan instead of nominating a separate candidate. Bryan was a powerful speaker. In an electrifying address in defense of silver, Bryan said "you shall not crucify mankind on a cross of gold." He carried his campaign across the country. But this crusade only irritated many immigrants and city people.

McKinley launched a "Front Porch Campaign." He greeted delegations at his home. Many employers warned workers that if Bryan won, businesses would fail and unemployment would rise. Most workers and business leaders supported the Republican Party. McKinley won the election. Bryan and the Democrats lost in the northeastern industrial region. The Populist Party declined after 1896. Some of the reforms they favored were adopted later.

Answer these questions to check your understanding of the entire section.

1. Why did the farmers form cooperatives after the Civil War? How successful were these organizations?

_____

_____

_____

2. Who joined the Populist Party and what were its goals?

_____

_____

_____

In the space provided, write an encyclopedia entry explaining the events that led to the rise of the Populist Party.

_____

_____

_____

_____

_____

_____

_____

_____

_____

_____

_____

The Rise of Segregation

Big Idea

As you read pages 248–253 in your textbook, complete this web diagram by listing the ways that states disenfranchised African Americans and legalized discrimination.

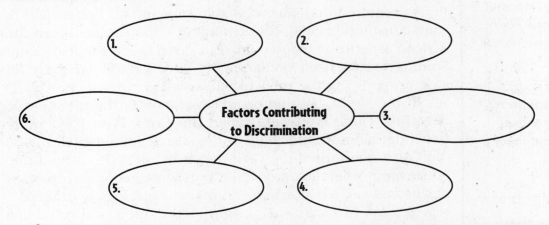

1.

2.

6.

Factors Contributing to Discrimination

3.

5.

4.

 **Notes**

Read to Learn

Resistance and Repression (page 248)

Analyzing Information

Why did Democratic Party leaders fear the coalition of poor whites and African American Populists?

_____

_____

_____

_____

_____

_____

_____

After Reconstruction, many African Americans were very poor and lived under great hardship. Most were sharecroppers, or landless farmers. They worked the land and turned over a large part of their crop to the landlord to pay for rent and supplies.

In 1879, Benjamin "Pap" Singleton, who had formerly been enslaved, organized a large migration of African Americans from the rural South to Kansas. They became known as the Exodusters. Some African Americans joined with the poor white farmers in the Farmers' Alliance. In 1886, a group formed the Colored Farmers' National Alliance. Many African Americans joined the Populist Party in 1891.

Democrats feared the coalition of poor whites and African American Populists. To break it up, Democratic leaders began to appeal to racism. They warned southern whites that the Populist Party would bring back "Black Republican" rule. They made it sound like the return of the Reconstruction period. In addition, election officials found ways to make it difficult for African Americans to vote.

Imposing Segregation *(page 250)*

Drawing Conclusions

Draw a conclusion based on these facts:

Fact: States imposed poll taxes and literacy requirements on voters.

Fact: Election officials were not strict in applying these rules to white voters.

Conclusion:

_____

_____

_____

The Fifteenth Amendment prohibited states from denying people the right to vote based on race, color, or former servitude, but not based on other grounds. Soon, states began imposing other voting restrictions that were intended to keep African Americans from voting. Mississippi charged a $2 **poll tax,** a sum beyond the means of most poor African Americans. It also required that voters be able to read and understand the state constitution. With few schooling opportunities, even those African Americans who could read often failed the tests. Other Southern states used similar tactics. Election officials were less strict in applying the rules to white voters.

In the South, laws enforced separation of the races, or **segregation.** These laws were called **Jim Crow laws.** Two Supreme Court decisions set the stage for legalized segregation. In 1883, the Court overturned the Civil Rights Act of 1875. It held the Fourteenth Amendment covered only state actions, so private businesses such as hotels or railroads could legally practice segregation. In *Plessy* v. *Ferguson* (1896), the Court ruled that "separate but equal" facilities were legal. Separate facilities were often far from equal.

The African American Response *(page 252)*

Comparing and Contrasting

As you read, complete the sentences.

Booker T. Washington thought African Americans should

_____

_____

W.E.B. Du Bois believed African Americans should

_____

_____

African Americans increasingly faced mob violence or **lynchings.** These executions by mobs occurred without proper court action. In 1892, Ida B. Wells, an African American woman from Tennessee, started a campaign against lynching. She published a book condemning the mob violence. Wells called for a fair trial for those accused of crimes. The number of lynchings decreased in the 1900s due in part to her work.

Booker T. Washington was a well-known African American educator. He believed African Americans should try to achieve economic rather than political goals. In 1895, Washington summed up his views in a speech called the Atlanta Compromise. He urged African Americans to delay the fight for civil rights. He said they should focus instead on vocational education to prepare themselves for equal treatment.

Other African American leaders such as W.E.B. DuBois rejected Washington's ideas. DuBois believed African Americans could achieve equality only by demanding their rights, especially voting rights. Many African Americans continued to work to restore the right to vote and to end discrimination.

Section Wrap-up

Answer these questions to check your understanding of the entire section.

1. How were African Americans in the South prevented from exercising their voting rights?

_____

_____

_____

2. What was the Supreme Court's role in legalizing segregation?

_____

_____

_____

Write a journal entry giving your reaction to a speech by a major African American leader from the late 1800s about racial discrimination in the United States.

_____

_____

_____

_____

_____

_____

_____

_____

_____

_____

_____

The Imperialist Vision

Big Idea

As you read pages 262–267 in your textbook, complete the outline below using the major headings of the section.

The Imperialism Vision

I. Building Support for Imperialism

   A. _____

   B. _____

   C. _____

II. _____

   A. _____

   B. _____

III. _____

 **Notes**

Read to Learn

Building Support for Imperialism *(page 262)*

Determining Cause and Effect

List three causes of European expansion.

1. _____
_____
_____

2. _____
_____
_____

3. _____
_____
_____

In the 1800s, nations in Europe expanded overseas. This growth became known as the New Imperialism. **Imperialism** is a strong nation's economic and political domination over weaker ones. It had several causes. Europe needed more raw materials than it could produce. Tariffs hurt trade between industrial countries. These countries looked overseas for new markets. Europe was also running out of investment opportunities, so Europeans invested in other countries. To protect these investments, Europe made the countries into colonies and **protectorates.** In a protectorate, the imperial power let local rulers stay in control.

The United States also wanted to find new markets in other countries. Some Americans used the ideas of Social Darwinism to justify expansion. Others believed that English-speaking countries were naturally superior and should control other countries.

American leaders thought the United States needed a powerful navy. A navy could protect the country's merchant ships and defend its right to trade with other countries. By the late 1890s, the United States was becoming a great naval power.

American Expansion in the Pacific *(page 265)*

Predicting

Complete the statement.

If Queen Liliuokalani had held on to power in Hawaii,_____

_____

_____

_____

_____

_____

_____

_____

_____

In the 1800s, Japan traded only with the Chinese and the Dutch. In 1853, President Fillmore decided to force Japan to trade with the United States. He sent a naval expedition to negotiate a treaty. When they saw the four warships, the Japanese knew they could not compete against such technology. Japan opened two ports to American trade.

Americans were also interested in Hawaii. Sugarcane grew well in Hawaii's climate. By the mid-1800s, there were many sugarcane plantations. In 1875, the United States removed tariffs on Hawaiian sugar. The islands' sugar industry boomed. Planters grew wealthy. In 1887, the planters made the Hawaiian king sign a constitution limiting his power. An 1890 tariff gave subsidies to U.S. sugar growers. Hawaiian sugar became more expensive than American sugar. Sales of Hawaiian sugar decreased, and the Hawaiian economy weakened.

In 1891, Queen Liliuokalani became the ruler of Hawaii. She disliked American influence in Hawaii and tried to create a new constitution that reestablished her authority. The planters responded by overthrowing the government and forcing the queen to give up power. Then they set up their own government. The United States annexed Hawaii five years later.

Diplomacy in Latin America *(page 267)*

Problems and Solutions

Write the solution James G. Blaine proposed.

Problem: Latin America was not buying enough products from the United States.

Solution:

_____

_____

_____

The United States wanted more influence in Latin America. While the United States bought many raw materials from Latin American countries, those countries got most of their manufactured goods from Europe. The United States wanted to sell more products in Latin America. It also wanted Europeans to see the United States as the main power in the region. The idea that the United States and Latin American countries should work together became known as Pan-Americanism.

In 1889, the United States invited Latin American countries to a conference in Washington, D.C. James G. Blaine was secretary of state at that time. He had two goals for the conference. He wanted a customs union that would allow the countries to trade freely. He also wanted a system to solve disagreements among American nations. Latin American countries rejected these ideas. They did agree to create an organization to help countries in the Western Hemisphere work together. It was called the Commercial Bureau of the American Republics. Today it is known as the Organization of American States.

Section Wrap-up

Answer these questions to check your understanding of the entire section.

1. How did a desire for more trade and markets change the way the United States acted toward other countries?

   _____

   _____

   _____

2. What were the motivations for American expansion in the Pacific?

   _____

   _____

   _____

In the space provided, write a journal entry about the planters' overthrow of Queen Liliuokalani. Write from the point of view of either a planter or a native Hawaiian loyal to the queen.

_____

_____

_____

_____

_____

_____

_____

_____

_____

The Spanish-American War

Big Idea

As you read pages 268–275 in your textbook, complete this graphic organizer by listing the circumstances that contributed to war with Spain.

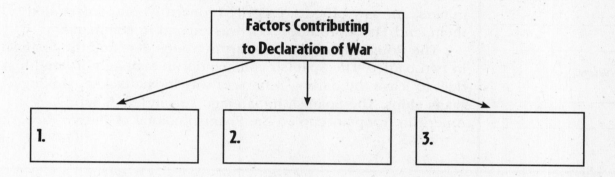

Factors Contributing to Declaration of War

1.

2.

3.

 **Notes**   **Read to Learn**

The Coming of War (page 268)

Drawing Conclusions

Complete the sentence.

Spain offered Cuba autonomy because

_____

_____

_____

_____

_____

_____

_____

_____

Cuba began fighting for independence from Spain in 1868. In 1878, the rebellion collapsed. Many rebels fled to the United States. Americans had invested millions of dollars in Cuba's railroads and sugar plantations. They bought Cuban sugar. Then a new tariff on sugar caused the sale of Cuban sugar to fall. This hurt Cuba's economy. Rebels rose up against Spain again in February 1895 and declared Cuba independent.

Americans read stories of Spanish brutality in newspapers. This sensational reporting became known as **yellow journalism.** Although many stories were exaggerated, Cubans suffered greatly. President McKinley warned Spain that the United States might intervene. Spain removed the Spanish governor of Cuba and offered Cuba **autonomy,** or self-rule, if it agreed to remain part of the Spanish empire. The Cubans refused.

In 1898, riots started in Havana. McKinley sent the battleship *Maine* to evacuate Americans in Cuba. When it exploded in Havana's harbor, Americans blamed Spain. **Jingoism,** or aggressive nationalism contributed to the push for war. Congress declared war on Spain on April 19.

Notes | Read to Learn

A War on Two Fronts *(page 271)*

Comparing and Contrasting

Compare how the U.S. Army and Navy performed during war.

U.S. Army:_____

_____

_____

U.S. Navy:_____

_____

_____

Spain was not prepared for war, but the U.S. Navy was. A U.S. Navy fleet blockaded Cuba. Another fleet attacked and destroyed the Spanish fleet in the Philippines. With the help of local rebels, the navy fleet took control of the Filipino capital, Manila.

The U.S. Army was not as ready for war as the navy was. However, on June 14, 1898, about 17,000 soldiers landed in Santiago, Cuba. A volunteer cavalry regiment called the "Rough Riders" accompanied them. They were a group of cowboys, miners, and law officers. Colonel Leonard Wood commanded them, and Theodore Roosevelt was second in command.

The Rough Riders and the army troops defeated the Spanish in two battles. The Spanish commander in Santiago ordered his fleet to leave the harbor. American warships attacked, sinking many ships. The Spanish in Santiago surrendered. Soon American troops occupied the Spanish colony of Puerto Rico.

An American Empire *(page 273)*

Making Generalizations

Make a generalization about nations living under imperialist rule.

_____

_____

_____

_____

_____

_____

_____

_____

_____

After the war, Cuba obtained its freedom, and the United States annexed Guam and Puerto Rico. The question of what to do with the Philippines remained open. Some Americans pushed for annexing the Philippines. Others opposed it. When the United States signed the Treaty of Paris with Spain in 1898, it agreed to pay $20 million to annex the Philippines.

Although Cuba became independent, President McKinley made sure it remained tied to the United States. He allowed Cuba to set up a new constitution under conditions that effectively made Cuba a protectorate of the United States. These conditions became known as the Platt Amendment. Cuba reluctantly added the amendment to its constitution.

The United States had to decide how to govern Puerto Rico. At first it was governed by a U.S.-appointed official. Congress gradually gave Puerto Rico more self-government. The debate over whether Puerto Rico should become a state, an independent country, or remain a commonwealth continues today.

In the Philippines, rebels fought the United States for control of the islands. The United States responded by treating the Filipinos much like Spain had treated the Cubans. Thousands died in reconcentration camps. The United States instituted reforms in the Philippines, which eased Filipino hostility toward it. Over the years, the United States gave the Filipinos more control. It finally granted independence to the Philippines in 1946.

Section Wrap-up

Answer these questions to check your understanding of the entire section.

1. What were two reasons that the United States went to war with Spain in 1898?

_____

_____

_____

2. How did the war make the United States a world power?

_____

_____

_____

In the space provided, write a newspaper editorial from the point of view of a person living in the United States in 1898. Express an opinion for or against annexing the Philippines. Give reasons to support your position.

_____

_____

_____

_____

_____

_____

_____

_____

_____

_____

New American Diplomacy

Big Idea

As you read pages 276–283 in your textbook, complete this graphic organizer by listing the reasons the U.S. wanted a canal through Central America.

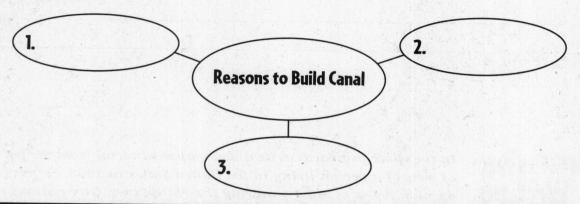

1.

2.

Reasons to Build Canal

3.

 **Notes**   **Read to Learn**

American Diplomacy in Asia *(page 276)*

Identifying the Main Idea

Write the main idea of the first paragraph.

_____

_____

_____

_____

_____

_____

_____

In 1894 China and Japan went to war over Korea, part of the Chinese empire. Japan easily defeated China. The peace treaty gave Japan a region of China called Manchuria. Russia opposed this because Manchuria bordered Russia. The Russians forced Japan to return Manchuria, then demanded that China lease it to Russia. The territory would still belong to China but be under Russian control. Then Germany, France, and Britain also wanted China to lease territory to them. Each leased area became the center of a **sphere of influence** where a foreign nation controlled economic development.

The United States supported an **Open Door policy** in which all countries could trade with China. The U.S. Secretary of State asked nations with leaseholds in China to allow other nations to trade freely within China. In the meantime, secret Chinese societies such as the Boxers were working to rid China of foreign control. In the 1900 Boxer Rebellion, the Boxers seized foreign embassies in Beijing and killed more than 200 foreigners. An international force crushed the rebellion.

Notes | Read to Learn

Roosevelt's Diplomacy (page 278)

Formulating Questions

Write a question you have about dollar diplomacy.

_____

_____

_____

_____

_____

_____

_____

_____

_____

In the election of 1900, Theodore Roosevelt was President McKinley's running mate. They won. On September 6, 1901, McKinley was shot by an anarchist. He died a few days later. At 42, Roosevelt became the youngest president ever. Roosevelt supported the Open Door policy in China. He also helped to end a war between Japan and Russia in 1905.

In 1903, Roosevelt decided to build a canal through Panama, which was then part of Colombia. The United States offered Colombia $10 million and a yearly rent for the right to build the canal. Colombia refused the offer. The people of Panama, however, wanted the benefits of having a canal. They also wanted independence from Colombia. Officials in Panama planned an uprising. Roosevelt sent ships to prevent Colombia from interfering. The United States recognized Panama's independence, and the two nations signed a treaty allowing the canal to be built.

Roosevelt's approach to diplomacy came to be called the Roosevelt Corollary. It stated that the United States would intervene in Latin America when necessary to help the Western Hemisphere stay stable. President Taft continued Roosevelt's policies but focused more on industry development than military force. This became known as **dollar diplomacy.**

Woodrow Wilson's Diplomacy in Mexico (page 282)

Analyzing Information

List three reasons why Wilson's diplomacy in Mexico was unsuccessful.

1. _____

_____

2. _____

_____

3. _____

_____

Porfirio Díaz ruled Mexico until 1911. Under his rule, most Mexicans were poor and landless. They revolted. Francisco Madero replaced Díaz, but he proved to be a poor leader. General Victoriano Huerta had Madero murdered and seized power. President Wilson opposed imperialism, but he believed that the United States should promote democracy. He therefore refused to recognize Huerta's government. In April 1914, American sailors visiting Mexico were arrested for entering a restricted area. Mexico quickly released them, but refused to apologize. Wilson used this as an opportunity to overthrow Huerta. Anti-American riots followed this action. Venustiano Carranza became the Mexican president.

Mexican forces opposed to Carranza carried out raids into the United States. **Guerrillas** led by Pancho Villa burned the town of Columbus, New Mexico. Sixteen Americans died. Guerrilla fighters use surprise attacks and sabotage instead of open warfare. Wilson sent troops into Mexico to capture Villa, but they failed. Wilson's actions in Mexico damaged U.S. foreign relations. However, Wilson continued to intervene in Latin American countries in an attempt to promote democracy.

Section Wrap-up

Answer these questions to check your understanding of the entire section.

1. How did Theodore Roosevelt's foreign policy affect the role of the United States in the world?

_____

_____

_____

2. What was the Open Door policy?

_____

_____

_____

In the space provided, compare Roosevelt's approach to diplomacy with Wilson's dealings with Mexico.

_____

_____

_____

_____

_____

_____

_____

_____

_____

_____

The Roots of Progressivism

Big Idea

As you read pages 292–299 in your textbook, complete this graphic organizer by filling in the beliefs of the Progressives.

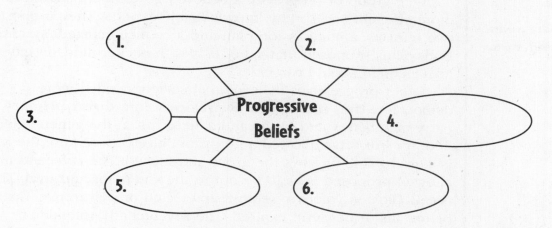

1.

2.

3.

Progressive Beliefs

4.

5.

6.

Notes   Read to Learn

The Rise of Progressivism *(page 292)*

Evaluating Information

Were muckrakers good for society? Circle your answer. Underline parts of the text that support your answer.

Yes   No

Progressivism was a mix of ideas and views about how to fix the nation's problems. Most progressives believed that industrialism and urbanization had caused many social problems. Although they focused on different issues, they all believed that the government should play an active role in solving most of society's problems. They also believed people should fix society's problems by applying scientific principles to them.

Journalists were the first to express Progressive ideas. These journalists, known as **muckrakers,** examined social conditions and political corruption. They uncovered corruption in many areas. Some looked into the unfair practices of large corporations. Ida Tarbell published articles about the practices of the Standard Oil Company. Some investigated the government. Lincoln Steffens reported on vote stealing and other corrupt political practices. Others focused on social problems. Jacob Riis wrote about the poverty and disease that were part of many immigrant neighborhoods in New York City. The work of muckrakers pressured politicians to start reforms.

Reforming Government *(page 294)*

Distinguishing Fact from Opinion

Underline one opinion held by progressives.

Circle one fact about progressive reforms.

In most cities, the mayor or city council chose the heads of city departments. They often hired political supporters and friends. These people often knew nothing about managing city services. Bosses of political parties controlled who ran for office. Political machines influenced the election of senators.

One group of progressives believed government should be more efficient and run by knowledgable experts. They proposed two reforms: a commission plan and a council-manager system. Both plans proposed that specialists with backgrounds in city management should run cities.

Other progressives believed that society needed more democracy. They introduced five reforms. In a **direct primary,** party members voted for a candidate to run in the general election. An **initiative** allowed a group of citizens to require the legislature to vote on laws the group introduced. The **referendum** allowed proposed laws to be put to the voters for approval. The **recall** allowed voters to remove an elected official from office before his or her term expired. The Seventeenth Amendment gave voters the right to elect their senators directly.

Suffrage *(page 296)*

Comparing and Contrasting

Tell how each group wanted to achieve women's suffrage.

National Woman Suffrage Association:

_____

_____

_____

American Woman Suffrage Association:

_____

_____

_____

The first women's rights convention met in Seneca Falls, New York, in 1848. It launched the **suffrage** (right to vote) movement. The convention's top goal, and that of many women progressives, was getting women the right to vote.

The movement got off to a slow start. It split into two groups when Congress passed the Fourteenth and Fifteenth Amendments to the Constitution. These amendments aimed to protect voting rights of African Americans. The National Woman Suffrage Association wanted Congress to pass an amendment guaranteeing women the right to vote. The American Woman Suffrage Association wanted state governments to grant women suffrage.

In 1890 the two groups joined to form the National American Woman Suffrage Association (NAWSA). NAWSA started slowly, but many women realized that they needed suffrage to push for social reform and for labor laws to protect them.

NAWSA threw its support behind President Wilson in the election of 1916. However, support for an amendment began to grow in Congress. In 1919, the Senate passed the Nineteenth Amendment guaranteeing women the right to vote. The states ratified it in 1920.

Chapter 8, Section 1

Reforming Society *(page 298)*

Problems and Solutions

List three social problems that concerned progressives.

1. _____
   _____

2. _____
   _____

3. _____
   _____

Many progressives focused on specific social problems. One was child labor. Many children worked in dangerous and unhealthy conditions. States began passing laws setting age and hour limits for working children. Progressives also pushed for health and safety codes for workers of all ages, such as laws to protect workers injured on the job. Some progressives believed alcohol caused many problems in American life. The temperance movement supported the moderation or elimination of alcohol consumption. The temperance movement later pushed for **prohibition,** or laws making it illegal to make, sell, or consume alcohol.

Many progressives wanted to reform the economy. They believed big businesses needed regulation and pushed the government to break up large companies. Some went further and supported socialism. This was the idea that the government should own and operate industry.

Section Wrap-up

Answer these questions to check your understanding of the entire section.

1. Why did the Progressive movement arise?

_____

_____

2. How were the Progressive and suffrage movements alike?

_____

_____

In the space provided, write a brief paragraph to include in a Progressive Era pamphlet either in favor of or against woman suffrage.

_____

_____

_____

_____

_____

_____

_____

Roosevelt and Taft

Big Idea

As you read pages 300–307 in your textbook, use the major headings of the section to complete the outline below.

Roosevelt in Office

I. **Roosevelt Revives the Presidency**
   A. _____
   B. _____
   C. _____

II. _____
   A. _____

III. _____
   A. _____
   B. _____
   C. _____
   D. _____

Notes

Read to Learn

Roosevelt Revives the Presidency (page 300)

Identifying the Main Idea

Write the main idea in this passage.

_____
_____
_____
_____
_____
_____
_____
_____

President Roosevelt believed in both progressivism and **Social Darwinism.** He thought large corporations, helped the United States prosper. He also thought the government should balance the needs of groups in American society. His reforms programs were known as the Square Deal.

Roosevelt did not hesitate to enforce the law. When the railroad company Northern Securities tried to form a monopoly, Roosevelt sued them under the Sherman Antitrust Act. Other times he negotiated. He struck a deal with U.S. Steel that allowed the government to go over its books privately. This prevented a lawsuit and the disruption of the economy.

Roosevelt also felt it was his duty as the nation's "head manager" to prevent conflict. A union of coal mine workers—the United Mine Workers—launched a strike in eastern Pennsylvania. It led to a potential crisis in the supply of the nation's coal. As the strike wore on, Roosevelt asked the union and the owners to agree to **arbitration**—a settlement imposed by an outside party. The owners eventually agreed to a settlement.

Conservation *(page 304)*

Detecting Bias

Put an X by the statement Roosevelt would most likely agree with.

____ *The need for timber now outweighs the health of timber supplies.*

____ *Protecting the environment is an investment in the future.*

Roosevelt also cared about environmental conservation. He was alarmed at the rate at which natural resources were being used. He introduced reform to save the nation's forests through timber management. He also added over 100 million acres to the protected national forests, established five new national parks, and established 51 federal wildlife reserves.

Taft's Reforms *(page 305)*

Making Generalizations

Make a generalization about Taft's presidency.

_____

_____

_____

_____

_____

_____

_____

_____

_____

_____

President Roosevelt and President Taft agreed on many Progressive issues and were close friends. However, they disagreed on some subjects. One was tariffs. Taft believed high tariffs limited competition and protected trusts. His attempt to lower tariffs divided progressives and conservative Republicans. Taft signed the Payne-Aldrich Tariff into law, but it reduced some tariffs only a little and actually raised others.

Taft replaced Roosevelt's conservationist secretary of the interior with a more conservative corporate lawyer, Richard A. Ballinger. This made some progressives unhappy. One official, Gifford Pinchot, accused Ballinger of wrongdoing. Although the attorney general found his charges groundless, Pinchot leaked the story to the press. Taft fired Pinchot for **insubordination,** or disobedience.

Taft did have some successes. He pursued progressive policies on child labor and established the Children's Bureau. Like Roosevelt, Taft was a dedicated conservationist. He expanded national forests and protected waterpower sites.

Yet his friendship with Roosevelt was damaged. Roosevelt was so annoyed by some of Taft's policies, he ran for president again in the 1912 election. Both he and Taft lost to Woodrow Wilson.

Answer these questions to check your understanding of the entire section.

1. What efforts did Roosevelt make to regulate concentrated corporate power?

   _____

   _____

   _____

2. How did both Roosevelt and Taft promote environmental conservation?

   _____

   _____

   _____

Descriptive Writing

Suppose you are a journalist interviewing President Roosevelt about his political beliefs. Write a brief summary of your interview.

_____

_____

_____

_____

_____

_____

_____

_____

_____

_____

The Wilson Years

Big Idea

As you read pages 308–313 in your textbook, complete this chart by listing Wilson's progressive economic and social reforms.

Economic Reforms	Social Reforms
1.	5.
2.	6.
3.	7.
4.	

Notes

Read to Learn

The Election of 1912 (page 308)

Formulating Questions

Write one question you have based on the passage. Then write a short answer to it.

Question:

_____

_____

Answer:

_____

_____

_____

The election of 1912 featured a current president, a former president, and an academic with limited political experience. Former President Roosevelt was disappointed with President Taft's performance. He decided to run as the leader of the newly formed Progressive Party. Because Taft had alienated so many groups, the race was truly between Roosevelt and Woodrow Wilson.

Both Roosevelt and Wilson supported progressivism. Yet they each had their own approach to reform. Roosevelt accepted the trusts as a fact of life. Roosevelt called his reform the New Nationalism. Wilson countered with his plan, the New Freedom. He argued that Roosevelt's approach gave the government too much power in the economy and did nothing to facilitate competition. He promised to restore this competition by breaking up the monopolies.

Roosevelt and Taft wound up splitting the Republican vote. This enabled Wilson to win the Electoral College and the election, even though he only won 42% of the popular vote.

Wilson's Reforms (page 310)

Copyright © Glencoe/McGraw-Hill, a division of The McGraw-Hill Companies, Inc.

Determining Cause and Effect

Write the effects of these three acts.

Underwood Tariff Act

_____

_____

_____

Federal Reserve Act

_____

_____

_____

Adamson Act

_____

_____

_____

As president, Wilson continued to push for progressive reform. He reduced tariffs and levied an **income tax**—a direct tax on the earnings of individuals—with the Underwood Tariff Act, reformed the banks with the Federal Reserve Act, and created the Federal Trade Commission to help regulate the trusts. He also signed the Adamson Act, which established the eight-hour work-day for railroad workers.

He lobbied members of Congress personally to pass the tariff act. The act reduced most tariffs by 30%, which Wilson believed would benefit the American economy. The Federal Reserve Act established regional federal banks, where other banks could put a portion of their deposits to protect them against losses.

Once Wilson was in office, he came to agree with Roosevelt's view regarding trusts. He felt that regulating the trusts was more efficient and safer than trying to break them up. To help do this, Wilson established the Federal Trade Commission (FTC). The FTC was a board that had the power to investigate companies and issue "cease and desist" orders to companies engaging in **unfair trade practices,** or those which hurt competition. Companies that disagreed with the FTC could take the commission to court.

Some progressives, unsatisfied by Wilson's approach, passed the Clayton Antitrust Act in 1914, which outlawed certain practices that restricted competition.

Progressivism's Legacy and Limits (page 312)

Analyzing Information

Explain one way Progressivism was limited.

_____

_____

_____

_____

_____

_____

Like Roosevelt, Wilson expanded the role of the president. He also broadened the role of the federal government. Before the Progressive Era, most Americans did not expect the government to pass laws to protect workers. They also did not expect it to regulate big business. In fact, many courts reversed such laws. However, by the end of the era both public opinion and legal opinion had shifted. Americans came to expect the federal government to play an active role in regulating the economy. They also expected the government to solve social problems.

Despite its successes, the Progressive movement failed to address racial issues. Even so, African Americans began to demand changes. In 1905 W.E.B. Du Bois and other African Americans met at Niagra Falls. They wanted to develop a plan that would help African Americans gain full rights. This meeting led to the founding of the National Association for the Advancement of Colored People (NAACP) in 1909. Du Bois, as well as other NAACP founders, worked to ensure African Americans voting rights and to end lynching.

Answer these questions to check your understanding of the entire section.

1. What were President Wilson's social and economic reforms?

_____

_____

_____

2. How would you evaluate the legacy of the Progressive movement?

_____

_____

_____

In the space provided, write a short address President Wilson might have given toward the end of his time in office. Explain how the president's views on trusts changed during his presidency.

_____

_____

_____

_____

_____

_____

_____

_____

_____

_____

_____

The United States Enters World War I

Big Idea

As you read pages 320–327 in your textbook, complete this graphic organizer by identifying some factors that contributed to the conflict.

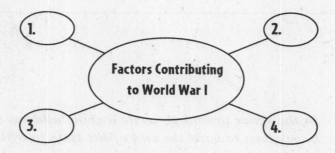

1.
2.
3.
4.

Factors Contributing to World War I

Notes   Read to Learn

World War I Begins (page 320)

Making Inferences

Explain why the heir to the Austro-Hungarian throne was killed.

_____

_____

_____

_____

_____

_____

_____

_____

_____

In the late 1800s, Germany and France were enemies. Germany joined Italy and Austria-Hungary in the Triple Alliance. France, Russia, and Great Britain formed the Triple Entente. This system of alliances encouraged **militarism**—the buildup of armed forces.

Nationalism is intense pride in one's homeland. Imperialism led European powers to form empires. These factors led to conflict in southeastern Europe between the ruling Ottoman and Austro-Hungarian empires and the newly independent nation of Serbia. Austria-Hungary took control of the nation of Bosnia to stop the Serbs from uniting with it. The Serbs were angry. In June 1914, a Bosnian member of a Serbian nationalist group killed the heir to the Austro-Hungarian throne.

Several nations became involved. They formed alliances and declared war. France, Russia, Great Britain, and Italy became the Allies. Germany, Austria-Hungary, the Ottoman Empire, and Bulgaria became the Central Powers. Eventually, both sides became locked in a stalemate in France. In Russia, the Germans and Austrians swept across hundreds of miles of land and took thousands of prisoners.

America Declares War (page 324)

Drawing Conclusions

List two reasons Americans supported the Allies as World War I began.

1. _____

_____

_____

2. _____

_____

_____

Write a conclusion about how this influenced U.S. policy.

3. _____

_____

_____

_____

Determining Cause and Effect

Underline the sentence that describes why Americans became so angry about the Zimmerman Telegram.

As World War I began, President Wilson declared the United States neutral. However, many Americans supported one side or the other. Most Americans favored the Allies. Most of President Wilson's cabinet supported the Allies, too. The British worked to win U.S. support. They used **propaganda,** information designed to influence opinion. Britain also cut the transatlantic telegraph cable from Europe to the United States. This limited the news about the war mainly to British communications. Although many reports were exaggerated, many Americans believed them.

Businesses also supported the Allies because they had ties with businesses in the Allied countries. Many American banks loaned the Allies money. If the Allies won, the money would be paid back. If they lost, the money would be, too.

Although most Americans did not want to enter the war, many events drew the United States into it. The British navy had blockaded Germany. They stopped neutral ships to inspect them for **contraband,** or prohibited materials, headed for Germany or its allies. In response, Germany announced that it would sink without warning any ships in the waters around Britain. Attacking civilian ships without warning was against international law. In May, the British passenger ship *Lusitania* entered the war zone. A German U-boat—or submarine—sank the ship, killing nearly 1,200 people. About 128 were Americans.

President Wilson still tried to stay out of the war. However, he did send notes to Germany telling it to stop endangering the lives of civilians in war zones. After a U-boat shot at the French passenger ship *Sussex,* Wilson warned Germany to stop its submarine warfare or risk war with the United States. Germany did not want the United States to join the Allies. In the Sussex Pledge, Germany promised not to sink any merchant ships without warning.

In January 1917, a German official named Arthur Zimmermann told the German ambassador to Mexico to ask Mexico to ally itself with Germany in case of war between Germany and the United States. In return, Mexico would get back the territory it once held in Texas, New Mexico, and Arizona. The British intercepted the Zimmermann telegram. It was leaked to American newspapers. Many Americans now believed that war with Germany was necessary. In February 1917, Germany again began unrestricted submarine warfare. Finally, after Germany sank six American merchant ships, Wilson asked Congress to declare war on Germany. It did so on April 6, 1917.

Section Wrap-up

Answer these questions to check your understanding of the entire section.

1. How did intricate alliances contribute to the start of World War I?

_____

_____

_____

2. Why did the United States eventually enter World War I?

_____

_____

_____

In the space provided, write a journal entry describing how you would react to reading the Zimmermann telegram for the first time in the newspaper.

_____

_____

_____

_____

_____

_____

_____

_____

_____

_____

_____

The Home Front

Big Idea

As you read pages 328–333 in your textbook, use the major headings of the section to complete the outline below.

The Home Front

I. **Organizing the Economy**

   A. _____

   B. _____

   C. _____

II. _____

   A. _____

   B. _____

 **Notes** | **Read to Learn**

Organizing the Economy *(page 328)*

Identifying the Main Idea

Write the main idea of the passage.

_____

_____

_____

_____

_____

_____

_____

_____

Congress created special agencies to prepare the economy for war. The War Industries Board (WIB) coordinated the production of war materials. The Food Administration encouraged Americans to grow their own vegetables in **victory gardens.** The Fuel Administration introduced daylight savings time and shortened workweeks to conserve energy. The government raised money for the war through taxes and bonds.

The National War Labor Board (NWLB) tried to avoid labor strikes. For workers, it pushed for wage increases, an eight-hour workday, and the right to organize unions. In return, labor leaders agreed not to strike. Women took over many now-open industry jobs. In the "Great Migration," many African Americans left the South to take jobs in northern factories. Many Mexicans came to the American Southwest to work for farmers and ranchers.

The Committee on Public Information (CPI) hired advertisers, artists, and others to sway public opinion in favor of the war. The government limited opposition to the war and **espionage,** or spying. Some civil liberties were suppressed.

Notes | Read to Learn

Building the Military (page 332)

Distinguishing Fact from Opinion

1. Underline one fact about draft boards.

2. Circle one opinion about draft boards.

Formulating Questions

Write two questions you have after reading the passage.

_____

_____

_____

_____

_____

_____

_____

_____

_____

When the United States entered the war in 1917, it did not have enough soldiers. Although many people volunteered, more were needed. Many progressives believed that conscription, or forced military service, was against democratic principles. Congress, however, believed conscription was necessary. It set up a new system of conscription called selective service. It required all men between 21 and 30 to register for the draft. A lottery then randomly decided the order in which individuals were called before local draft boards. These boards selected or exempted men from military service. The members of the draft boards were local civilians. Progressives believed these community members could better decide which men to draft.

Eventually about 2.8 million Americans were drafted. About 2 million more volunteered. Some wanted to fight after hearing about German atrocities. Others wanted to fight for democracy. Many saw World War I as an opportunity for adventure and wanted to fight for their country. Troop morale was high for American soldiers during World War I, despite losses. During the war 50,000 Americans died in combat and more than 200,000 were wounded.

About 42,000 of the 400,000 African Americans who were drafted served in the war overseas. African American soldiers faced discrimination and prejudice in the army. They served in racially segregated units. They were almost always under the control of white officers. Despite this, many African Americans fought with distinction in the war. Two African American divisions fought in battles along the Western Front.

Women officially served in the armed forces for the first time in World War I. They served in noncombat positions. With men serving in combat, the armed forces faced a shortage of clerical workers. The navy enlisted women to serve as clerical workers, radio operators, electricians, chemists, and other occupations. The army, however, refused to enlist women. It hired women as temporary employees to fill clerical jobs. The only women to actually serve in the army were the army nurses. Women served as nurses in the navy, too.

Section Wrap-up

Answer these questions to check your understanding of the entire section.

1. How did the United States raise an army for World War I?

_____

_____

_____

2. How did the government control the U.S. economy to support the war?

_____

_____

_____

Informative Writing

Suppose you are serving in the military during World War I. In the space provided write a letter telling how you came to serve in the military.

_____

_____

_____

_____

_____

_____

_____

_____

_____

_____

_____

_____

Chapter 9, Section 3 (Pages 336–345)
A Bloody Conflict

Big Idea

As you read pages 336–345 in your textbook, complete this graphic organizer by listing some kinds of warfare and technology used in the fighting.

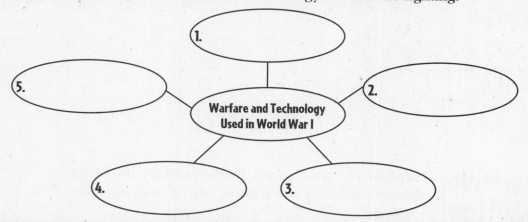

1.

2.

3.

4.

5.

Warfare and Technology Used in World War I

Notes

Read to Learn

Combat in World War I (page 336)

Making Inferences

Explain why the land between the trenches was called "no man's land."

_____

_____

_____

_____

_____

_____

During World War I, troops began using powerful artillery guns that hurled huge explosive shells long distances. They also used machine guns. Troops dug trenches to protect themselves from artillery. On the Western Front, troops dug a network of trenches that stretched from the English Channel to the Swiss border. The space between the opposing trenches became known as "no-man's-land." Soldiers from either side would race across no-man's-land while trying to dodge gunfire. Once across, they battled the enemy with grenades, bayonets, and sometimes even their fists. Combat was often brutal.

Both sides developed new technologies. The Germans began using poison gas. The fumes caused vomiting, blindness, and suffocation. The Allies also began using poison gas, and gas masks became necessary equipment. The British introduced the tank, which could roll over barbed wire and trenches. Airplanes were first used in World War I, first to observe enemy activities and then to shoot down German zeppelins and bomb enemy lines. Eventually, aircraft were used to shoot down other aircraft in air battles known as dogfights.

 **Notes** | **Read to Learn**

The Americans Arrive (page 338)

Copyright © Glencoe/McGraw-Hill, a division of The McGraw-Hill Companies, Inc.

Determining Cause and Effect

Write one effect of each cause.

1. Cause: U.S. ships traveled in convoys.

Effect:

_____

_____

2. Cause: Russia left World War I.

Effect:

_____

_____

About 2 million American soldiers fought in World War I. Although mostly inexperienced, they boosted the morale of the Allied forces. The admiral of the U.S. Navy suggested that merchant ships and troop transports headed for Europe be gathered in groups called **convoys.** Warships escorted the convoys. This system reduced shipping and troop losses.

In March 1917, riots broke out in Russia and its leader stepped down. A temporary government was unable to deal with the country's major problems. The Bolshevik Party led by Vladimir Lenin overthrew the Russian government. Lenin immediately pulled Russia out of the war, allowing Germany to concentrate its troops on the Western Front.

Germany launched a massive attack and pushed deeply into Allied lines. American and French troops twice blocked German drives on Paris. In September of 1918, American troops began a huge offensive against the Germans. By November, the Americans had destroyed the German defenses and pushed a hole in the German lines. Finally, on November 11, 1918, Germany signed an **armistice,** or cease-fire, that ended the war.

A Flawed Peace (page 342)

Analyzing Information

List reasons why this lesson is called "A Flawed Peace."

_____

_____

_____

_____

_____

_____

_____

_____

_____

The peace conference started in January 1919 at the Palace of Versailles in France. The resulting treaty was called the Treaty of Versailles. The main people involved, known as the Big Four, were leaders of the Allied nations. President Wilson made a plan for peace known as the Fourteen Points. Five points sought to eliminate the causes of war. Eight addressed the right to **national self-determination.** The final point called for the formation of a League of Nations to keep peace and prevent future wars. The other Allied governments believed Wilson's plan was too easy on the Germans.

The Treaty of Versailles included many terms to weaken and punish Germany. It reduced Germany's military and forced it to pay **reparations,** or war damages. The war led to the end of the Russian, Ottoman, German, and Austro-Hungarian empires and the establishment of several new nations. The Treaty of Versailles did include Wilson's plan for the League of Nations, but many U.S. Congress members opposed it for that reason. They believed it would force the United States into many conflicts. After voting twice, the U.S. Senate refused to ratify the treaty. The League of Nations started without the United States.

Section Wrap-up

Answer these questions to check your understanding of the entire section.

1. What fighting techniques were used in World War I?

_____

_____

_____

2. What was the American response to the Treaty of Versailles?

_____

_____

_____

In the space provided, write a paragraph explaining the potential advantages and disadvantages to the United States of ratifying the Treaty of Versailles.

_____

_____

_____

_____

_____

_____

_____

_____

_____

_____

_____

The War's Impact

Big Idea

As you read pages 348–353 in your textbook, complete this graphic organizer by listing some effects of the end of World War I on the American economy.

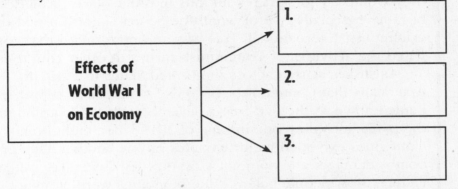

Effects of World War I on Economy

1.

2.

3.

 **Notes**   **Read to Learn**

An Economy in Turmoil *(page 348)*

Making Generalizations

The labor strikes of 1919 were

____ *very*

____ *somewhat*

____ *not at all*

effective for the strikers.

After the war, the government removed economic controls. The result was inflation, which raised the **cost of living**—the cost of food, clothing, shelter, and other items people need to survive. Workers wanted higher wages, but business owners wanted to hold down operating costs. Unions were larger and more organized than before. As a result, there were many strikes in 1919.

Shipyard workers in Seattle organized the first big strike. Soon it became a **general strike,** or a strike that involves all workers in a location, not just workers in one industry. Although the strikers made no gains, the general strike worried many people because it was a technique used by radicals in Europe. When police officers in Boston went on strike, riots broke out in the city. The police commissioner fired the strikers and hired a new police force. A strike by workers at U.S. Steel was one of the largest strikes. The company hired replacement workers and the strike failed.

Many soldiers returned home looking for work. Many African Americans had moved to the North during the war to take factory jobs. Racism and frustration erupted into riots.

Notes | Read to Learn

The Red Scare (page 351)

Predicting

Before you read, complete this sentence.

I think the term "Red Scare" will mean

_____

_____

_____

_____

Synthesizing Information

Explain why the Palmer raids targeted immigrants.

1. _____

_____

_____

_____

2. _____

_____

_____

_____

The strikes in 1919 led many people to believe that Communists were trying to start a revolution in the United States. Many Americans felt betrayed when Russia withdrew from the war. Since the late 1800s, many Americans blamed immigrants for bringing Communist ideas into the United States. They also blamed immigrants for labor problems and violence. When Communists took control of Russia, Americans feared they would try to start revolutions in other places. Americans became especially fearful when the Soviet Union formed the Communist International. This was an organization that coordinated the activities of Communist parties in other countries.

As strikes started across the United States in 1919, the fear of Americans that Communists, or "reds," would seize power led to a panic known as the Red Scare. Several incidents contributed to the panic, including one in June of 1919 when eight bombs in eight cities exploded within minutes of one another. One of these bombs damaged the home of U.S. Attorney General A. Mitchell Palmer. Most people believed the bombings were the work of radicals trying to destroy the American way of life.

Palmer set up a special division within the Justice Department. The General Intelligence Division was headed by J. Edgar Hoover, and it later became the Federal Bureau of Investigation (FBI). Although evidence pointed to no one group as the bombers, Palmer organized raids on the foreign-born and on radicals. Palmer rounded up many immigrants and had them **deported,** or expelled from the country.

The Palmer raids were carried out without concern for people's civil rights. Homes were entered without search warrants. People were jailed indefinitely and not allowed to talk to their attorneys. Palmer was first praised for his work. However, when he failed to find any real evidence of a revolutionary conspiracy, his popularity faded. The Red Scare led to anti-immigrant feelings and a call for Congress to limit immigration.

By 1920, most Americans wanted an end to the unrest within the country. In the 1920 election, the Democrats ran James M. Cox and Franklin D. Roosevelt. They ran on the ideals of progressivism. The Republicans ran Warren G. Harding. He called for a return to "normalcy." He wanted the United States to return to the simpler days before the Progressive Era reforms. Many voters agreed with Harding, and he won by a landslide.

Section Wrap-up

Answer these questions to check your understanding of the entire section.

1. What were the main causes of the wave of strikes after World War I?

_____

_____

_____

2. What were the causes of and reaction to the Red Scare?

_____

_____

_____

Persuasive Writing

In the space provided, write a short campaign speech Warren Harding might have given to persuade voters to vote for him in the 1920 election.

_____

_____

_____

_____

_____

_____

_____

_____

_____

_____

_____

_____

The Politics of the 1920s

Big Idea

As you read pages 362–367 in your textbook, complete the outline using the major headings of the section.

The Politics of the 1920s

I. **The Harding Administration**

   A. _____

   B. _____

II. _____

III. _____

   A. _____

   B. _____

   C. _____

   D. _____

 **Notes** | **Read to Learn**

The Harding Administration *(page 362)*

Determining Cause and Effect

Write the cause.

Cause:

_____

_____

_____

_____

_____

_____.

Effect: Scandals plagued the Harding administration.

Warren G. Harding was elected president in 1920. He ran on the campaign promise to return the country to normalcy. This meant a return to "normal" life after the war. Harding appointed many friends from Ohio to cabinet positions and high-level jobs. They were known as the Ohio Gang. Some used their positions to sell jobs, pardons, and protection from prosecution. They caused several scandals.

The most famous was Teapot Dome. Secretary of the Interior Albert B. Fall secretly allowed private companies to lease lands containing Navy oil reserves. Fall became the first cabinet officer to go to prison. Another scandal involved Attorney General Daugherty. He was suspected of taking bribes from a German agent.

In a 1923 tour of the West, President Harding fell ill and died. Vice President Calvin Coolidge became president and distanced himself from corruption. He restored integrity to the presidency. Coolidge believed his job was to make sure government interfered as little as possible with business. In 1924 he easily won the election.

Read to Learn

Policies of Prosperity *(page 365)*

Problems and Solutions

Complete the sentences.

1. To balance the budget, Mellon

_____

_____

_____.

2. To provide extra income to people and businesses, Mellon

_____

_____

_____.

Presidents Harding and Coolidge both opposed government regulation of business. Harding appointed two cabinet members who contributed to the economic growth and prosperity of the 1920s: Andrew Mellon and Herbert Hoover.

Mellon had three major goals as secretary of the treasury: balance the budget, reduce government debt, and cut taxes. Mellon convinced Congress to create agencies to prepare the budget and track expenses. He then cut government spending. Mellon argued that if taxes were lower, businesses and consumers would spend and invest more. As the economy grew, the government would collect more taxes at a lower rate than if taxes were high. This idea is known today as **supply-side economics.** In 1928 Congress drastically cut tax rates.

Secretary of Commerce Hoover tried to encourage economic growth. His policy of **cooperative individualism** encouraged businesses to form trade associations. These groups would then share information with the government. Hoover believed this would reduce costs and increase efficiency. Hoover also tried to help companies find new markets and supported the growth of the airline and radio industries.

Trade and Arms Control *(page 366)*

Synthesizing Information

Complete the statement based on the last paragraph. After World War I, many countries

_____

_____

_____

_____

_____

_____.

Before World War I, the United States was a debtor nation. By the end of the war, allies owed the United States more than $10 billion. Many Americans at this time favored **isolationism.** This was a policy of staying out of world affairs. However, the nation was too involved economically and politically with other countries to be truly isolationist. America's former allies struggled to repay their war debts. High import taxes made it hard for foreign countries to sell products in the United States. The war reparations, Germany paid to European nations crippled its economy. In 1924 a U.S. diplomat negotiated the Dawes Plan. American banks loaned Germany money to pay reparations. Britain and France agreed to accept less in reparations and to pay more on their war debts.

Secretary of State Charles Evans Hughes spoke to the major world powers at a conference in Washington. The conference led to a treaty between Britain, France, Italy, Japan, and the United States to reduce the naval arms race. This supported the idea that written agreements could end war. The United States and fourteen other nations signed the Kellogg-Briand Pact. In it they agreed to settle all disputes peacefully.

Section Wrap-up

Answer these questions to check your understanding of the entire section.

1. How did two of President Harding's cabinet appointees contribute to the economic growth and prosperity of the 1920s?

_____

_____

_____

2. Why was it impossible for the United States to maintain an isolationist stand after World War I?

_____

_____

_____

Descriptive Writing

In the space provided, write a newspaper obituary for Warren G. Harding. Use words that reflect feelings about him and his administration at the time of his death.

_____

_____

_____

_____

_____

_____

_____

_____

_____

_____

_____

A Growing Economy

Big Idea

As you read pages 368–375 in your textbook, complete this graphic organizer to analyze the causes of economic growth and prosperity in the 1920s.

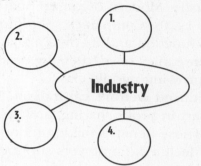

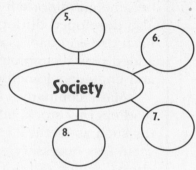

Notes | Read to Learn

The Rise of New Industries *(page 368)*

Making Generalizations

Complete the statement.

During the 1920s,

_____

_____

_____

_____

_____

_____

_____

_____.

During the 1920s, Americans earned more money than ever before while working fewer hours. **Mass production,** or large-scale product manufacturing done mainly by machinery, made more products available and lowered costs. This reshaped American economics and industry.

Henry Ford used the **assembly line** to build cars. This system divided operations into simple tasks unskilled workers could do. It reduced the time needed and the cost. By lowering the price of his mass-produced car, the **Model T,** Ford created a huge demand. The automobile reduced the isolation of rural areas and allowed people to live farther from work.

With their greater incomes, people bought new products such as frozen foods, household cleaners, washing machines, and cosmetics. During the 1920s, the airlines and radio industries expanded. The government used airlines to deliver mail and began building airports. Lindbergh's transatlantic solo flight gave the idea of commercial flights a boost. NBC and CBS began creating networks of radio stations.

The Consumer Society (page 372)

Making Inferences

Make two inferences based on the passage.

1. _____

_____

_____

2. _____

_____

_____

Before the 1920s, most Americans thought that going into debt was shameful. This attitude changed, and more Americans went into debt to buy items such as furniture and bought cars on credit.

Inventors at this time had trouble getting people to buy products they did not know they needed. Advertising stepped in to convince consumers to buy new products and itself soon became an important industry. Modern organizational structures also developed during the 1920s. Companies split into divisions. Each division had its own function and its own manager. As they added new technology, companies needed engineers. Managers and engineers joined the growing middle class.

Many companies introduced **welfare capitalism.** They let workers buy stock, take part in profit sharing, and receive benefits such as medical care. These benefits made union membership seem less necessary, so it declined. Employers supported **open shops,** which did not require union membership. Not all Americans shared in the economic boom. African Americans, Native Americans, women, immigrants, and farmers struggled.

The Farm Crisis (page 375)

Drawing Conclusions

Draw a conclusion about how tariffs affected American farmers.

_____

_____

_____

_____

_____

_____

_____

During the war, the government had encouraged farmers to grow more to meet the need for food in Europe. Many farmers went into debt to buy more land and machinery to raise more crops. Sales and prices were high, so farmers prospered. After the war, Europeans began producing more farm products, so profits fell for American farmers. New technologies such as fertilizers, machinery, and new seed varieties allowed farmers to produce more, but demand for the products did not increase, so farmers received lower prices for their goods.

In 1922 Congress passed the Fordney-McCumber Act. This law raised tariffs to protect American industries from competition. Europeans reacted by buying fewer American agricultural products. Prices dropped even more when farmers could not sell their products overseas.

Some congressmen tried to help the farmers sell their surpluses. They proposed a plan in which the government would buy the crop surpluses to sell abroad at a loss. However, President Coolidge vetoed the bill. He thought it would encourage farmers to produce greater surpluses. As a result, American farmers stayed in a recession throughout the 1920s.

Section Wrap-up

Answer these questions to check your understanding of the entire section.

1. How did the growth of the automobile industry and the rise of other new industries improve Americans' standard of living?

   _____

   _____

   _____

2. What factors contributed to the economic crisis in farming during the 1920s?

   _____

   _____

   _____

In the space provided, write an advertisement for a 1920s Ford Model T.

_____

_____

_____

_____

_____

_____

_____

_____

_____

A Clash of Values

Big Idea

As you read pages 376–381 in your textbook, complete this graphic organizer by filling in some causes and effects of anti-immigrant prejudices.

1. _____

2. _____   **Anti-Immigrant**

3. _____   **Prejudices**

4. _____

5. _____

6. _____

 **Notes** | **Read to Learn**

Nativism Resurges (page 376)

Synthesizing Information

Write two reasons Mexican immigrants filled agriculture, mining, and railroad jobs.

1. _____

_____

_____

2. _____

_____

_____

During the 1920s, anti-immigrant feelings grew because of an influx of immigrants, cultural tensions, and recession. **Nativism,** the belief that one's native land needs to be protected against immigrants, also grew. In 1920 two Italian immigrants named Nicola Sacco and Bortolomeo Vanzetti were arrested for armed robbery and murder. It was widely reported that they were **anarchists,** people who oppose all forms of government. Despite thin evidence, Sacco and Vanzetti were found guilty and later executed. One of the biggest efforts to restrict immigration came from the Ku Klux Klan. It targeted groups it felt did not represent traditional American values.

In 1921 Congress passed the Emergency Quota Act to limit immigration. The National Origins Act of 1924 made the quotas stricter and permanent. These acts favored people from northwestern Europe and exempted those from Central and South America. The reduction in immigration caused a shortage of workers for agriculture, mining, and railroad work. Mexican immigrants filled these jobs. Large numbers arrived after the Newlands Reclamation Act of 1902 funded projects in the Southwest.

 **Notes** | **Read to Learn**

A Clash of Cultures *(page 378)*

Identifying the Main Idea

Write the main idea.

_____

_____

_____

_____

_____

Distinguishing Fact from Opinion

Write one opinion held by Fundamentalists in the 1920s. Then write one fact about them.

Opinion:

_____

_____

_____

Fact:

_____

_____

_____

_____

During the 1920s, a "new morality" took over the nation. The new morality challenged traditional ways of thinking. It glorified youth and personal freedom and changed American society.

Women won the right to vote in 1920. This encouraged many women to break free of their traditional roles and behaviors. Attitudes toward marriage changed. The ideas of romance, pleasure, and friendship became linked to successful marriages. The automobile also played a part in the new morality. It gave young people more freedom. Single women began working for their own financial independence as employment opportunities increased during the 1920s. Women's colleges encouraged students to pursue careers. Many professional women made contributions in fields such as science, medicine, law, and literature.

Many groups wanted to preserve traditional values against the new morality. A religious movement called Fundamentalism stressed the teachings of the Bible as literally true history. Fundamentalists rejected the theory of **evolution,** which argued that human beings had developed from lower forms of life over the course of millions of years. Fundamentalists believed in **creationism,** which says that God created the world as described in the Bible. In 1925 Tennessee outlawed the teaching of evolution. A high school biology teacher named John T. Scopes was tried and convicted of breaking this law. The Scopes Trial helped illustrate the struggle between the new morality and traditional beliefs.

In January of 1920 the Eighteenth Amendment went into effect. This amendment prohibited, or banned, the sale of alcohol. Many people felt prohibition would reduce unemployment, violence, and poverty. Congress passed the Volstead Act to enforce the law, but many Americans violated it. Organized crime supplied illegal alcohol to secret bars called **speakeasies.** In 1933 the Twenty-first Amendment later repealed prohibition.

Section Wrap-up

Answer these questions to check your understanding of the entire section.

1. What factors contributed to the rise in nativism during the 1920s?

_____

_____

_____

2. How did the status of women change during the 1920s?

_____

_____

_____

In the space provided, write a magazine article in favor of or against the new morality. Give reasons to support your position.

_____

_____

_____

_____

_____

_____

_____

_____

_____

_____

_____

Cultural Innovations

Big Idea

As you read pages 382–385 in your textbook, complete this chart by filling in the main characteristics of art, literature, and popular culture from the 1920s.

Cultural Movement	Main Characteristics
Art	1.
Literature	2.
Popular Culture	3.

Notes | Read to Learn

Art and Literature (page 382)

Making Generalizations

Make a generalization about art and literature of the 1920s.

_____
_____
_____
_____
_____
_____
_____
_____

Many artists and writers of the 1920s were attracted by the lifestyle of Manhattan's Greenwich Village and Chicago's South Side. This unconventional and artistic lifestyle was known as **bohemian.** Artists explored the meaning of the modern world.

European art movements influenced American art. American artists expressed modern experiences in a diverse range of styles. Painter John Marin was inspired by both nature and urban New York. Edward Hopper painted haunting, realistic scenes. Georgia O'Keeffe painted landscapes and flowers.

Poets and writers of the 1920s also varied greatly in their styles and subject matter. Poet Carl Sandburg used common speech to glorify the Midwest. Edna St. Vincent Millay wrote about women's equality. Playwright Eugene O'Neill wrote about realistic characters in tragic situations. Ernest Hemingway described the experience of war. Sinclair Lewis wrote about the follies of small town America. F. Scott Fitzgerald's novel *The Great Gatsby* exposed the emptiness of modern society.

Popular Culture *(page 384)*

Determining Cause and Effect

List three effects of the prosperity of the 1920s.

1. _____

_____

2. _____

_____

3. _____

_____

Formulating Questions

Write one question you have based on the passage.

_____

_____

_____

_____

Many Americans in the 1920s had more leisure time and spending money than before. They used this time to watch sports and enjoy movies, radio, and other types of popular entertainment.

Motion pictures were very popular during the 1920s. People rushed to see films starring Mary Pickford, Charlie Chaplin, Rudolph Valentino, and Douglas Fairbanks. Theaters hired piano players to provide music during silent pictures. Subtitles told the storyline. In 1927 the first "talking" movie was produced.

Radio was also popular at this time. Radio stations broadcast popular music as well as radio shows such as *Amos 'n' Andy.* Radio, movies, newspapers, and magazines, or the **mass media,** did more than entertain people. They helped spread new ideas and unify the nation.

Radio and films also popularized sports such as baseball and boxing. Baseball star Babe Ruth became a national hero. Sports fans idolized boxer Jack Dempsey. They followed his heavyweight matches against Gene Tunney. Newspaper coverage helped create interest in college football stars such as Red Grange. He was called the "Galloping Ghost" because of his speed and agility. Other sports celebrities included golfers, tennis players, and even swimmers.

1. How did the art and literature of the 1920s reflect the disillusionment of the era?

_____

_____

_____

2. How did many Americans spend their leisure time during the 1920s?

_____

_____

_____

In the space provided, write a paragraph comparing the sports stars, movies, or radio of the 1920s with those of today.

_____

_____

_____

_____

_____

_____

_____

_____

_____

_____

African American Culture

Big Idea

As you read pages 388–393 in your textbook, complete this graphic organizer by filling in some causes and effects of the Harlem Renaissance.

Causes

Efffects

1.

Harlem Renaissance

2.

3.

4.

Notes

Read to Learn

The Harlem Renaissance (page 388)

Comparing and Contrasting

List major figures in these genres of the Harlem Renaissance.

Literature:

_____

_____

Music:

_____

_____

Theater:

_____

_____

Many African Americans joined the Great Migration from the rural South to northern cities. They hoped to escape segregation, find jobs, and improve their lives. As the North's African American population grew, it influenced culture and the arts. New York City's Harlem neighborhood became the center for the flowering of African American arts known as the Harlem Renaissance. Two of its writers were Claude McKay and Langston Hughes. McKay's verses reflect defiance and contempt for racism, which were major characteristics of the movement. Hughes became the leading voice of the African American experience.

Louis Armstrong introduced an early improvisational style of **jazz** music influenced by Dixieland and ragtime. Bandleader Duke Ellington got his start at the Harlem Cotton Club. He soon created his own sound. Bessie Smith performed the **blues,** soulful music evolved from spirituals.

The theater also thrived. Paul Robeson gained fame for his roles in *Emperor Jones* and *Show Boat*. Josephine Baker was a well-known singer and dancer. This artistic flowering inspired pride in African American culture and its roots.

African Americans and 1920s Politics *(page 391)*

Predicting

Skim the passage. Make a prediction about what you will learn.

_____

_____

_____

_____

Analyzing Information

Give two reasons why middle class African Americans may have distanced themselves from Garvey.

1. _____

_____

_____

2. _____

_____

_____

_____

The Great Migration influenced politics in the North. The African American population became an important voting bloc that often affected the outcomes of elections in the North.

Many African Americans voted for Republicans, the party of Abraham Lincoln. In 1928 African American voters in Chicago elected Oscar DePriest to Congress. He was the first African American congressman from a Northern state. DePriest introduced laws against racial discrimination and lynching.

The National Association for the Advancement of Colored People (NAACP) worked against segregation and injustice. Its main tactic was lobbying politicians, but it also worked through the courts. In 1922 the NAACP helped get an anti-lynching law passed in the House of Representatives. The Senate did not pass the bill, but the NAACP's work kept the issue in the news. In 1930 the NAACP helped defeat a Supreme Court nominee known for his racist positions. His nomination was defeated. This proved the NAACP had the political strength to affect national politics.

Other groups stressed black pride and nationalism. Marcus Garvey was a dynamic leader from Jamaica. He founded a group called the Universal Negro Improvement Association (UNIA). Garvey believed African Americans could gain economic and political power through education. He also called for separation from white society. Garvey planned to lead his followers back to Africa.

The growing African American middle class distanced itself from this movement. The FBI thought the UNIA was dangerous. Garvey insulted some key figures in the Harlem Renaissance. Garvey was convicted of mail fraud in 1923, and in 1927 President Coolidge had him deported. In the end, Garvey's movement inspired many people with pride in their African heritage.

Section Wrap-up

Answer these questions to check your understanding of the entire section.

1. How did the Harlem Renaissance lead to a rediscovery of African American cultural roots?

_____

_____

_____

2. Why was there an increase in African American political activism in the postwar period?

_____

_____

_____

In the space provided, write letter as someone living in Harlem during the 1920s. Describe your reactions to Marcus Garvey's back to Africa proposal.

_____

_____

_____

_____

_____

_____

_____

_____

_____

_____

_____

The Causes of the Great Depression

Big Idea

As you read pages 400–405 in your textbook, complete this graphic organizer by comparing the backgrounds and issues of the presidential candidates.

1928 Presidential Campaign		
Candidate	Background	Issue
1.	2.	3.
4.	5.	6.

 **Notes**

Read to Learn

The Long Bull Market (page 400)

Making Inferences

Read the third paragraph again. Make an inference about 1920s stock prices compared with their actual values.

_____

_____

_____

_____

_____

_____

In the 1928 presidential election, Herbert Hoover ran as the Republican nominee. The Democrats nominated Alfred E. Smith, a Catholic. Many Protestants feared the Catholic Church would rule the White House if he was elected. Hoover and the Republicans also took credit for the prosperity of the 1920s. As a result, Hoover won.

After the election, stock prices continued to increase. The **stock market** was a system for buying and selling shares of companies. The late 1920s saw a **bull market,** or a long period of rising stock prices. Many investors began buying stocks on **margin.** They made a small down payment on the stock and took out a loan from a stockbroker to pay for the rest. If stock prices fell, the stockbroker issued a **margin call,** a demand for the investor to repay the loan.

Before the late 1920s, the prices that investors paid for stocks had to do with the company's profits. This was no longer true by the late 1920s. Many buyers hoped to make a quick profit and practiced **speculation.** They were betting that the stock market would continue to climb.

Notes | Read to Learn

The Great Crash *(page 402)*

Determining Cause and Effect

List two causes of bank closures. Then list two effects of the closures.

Causes: _____

_____

_____

_____

Effects: _____

_____

_____

_____

By mid-1929, the stock market was running out of new customers. Professional investors began selling off their holdings. Prices decreased. Other investors sold their shares to pay the interest on loans from brokers. Prices fell further. On October 29, 1929, which became known as Black Tuesday, stock prices took their steepest dive. The crash was not a major cause of the Great Depression, but it undermined the economy.

Many banks had lent money to stock speculators. They had also invested depositors' money in the stock market. When stock prices fell, many banks lost money on their investments, and speculators could not repay their loans. The banks had to cut back on the number of loans they made. As a result, people could not borrow as much money as they once did. This helped send the economy into a recession.

Many banks were forced to close. People who had deposits in these banks lost all their savings. Some Americans began **bank runs.** This takes place when many people withdraw money at the same time out of fear the banks will close. This caused many more banks to collapse.

The Roots of the Great Depression *(page 404)*

Identifying the Main Idea

What is the main idea of the passage?

_____

_____

_____

_____

_____

_____

_____

_____

_____

_____

The Great Depression had several causes. One was overproduction. Most Americans did not have enough money to buy all the goods that were made. During the 1920s, many Americans bought high-cost items on the **installment** plan. This allowed people to pay for items in monthly installments. Some people had to reduce their purchases in order to pay their debts. When sales slowed, manufacturers cut production and laid off employees. This effect rippled through the economy.

Americans were also not selling many goods to foreign countries. In 1930, Congress passed the Hawley-Smoot Tariff. It raised the tax on many imports. Foreign countries then raised their tariffs against American goods, which caused fewer American products to be sold overseas.

The Federal Reserve had kept interest rates low in the 1920s, encouraging banks to make risky loans. Low rates also misled many business leaders into thinking that the economy was still growing. They borrowed more money to expand production. This led to overproduction when sales were actually decreasing. When the Depression hit, companies had to lay off workers to cut costs.

Answer these questions to check your understanding of the entire section.

1. How did buying stocks on margin cause problems?

_____

_____

_____

2. How did overproduction cause unemployment to rise?

_____

_____

_____

In the space provided, write a letter describing what happened on Black Tuesday. Imagine that you are someone who witnessed the events of the day firsthand.

_____

_____

_____

_____

_____

_____

_____

_____

_____

_____

Life During the Great Depression

Big Idea

As you read pages 406–409 in your textbook, use the major headings of the section to complete the outline.

Life During the Great Depression

I. **The Depression Worsens**
  A. _____
  B. _____
II. _____
  A. _____
  B. _____
  C. _____

Notes

Read to Learn

The Depression Worsens (page 406)

Evaluating Information

Which paragraph contains the best information about the Depression's impact on farmers?

_____

_____

_____

_____

_____

_____

The Depression grew worse during Hoover's administration. Thousands of banks failed, and thousands of companies went out of business. Millions of Americans were unemployed. Many relied on bread lines and soup kitchens for food.

Many people could not afford to pay their rent or mortgage and lost their homes. Court officers, called **bailiffs,** evicted non-paying tenants. Homeless people put up shacks on public lands, forming shantytowns throughout the country. Many called the shantytowns "Hoovervilles" because they blamed the president for their problems. Some homeless and unemployed people wandered around the country. Known as **hobos,** they traveled by sneaking onto open boxcars on freight trains.

Great Plains Farmers soon faced a new problem. When crop prices decreased in the 1920s, farmers left many fields unplanted. In 1932, the Great Plains experienced a severe drought. The unplanted soil turned to dust. Much of the Plains became a Dust Bowl. Many families packed their belongings and headed west to California. Still, many remained homeless and poor.

Art and Entertainment *(page 408)*

Making Generalizations

Make a generalization about how movies and radio affected people's lives during the Depression.

_____

_____

_____

_____

_____

_____

_____

Analyzing Information

Give two examples of how art and literature reflected the realities of the Great Depression.

1. _____

_____

_____

_____

2. _____

_____

_____

_____

Americans turned to entertainment to escape the hardships of the Depression. Many went to the movies. Comedies featuring child stars such as Shirley Temple provided people with a way to escape their daily worries. Americans also enjoyed cartoons. Walt Disney produced the first feature-length animated film in 1937. Even films that focused on the serious side of life were generally optimistic.

Two movies from this period were *The Wizard of Oz* and *Gone with the Wind*, both produced in 1939. *Gone with the Wind* is a Civil War epic that won nine Academy Awards. One went to Hattie McDaniel, who won Best Supporting Actress. She was the first African American to win an Academy Award.

Americans also listened to the radio. They listened to news, comedy shows, and adventure programs like *The Lone Ranger*. Short daytime dramas were also popular. Some of these dramas were sponsored by the makers of laundry soaps and were nicknamed **soap operas.** Talking about the lives of radio characters provided Americans with a common ground.

Art and literature in the 1930s reflected the realities of life during the Depression. Painters such as Grant Wood showed traditional American values, particularly those of the rural Midwest and the South. His painting *American Gothic* is one of the most famous American works of art.

Novelists such as John Steinbeck wrote about the lives of people in the Depression. In *The Grapes of Wrath,* Steinbeck told the story of an Oklahoma farm family who fled the Dust Bowl to find a better life in California. He based his writing on visits to and articles about migrant camps in California.

Some writers during the Depression influenced literary style. In a technique known as stream of consciousness, William Faulkner showed what his characters were thinking and feeling without using conventional dialogue. Faulkner explored the issue of race in the American South.

Photographers traveled around the nation taking pictures of life around them. In 1936, *Life* magazine was introduced. It was a weekly magazine that showcased the work of photojournalists, such as Dorothea Lange and Margaret Bourke-White, who documented the hardships of the Great Depression.

Answer these questions to check your understanding of the entire section.

1. What was the Dust Bowl and what caused it?

_____

_____

_____

2. How did the Great Depression affect American families?

_____

_____

_____

In the space provided, write an essay comparing real life during the Depression to life as it was portrayed in movies and on radio programs.

_____

_____

_____

_____

_____

_____

_____

_____

_____

Hoover Responds to the Depression

Big Idea

As you read pages 412–415 in your textbook, complete this graphic organizer by listing President Hoover's major initiatives and their results.

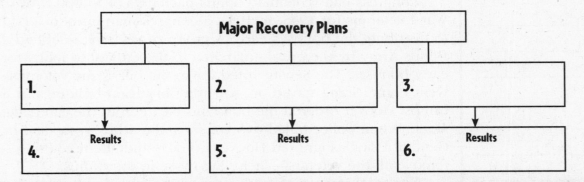

Major Recovery Plans

1.

2.

3.

Results
4.

Results
5.

Results
6.

Notes   Read to Learn

Promoting Recovery *(page 412)*

Identifying the Main Idea

What is the main idea of this passage?

_____

_____

_____

_____

_____

_____

_____

_____

Publicly, President Hoover declared the economy to be on the right track soon after Black Tuesday. Privately, he was worried. He brought together business, as well as government and labor leaders. Industry leaders promised not to cut factories or cut wages. By 1931, they had broken these promises.

Hoover increased **public works,** or government-financed building projects, to create jobs. It wasn't enough. For public works to make a dent, Hoover needed to massively increase government spending. He would have to either raise taxes or run a deficit. Either way, Hoover was afraid it would only delay economic recovery.

Hoover set up the National Credit Corporation and the Reconstruction Finance Corporation to provide money to banks and businesses, but neither met the nation's needs. Hoover opposed **relief,** money given directly to destitute families. By the spring of 1932, local and state governments were running out of money. Congress passed an act to provide loans to states for direct relief. Hoover signed it, but the program could not reverse the economy's downward spiral.

In an Angry Mood (page 414)

Determining Cause and Effect

What caused the Bonus March? What was an effect of the march?

Cause:

_____

_____

_____

Effect:

_____

_____

_____

Drawing Conclusions

What could you conclude about the mood of the public?

_____

_____

_____

_____

_____

_____

_____

_____

After the stock market crash in 1929, people were prepared to accept bad times. By 1931, people wanted more government help. The suffering nation grew restless and people began to revolt.

Farms were heavily mortgaged to pay for supplies. Many lost their farms when creditors **foreclosed** and took ownership. Other farmers began destroying crops, hoping the lack of supply would raise prices. Some even blocked food deliveries or dumped milk into ditches.

Congress had scheduled bonus payments of $1,000 to World War I veterans for 1945. In 1931, a congressman introduced a bill to distribute the bonuses early. A group of veterans—dubbed the Bonus Army by the press—marched to the Capitol to lobby for early bonuses. The Senate voted down the bill. Many veterans went home. Some stayed on, squatting in vacant buildings or in camps. Hoover ordered the buildings cleared but the camps left alone. When police killed two veterans, the army was called in. General Douglas ignored Hoover's orders and attempted to remove all the veterans—including those in the camps.

Newsreel images of troops assaulting veterans further damaged Hoover's reputation and haunted him throughout the 1932 campaign. Although Hoover failed to end the Depression, he expanded the role of the government more than any president before him.

Section Wrap-up

Answer these questions to check your understanding of the entire section.

1. How would you evaluate President Hoover's attempts to revive the economy?

_____

_____

_____

2. What were the limitations of Hoover's recovery plans?

_____

_____

_____

In the space provided, write a newspaper editorial arguing for or against the government's providing money for relief.

_____

_____

_____

_____

_____

_____

_____

_____

_____

_____

Chapter 12, Section 1 (Pages 422–431)
The First New Deal

Big Idea

As you read pages 422–431 in your textbook, complete this time line by recording the major problems Roosevelt addressed during his first 100 days in office.

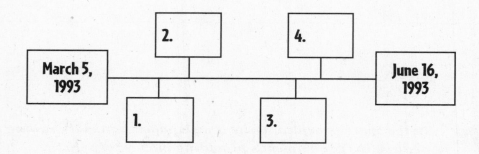

March 5, 1993

2.

1.

4.

3.

June 16, 1993

Notes   Read to Learn

Roosevelt's Rise to Power *(page 422)*

Determining Cause and Effect

Identify the cause.

Cause:

_____

_____

_____

Effect: Roosevelt's popularity paved the way for his presidential nomination.

The Republicans nominated Herbert Hoover to run for a second term. The Democrats choose the popular New York Governor Franklin D. Roosevelt. He pledged himself "to a new deal for the American people." The New Deal became the name for his policies to end the Depression.

Roosevelt was a distant cousin of President Theodore Roosevelt. He was born into a wealthy New York family and attended Harvard and Columbia Law School. After school, Roosevelt went into politics. He served in the New York legislature. Under President Wilson, he was assistant secretary of the navy. Roosevelt ran as the vice-presidential candidate in the 1920 election. He lost. A year later, Roosevelt came down with **polio**, a paralyzing disease. Eleanor Roosevelt, his wife, kept his political career alive through public speeches while he recovered.

By 1928, Roosevelt was active again in politics. As governor of New York, Roosevelt oversaw the creation of a relief agency to help the unemployed. His popularity paved the way for his presidential nomination. In November 1932, he won the election by a landslide.

 **Notes** | **Read to Learn**

The Hundred Days (page 424)

Distinguishing Fact from Opinion

Complete the sentences.

1. The opinion that Roosevelt would

_____

_____

led to bank runs.

2. It is a fact that under the gold standard

_____

_____

Between Roosevelt's election and his inauguration, unemployment continued to rise. Bank runs increased. Some people feared Roosevelt would lower the value of the dollar to fight the Depression. Under the **gold standard,** one ounce of gold equaled a set number of dollars. To lower the value of the dollar, the United States would have to stop exchanging dollars for gold. Depositors in American banks took out money. They wanted to convert deposits to gold before the dollar lost value. Thirty-eight state governors declared **bank holidays.** They closed banks before runs could put them out of business.

Roosevelt began his term by sending bill after bill to Congress. During the first three months of his administration, Congress passed 15 major acts to attack the economic crisis. Roosevelt chose advisors with different points of view. One group believed business and government should work together. A second group distrusted business and wanted government to run important parts of the economy. A third group wanted to break up companies to introduce competition.

Banks and Debt Relief (page 425)

Identifying the Main Idea

Write the main idea of the passage.

_____

_____

_____

_____

_____

_____

_____

President Roosevelt realized that one of the first things he needed to do was restore people's confidence in the banks. He declared a national bank holiday and then called a special session of Congress. On the day Congress met, the House and Senate passed the Emergency Banking Relief Act. The president signed it into law. It said federal officials would check the nation's banks and license those that were financially sound.

On March 12, Roosevelt addressed the nation on radio in the first of many **fireside chats**—talks in which he told the American people what he was trying to accomplish. He told them it was safe to put their money back into banks. The next day there were more deposits than withdrawals.

Roosevelt's advisors pushed for regulation of the bank industry and the stock market. The Securities Act of 1933 required companies to provide investors with complete and truthful information. The Glass-Steagall Banking Act created the Federal Deposit Insurance Corporation. It insured bank deposits up to a set amount. Roosevelt asked Congress to establish the Homeowners Loan Corporation to help people pay their mortgages. Congress also created the Farm Credit Administration to help farmers refinance their mortgages.

Farms and Industry *(page 428)*

Formulating Questions

Write two questions you have about the passage.

1. _____

_____

_____

2. _____

_____

_____

_____

To help farmers hurt by the Depression, Roosevelt started a new farm program. Under the program, the government paid farmers not to raise certain livestock and crops. The Agricultural Adjustment Administration ran the program. Over the next two years, the farm surplus fell sharply. Prices and farm income rose. The program mostly benefited large commercial farmers who grew one crop. Many poor tenant farmers became homeless.

In June 1933, Roosevelt turned his attention to industry. Congress enacted the National Industrial Recovery Act (NIRA). It suspended antitrust laws. It let business, labor, and government set up voluntary rules for each industry. These rules were known as codes of fair competition. Some codes set prices, minimum wages, and limited factories to two shifts per day. The National Recovery Administration (NRA) ran the program. Participating businesses displayed signs with the NRA symbol. NRA codes were difficult to administer and tended to favor large corporations. By the time the Supreme Court declared the NRA unconstitutional in 1935, it had lost much of its support.

Relief Programs *(page 430)*

Comparing and Contrasting

As you read, complete the sentences.

1. The PWA and the CWA both

_____

_____

2. Only the PWA

_____

_____

3. Only the CWA

_____

_____

Some presidential advisors thought the major cause of the Depression was a lack buying power. They supported work programs for the unemployed, which would get money into the hands of individuals. One such relief program was the Civilian Conservation Corps (CCC). The CCC employed young men 18 to 25 years old under the direction of the forestry service. They planted trees, fought forest fires, and built reservoirs. The young men lived in camps near their work areas, earning $30 per month. The program put about 3 million people to work.

Congress set up the Federal Emergency Relief Administration (FERA). The FERA provided federal money to state and local agencies to fund their relief projects. The Public Works Administration (PWA) was a federal relief agency. The PWA built highways, dams, sewer systems, schools, and government buildings. It gave contracts to construction companies. The PWA broke down racial barriers in construction trades.

The Civil Works Administration (CWA) hired workers directly and placed them on the federal payroll. It built roads, airports, schools, playgrounds, and parks before Roosevelt ordered it shut down. The New Deal programs inspired hope and restored faith in the country.

Answer these questions to check your understanding of the entire section.

1. What events and experiences were part of Franklin Roosevelt's early political career?

_____

_____

_____

2. Why did New Deal advisors feel it is sometimes necessary to regulate industry and labor?

_____

_____

_____

In the space provided, write a letter to President Roosevelt explaining whether he should or should not have signed NIRA into law. Give reasons for your position.

_____

_____

_____

_____

_____

_____

_____

_____

_____

_____

The Second New Deal

Big Idea

As you read pages 434–439 in your textbook, complete this graphic organizer by filling in Roosevelt's main Second New Deal legislative successes and their provisions.

Legislation	Provisions
1.	2.
3.	4.
5.	6.

Notes

Read to Learn

Launching the Second New Deal (page 434)

Analyzing Information

Why do you think Roosevelt asked Congress to fund the Second New Deal?

_____

_____

_____

_____

_____

_____

_____

By 1935, the New Deal was facing criticism from the right and the left. The right opposed Roosevelt's **deficit spending.** He borrowed money to finance programs. Other challenges came from the left. Three opponents threatened to draw enough votes to stop Roosevelt's reelection in 1936.

Roosevelt soon began a series of programs called the Second New Deal. He asked Congress for funds to provide work relief and jobs. One such program created a new federal agency called the Works Progress Administration (WPA). Its workers built highways, roads, public buildings, and parks. A program called Federal Program Number One gave jobs to artists, musicians, and writers. They created murals and sculptures and gave concerts. Writers recorded oral history and stories.

In May 1935, the Supreme Court struck down the National Recovery Administration, finding the NRA codes unconstitutional. Roosevelt called upon Congress to pass his new programs to keep the voters' support.

 **Notes** | # Read to Learn

Reforms for Workers and the Elderly *(page 437)*

Identifying the Main Idea

Complete the sentences to identify the main idea.

1. The Wagner Act protected workers' rights to

_____

_____

_____

2. One result of its passage was

_____

_____

_____

Synthesizing Information

Complete the statement.

The Social Security Act was meant to help

_____

_____

_____

_____

_____

_____

The Supreme Court ruling against the NRA also struck down the part of the NIRA that protected the right to form unions. The President and Congress knew the labor vote would be important in the 1936 election. They also believed higher union wages gave workers more money to spend to help the economy. Opponents argued that high wages meant higher costs and less money to hire workers.

In July 1935, Congress passed the National Labor Relations Act, or the Wagner Act. It guaranteed workers' rights to form unions and bargain collectively. It set up the National Labor Relations Board (NLRB), which organized secret ballots to form unions. The Wagner Act provided for **binding arbitration.** This meant that both sides to an argument could be heard by a third party who would decide the issue.

The Wagner Act stimulated more union activity. The United Mine Workers worked with other unions to organize other industrial workers. They formed the Committee for Industrial Organizations (CIO) in 1935. The CIO organized the automotive and steel workers.

Union organizers started using new tactics such as the **sit-down strike.** In this strike, workers stopped work inside the factory and refused to leave. Companies could not send in replacement workers. The United Auto Workers (UAW) union organized many successful sit-down strikes.

Roosevelt and his advisors spent months preparing the Social Security Act. They viewed it as an insurance measure. This law provided some security for older Americans and unemployed workers.

In the Social Security system, workers pay premiums. These premiums are a tax paid to the federal government. The government then distributes this money. Retired workers over the age of 65 could collect a monthly retirement benefit. Unemployed workers looking for jobs could receive temporary income. Poor mothers with children and the disabled could receive welfare payments.

The Social Security Act helped many people, but not all. It did not cover farmers and domestic workers. About 65 percent of African Americans fell into those two groups. Social Security established the idea that government should take care of those who were unable to work.

Section Wrap-up

Answer these questions to check your understanding of the entire section.

1. What challenges did Roosevelt face in the mid-1930s?

   _____

   _____

   _____

2. Why is the Social Security Act considered one of the most important laws passed by the New Deal?

   _____

   _____

   _____

Descriptive Writing

Write a journal entry in the voice of someone who was recently employed through the WPA. Describe the work you do and how it has affected your life.

_____

_____

_____

_____

_____

_____

_____

_____

_____

_____

The New Deal Coalition

Big Idea

As you read pages 440–445 in your textbook, complete this outline by using the major headings of the section.

The New Deal Coalition

I. Roosevelt's Second Term

   A. _____

   B. _____

   C. _____

II. _____

   A. _____

   B. _____

 **Notes** | **Read to Learn**

Roosevelt's Second Term *(page 440)*

Analyzing Information

Based on the passage, explain how government spending relates to recessions.

1. _____

_____

_____

_____

2. _____

_____

_____

_____

The New Deal caused shifts in party loyalties. People in the South had been the core of the Democratic Party. New supporters of the Democratic Party included farmers, industrial workers, immigrants, African Americans, women, and ethnic minorities. Roosevelt won the 1936 election against Alf Landon.

In 1936, the Supreme Court struck down the Agricultural Adjustment Act as unconstitutional. Other New Deal programs seemed threatened. Roosevelt proposed changing the balance of the Court by adding more justices. This **court-packing** plan was a political mistake. Roosevelt appeared to be threatening the Court's independence. Many people opposed the idea, and the court-packing bill never passed.

In 1937 the economy seemed on the verge of recovery. Roosevelt decided to balance the budget. Then unemployment surged again. This recession led to a debate in his cabinet. Treasury Secretary Morgenthau favored cutting spending. Others wanted to spend heavily to jump-start the economy. Roosevelt was reluctant to start deficit spending but decided to ask for more funds in 1938.

The New Deal Ends (page 444)

Identifying the Main Idea

Write the main idea of the passage.

_____

_____

_____

_____

_____

_____

Drawing Conclusions

Identify the three elements that contributed to the creation of the broker state.

1. _____

_____

2. _____

_____

3. _____

_____

In Roosevelt's second term, Congress passed laws to build low-cost housing, give loans to tenant farmers, abolish child labor, and set a 44-hour workweek.

The New Deal had only limited success in ending the Depression. Unemployment remained high until after World War II. The New Deal did give Americans a stronger sense of security. The Roosevelt recession enabled more Republicans to win seats in the 1938 elections. With some conservative Democrats, they began blocking New Deal legislation. By 1939, the New Deal had ended.

The New Deal worked by balancing competing interests. As a result, business leaders, farmers, workers, and consumers expected the government to protect their interests. Two Supreme Court rulings encouraged the government to take on this role. One was the 1937 case of *NLRB* v. *Jones and Laughlin Steel*. In it, the Court held that the interstate commerce clause gave the federal government authority to regulate production in states. Another case was *Wickard* v. *Filburn* in 1942. This time the Court allowed the government to regulate consumption. These decisions increased federal power over the economy and gave the government a mediator role. The New Deal set up this role of **broker state.** This means the government brokers, or works out, conflicts between different interest groups.

The biggest change brought about by the New Deal is Americans' view of government. New Deal programs created a **safety net** for average Americans. Safeguards and relief programs protected them against economic disaster. People wanted the government to keep this safety net in place. Some critics thought the New Deal gave the government too much power. People still debate today whether the government should intervene in the economy. Another issue still debated today is how much the government should support disadvantaged people.

Section Wrap-up

Answer these questions to check your understanding of the entire section.

1. What were the achievements and defeats of Roosevelt's second term?

   _____

   _____

   _____

2. What new role did the federal government take on during the New Deal era?

   _____

   _____

In the space provided, write a pamphlet to describe the coalition that helped reelect Roosevelt in 1936.

_____

_____

_____

_____

_____

_____

_____

_____

_____

_____

_____

America and the World

Big Idea

As you read pages 454–459 in your textbook, complete the outline below by using the major headings of the section.

America and the World

I. **The Rise of Dictators**

   A. _____

   B. _____

   C. _____

   D. _____

II. _____

   A. _____

   B. _____

   C. _____

 **Notes** | **Read to Learn**

The Rise of Dictators (page 454)

Analyzing Information

Read the first paragraph. How did Mussolini and Hitler rise to power?

_____

_____

_____

_____

_____

_____

_____

Many countries struggled economically after World War I. This made room for dictators in Europe, Russia, and Japan. Benito Mussolini founded Italy's Fascist Party. **Fascism** was an aggressive nationalist movement. It was also strongly anticommunist. Adolph Hitler rose to power in Germany when he worked to elect the Nazis to the Reichstag. He claimed Jews were responsible for Germany's defeat in the war. Mussolini and Hitler exploited people's fears and racism. By 1932, the Nazi party dominated the Reichstag. They later voted to give Hitler dictatorial powers.

Vladimir Lenin led the Communist Party in Russia. The party established communist control throughout the Russian Empire and renamed these territories. Setting up a one-party system, they suppressed individual rights and punished opponents. When Joseph Stalin came into power, he combined family farms and turned them into **collectives.** Between 8 and 10 million people died from hunger or false trials during Stalin's rule. Japan fell under military rule. Its army invaded Manchuria, a resource-rich region in China. Officers assassinated Japan's prime minister. The military now controlled Japan.

 **Notes** | # Read to Learn

American Neutrality *(page 458)*

Identifying the Main Idea

Identify the main idea in this passage.

_____

_____

_____

_____

_____

_____

Detecting Bias

What words tell you Roosevelt opposed the dictators' policies?

_____

_____

_____

_____

_____

_____

_____

_____

American isolationism grew after World War I. European nations could not repay the money they had borrowed during World War I. Books and articles claimed arms manufacturers had tricked the United States into going to war. This impression was only furthered when the Nye Committee held hearings that documented the huge profits these businesses made during the war. This suggested they had influenced the United States to enter the war. After the Nye Report, even more Americans turned toward isolationism.

In response to these feelings, Congress passed three neutrality acts between 1935 and 1937. The Neutrality Act of 1935 made it illegal for the United States to sell arms to any country at war. In 1936, a rebellion erupted in Spain, which quickly became a civil war. Hitler and Mussolini helped the rebels. A second neutrality act was passed after the Spanish Civil War began. The act made it illegal for the United States to sell arms to either side in a civil war.

Soon after, Italy, Germany, and Japan formed the Axis Powers. Congress passed the Neutrality Act of 1937 in response. This required warring nations to buy all nonmilitary supplies from the United States on a "cash and carry" basis. Loans were not allowed. The countries had to send their ships to the United States to pick up the supplies. This was to prevent attacks on neutral American ships that would pull the country into a European or global conflict.

President Roosevelt knew that ending the Depression was the nation's first priority. He understood his countrymen's feelings, but he was not an isolationist. Roosevelt believed in **internationalism,** the idea that trade between nations helped to prevent war. When Japan attacked Manchuria, Roosevelt decided to help China. He authorized the sale of weapons to China. He argued that the Neutrality Act did not apply, since neither country had declared war. He warned the nation that it was dangerous to stand by and let "an epidemic of lawlessness" infect the world.

Section Wrap-up

Answer these questions to check your understanding of the entire section.

1. How did postwar conditions contribute to the rise of antidemocratic governments in Europe?

   _____

   _____

   _____

2. Why did many Americans support a policy of isolationism in the 1930s?

   _____

   _____

   _____

Expository Writing

In the space provided, write an essay about the advantages and disadvantages of the United States following a policy of isolationism in the 1930s.

_____

_____

_____

_____

_____

_____

_____

_____

_____

_____

_____

World War II Begins

Big Idea

As you read pages 460–465 in your textbook, complete the time line below by recording the events leading up to the beginning of World War II.

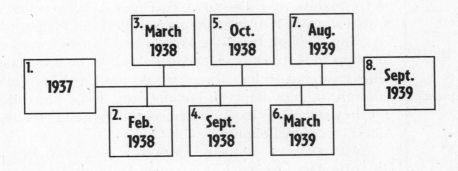

1. 1937
2. Feb. 1938
3. March 1938
4. Sept. 1938
5. Oct. 1938
6. March 1939
7. Aug. 1939
8. Sept. 1939

Notes | Read to Learn

Path to War (page 460)

Making Inferences

Make an inference about the success or failure of the policy of appeasement.

_____

_____

_____

_____

_____

_____

European leaders tried to avoid war by negotiating with Germany. In 1938, Hitler threatened to invade Austria unless Nazis were given important government posts. Austria's chancellor put the matter to a democratic vote. Fearing the outcome, Hitler sent troops into Austria and announced the unification of Austria and Germany. Then Hitler claimed the Sudetenland, a German-speaking area of Czechoslovakia. Though Czechoslovakia opposed his claim, Britain and France agreed to Hitler's demands at the Munich Conference. The resulting policy became known as **appeasement.**

Hitler next demanded German control of the Polish city of Danzig. This convinced Britain and France to prepare for a military intervention. They announced that they would aid Poland if it defended its territory. In May 1939, Hitler ordered his army to prepare to invade Poland. He also began negotiating with the USSR. Hitler proposed to Stalin a nonaggression treaty. Stalin agreed—shocking the world. However, Britain and France understood that Hitler was freeing himself to fight them. The pact also included a deal to divide Poland between Germany and the USSR.

Read to Learn

The War Begins *(page 462)*

Copyright © Glencoe/McGraw-Hill, a division of The McGraw-Hill Companies, Inc.

Determining Cause and Effect

1. What caused Hitler to invade through Belgium?

_____

_____

2. What were the effects of this invasion route?

_____

_____

Hitler invaded Poland on September 1, 1939. Two days later, Britain and France declared war on Germany. World War II had begun. Poland bravely resisted the invasion. Germany's new way of fighting **blitzkrieg,** or lightning war, proved too advanced for Poland's outdated army. By October 5, Germany had defeated Poland. Hitler prepared to invade France.

The British sent troops to France. Instead of attacking Germany, French forces waited behind the Maginot Line, along its German border. This allowed Hitler to concentrate on Poland. It also allowed him to maneuver around the Maginot Line by invading through Belgium. French and British forces raced into Belgium in response, which turned out to be a mistake. The Allies assumed Hitler's forces would not be able to make it through the mountains of Luxembourg and eastern Belgium—but they did. They easily smashed the French lines and trapped Allied forces in Belgium.

Britain was able to save more than 300,000 troops when Hitler hesitated to attack the port of Dunkirk. However, France surrendered to Germany in June of 1940. After installing a puppet government, Hitler then set his sights on Britain.

Britain Remains Defiant *(page 465)*

Predicting

Predict the fate of the British had they not had the advantage of radar.

_____

_____

_____

_____

_____

_____

_____

Hitler expected Britain to negotiate peace after France surrendered. For British Prime Minister Winston Churchill, however, the war was now a fight to defend civilization. When Hitler realized Britain would not surrender, he prepared to invade. Getting across the English Channel would be a challenge, though, for Germany did not have many transport ships. To invade, Hitler had to defeat the British Royal Air Force. In June 1940, the *Luftwaffe* launched a fierce air battle—the Battle of Britain—to destroy the British air force.

On August 23, German bombers accidentally bombed London, enraging the British, who in turn bombed Berlin the following night. Furious, Hitler then ordered the *Luftwaffe* to continue bombing London. Hitler's goal was now to terrorize the British people into surrendering. He failed. Londoners took refuge in the city's subway tunnels whenever German planes attacked.

Germany had thousands of fighter planes. Britain had a few hundred, but it also had radar, which let British fighters detect and intercept incoming German planes. The German air force suffered greatly as a result. On October 12, 1940, Hitler cancelled the invasion of Britain.

Section Wrap-up

Answer these questions to check your understanding of the entire section.

1. Why was Hitler able to take over Austria and Czechoslovakia?

_____

_____

_____

2. Describe the early events of the war. Why was Britain able to resist the Nazis?

_____

_____

_____

In the space provided, write a journal entry about the German air raids on London from the point of view of a British citizen living in London during World War II.

_____

_____

_____

_____

_____

_____

_____

_____

_____

_____

The Holocaust

Big Idea

As you read pages 466–471 in your textbook, complete the graphic organizer below by listing some examples of Nazi persecution of European Jews.

Examples of Persecution	
	1.
	2.
	3.
	4.
	5.

 **Notes**

Read to Learn

Nazi Persecution of the Jews (page 466)

Problems and Solutions

Identify two problems faced by Jewish immigrants who wanted to enter the United States.

_____

_____

_____

_____

_____

_____

_____

European Jews had experienced anti-Semitism before World War II. They had sometimes been set apart in ghettos and prohibited from owning land. Persecution of Jews during World War II reached alarming heights. In September of 1935, the Nuremberg Laws took citizenship away from Jewish Germans. It also banned marriage between Jews and other Germans. Soon after, Jewish people were barred from voting. Their passports were marked with a red "J." By 1938, they could not practice law or medicine or operate businesses.

On *Kristallnacht,* "the night of broken glass," anti-Jewish violence erupted in Germany and Austria. The result was 90 Jewish deaths and hundreds of serious injuries. The Gestapo arrested thousands of wealthy Jews. German and Austrian Jews now lived in terror.

The United States had huge backlogs of visa applications from Jews in Germany. U.S. immigration laws barred officials from granting visas to anyone "likely to become a public charge," a description custom officials felt fit Jewish immigrants who had to leave any wealth behind. As a result, millions of Jews remained trapped in Europe.

The Final Solution *(page 470)*

Making Inferences

What was meant by the term "final solution" to the Jewish question?

_____

_____

_____

_____

_____

Determining Cause and Effect

List three causes that help explain why the Holocaust occurred.

1. _____

_____

_____

2. _____

_____

_____

3. _____

_____

_____

In 1942, Nazi leaders met at the Wannsee Conference to determine the "final solution of the Jewish question." Previous "solutions" included rounding up Jews and other "undesirables," such as the disabled, Gypsies, and Slavs from conquered territories, and shooting them. They were then piled into mass graves. Nazis also forced Jewish people into trucks and piped in exhaust fumes to kill them. But the Nazis considered these methods slow and inefficient.

The Nazis made plans to round up Jews from areas of Nazi-controlled Europe. They built **concentration camps,** or detention centers throughout Europe. Healthy individuals from these camps worked 12-hour shifts as slave laborers in nearby factories until they dropped dead from the living conditions. The elderly, disabled, and young children, who could not work, were sent directly to **extermination camps.** Here, they were executed in huge gas chambers, where the whole process could be done more efficiently. The bodies of these victims were burned.

The first concentration camps, which the Nazis built in 1933, were used to jail their political opponents. Buchenwald was built in 1937 near the town of Weimar, Germany. It was one of the largest concentration camps of the World War II era. Even without gas chambers, hundreds of prisoners died there every month from exhaustion and harsh conditions.

Extermination camps did even more damage. Most were located in Poland. At these camps, including the infamous Treblinka and Auschwitz, Jews were the main victims. More than 1,300,000 Jews died at Auschwitz. In only a few years, Jewish culture was virtually wiped out in Nazi-controlled regions of Europe.

People continue to debate why and how the Holocaust happened. Most historians believe several factors contributed to it. The German people felt they had been unjustly treated by the harsh treaty terms of World War I. Germany faced severe economic problems. Hitler had a strong hold over Germany and people feared his secret police. Resistance was difficult and dangerous. Germany did not have a strong tradition of representative government before the Nazi era. Europe had a long history of anti-Jewish prejudice and discrimination, which fed into the Nazi propaganda and racial program.

Section Wrap-up

Answer these questions to check your understanding of the entire section.

1. Describe the early persecutions of Germany's Jewish population.

_____

_____

_____

2. What methods did the Nazis use to try to exterminate Europe's Jewish population?

_____

_____

_____

In the space provided, write a brief encyclopedia article about the Holocaust. Include an explanation of what led to this shocking episode in history.

_____

_____

_____

_____

_____

_____

_____

_____

_____

_____

America Enters the War

Big Idea

As you read pages 474–479 in your textbook, complete the graphic organizer by naming events that shifted American opinion toward helping the Allies.

```
┌─────────────────────────────┐
│  Events That Shifted American│
│          Opinion             │
└─────────────────────────────┘
        │              │
   ┌────────┐     ┌────────┐
   │ 1.     │     │ 2.     │
   └────────┘     └────────┘
```

Notes   Read to Learn

FDR Supports England *(page 474)*

Formulating Questions

What is a question you could ask to understand the Neutrality Act of 1939?

_____

_____

_____

_____

_____

_____

The United States was divided at the beginning of Germany's war with Britain and France. President Roosevelt declared the United States neutral two days after Britain and France declared war. Despite this, Roosevelt wanted to help the two nations in their struggle against Hitler. He asked Congress to revise the neutrality laws to eliminate the ban on arm sales to nations at war. The result was the Neutrality Act of 1939. The law was similar to the 1937 Neutrality Act governing the sale of nonmilitary items by allowing countries to buy weapons on a cash-and-carry basis. The public supported the president's decision to help the allies as long as the arms sales were not carried on American ships.

Soon U.S. neutrality would be tested. Britain had lost nearly half its naval destroyers. It needed to purchase destroyers from the United States, but lacked the cash. Roosevelt created a loophole. He exchanged 50 American destroyers for the right to build American bases in British-controlled parts of Bermuda and in the Caribbean. The act did not apply because the deal did not involve a sale or any purchases.

 **Read to Learn**

Edging Toward War (page 476)

Analyzing Information

How did the hemispheric defense zone concept help Britain?

_____

_____

_____

_____

_____

_____

_____

_____

After President Roosevelt was reelected, he began to expand the nation's role in the war. He removed the cash requirement of the Neutrality Act with the Lend-Lease Act. This allowed the United States to lend or lease arms to any country "vital to the defense of the United States." Congress passed the act by a wide margin. The United States began leasing weapons to Britain.

Technically, the United States was still neutral and could not protect British cargo ships, hindering getting the arms to Britain. Roosevelt then introduced the **hemispheric defense zone.** He declared the entire western half of the Atlantic to be neutral. This way, U.S. Navy ships could patrol the western Atlantic and reveal the location of German ships to Britain.

Winston Churchill and Roosevelt met to discuss the Atlantic Charter in 1941, an agreement that committed their nations to democracy and free trade. Fifteen other nations signed the charter that year. Soon after, a German submarine fired on an American destroyer. Roosevelt ordered American ships to "shoot on sight" German ships. Germany retaliated, and the United States found itself drawn further into the war.

Japan Attacks (page 477)

Problems and Solutions

As you read, write Roosevelt's solution to the following problem.

Problem: Great Britain's ships in Asia were threatened by Japanese attacks.

Solution:

_____

_____

_____

_____

_____

_____

Britain needed much of its navy in Asia to protect itself against a Japanese attack. Japan depended on the United States for key materials, including steel and oil. Wanting to hinder Japanese aggression, Roosevelt restricted the sale of **strategic materials,** including fuel and iron. Furious, the Japanese signed an alliance to become a member of the Axis.

Japan sent troops into Indochina, now a direct threat to Great Britain. Roosevelt responded by freezing Japanese assets in the United States. He reduced the amount of oil sent to Japan and sent General Douglas MacArthur to the Philippines to build American defenses there. Roosevelt made it clear the oil embargo would end only if Japan withdrew its troops from Indochina. Japan continued to prepare for war while it negotiated with the United States. Neither side would back down. On December 7, 1941, Japan attacked Pearl Harbor.

Although Germany and Japan were allies, Hitler was under no obligation to aid Japan. He was frustrated, though, with the American naval attacks on German submarines. He believed the time had come to declare war. On December 11, Germany and Italy both declared war on the United States. Hitler had greatly underestimated U.S. strength.

Section Wrap-up

Answer these questions to check your understanding of the entire section.

1. How did Roosevelt help Britain while maintaining official neutrality?

_____

_____

_____

2. What events led to increasing tension, and ultimately war, between the United States and Japan?

_____

_____

_____

Persuasive Writing

In the space provided, write a newspaper editorial arguing for or against the United States becoming involved in World War II.

_____

_____

_____

_____

_____

_____

_____

_____

_____

_____

_____

_____

Mobilizing the War

Big Idea

As you read pages 486–493 in your textbook, complete the graphic organizer below by filling in the agencies that the U.S. government created to mobilize the nation for war.

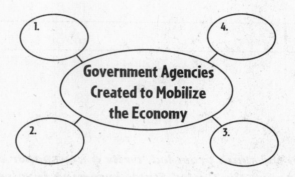

1.
4.

Government Agencies Created to Mobilize the Economy

2.
3.

 **Notes** | **Read to Learn**

Converting the Economy (page 486)

Identifying the Main Idea

What is the main idea of this passage?

_____
_____
_____
_____
_____
_____
_____

Even before the attack on Pearl Harbor, the United States had begun to mobilize the economy. When the German blitzkrieg hit France in May 1940, President Roosevelt declared a national emergency. He announced a plan to build 50,000 warplanes a year.

Roosevelt and his advisors believed that giving industry an incentive to move quickly was the best way to convert the economy to war production. Normally, companies would bid for a contract to make military equipment. That system was now too slow. Instead, the government signed **cost-plus** contracts, agreeing to pay a company whatever it cost to make a product, plus a guaranteed percentage of the cost as profit. Under this system, the more a company produced and the faster it did the work, the more money it would make.

Congress gave the Reconstruction Finance Corporation (RFC) new authority. Congress did this to help convince companies to switch their factories to make military goods. The government gave the agency permission to make loans to companies to help them cover the cost of converting to war production.

Notes | Read to Learn

American Industry Gets the Job Done *(page 488)*

Determining Cause and Effect

Fill in the effect.

Cause: Clashes occurred between the WPB and the military.

Effect: _____

_____

_____

_____

_____

By the summer of 1942, most major industries had changed to war production. Automobile companies began to make trucks, jeeps, and tanks. They also made rifles, mines, helmets, and other military equipment. The Ford Company created an assembly line to build the B-24 bomber. By the end of the war, the company had built more than 8,600 aircraft.

Henry Kaiser's shipyards built ships. They were best known for making Liberty ships. These were the basic cargo ships used during the war. They were welded instead of riveted, making them cheap, easy to build, and difficult to sink.

To make mobilization more efficient, President Roosevelt set up the War Production Board (WPB). This agency had the authority to set priorities and production goals. It also controlled the distribution of raw materials and supplies. Almost immediately, the WPB clashed with the military. Military agents continued to sign contracts without consulting the WPB. In 1943, Roosevelt set up the Office of War Mobilization (OWM) to settle arguments among the different agencies.

Building an Army *(page 490)*

Drawing Conclusions

How did the participation of women and minorities affect the U.S. war effort?

_____

_____

_____

_____

_____

_____

_____

Before the defeat of France, Congress had opposed a peacetime draft. Congress approved the Selective Service and Training Act in September 1940. This peacetime draft prepared people to fight the war.

The military was segregated. Minorities served in noncombat roles. Because they were **disenfranchised,** or could not vote, some African Americans did not want to support the war. African American leaders launched the "Double V Campaign." This campaign urged African Americans to support the war effort in order to fight racism abroad and at home. Roosevelt had to order the military to recruit women and minorities.

The 99th Pursuit Squadron was the army's first African American unit. The pilots trained in Tuskegee, Alabama. They became known as the Tuskegee Airmen and helped win the Battle of Anzio in Italy. Later, three new African American squadrons, the 332nd Fighter Group, protected American bombers without losing a single aircraft to enemy forces.

The Women's Army Corps (WAC) brought women into the army, although women were barred from combat. Oveta Culp Hobby was assigned the rank of colonel. The Women Airforce Service Pilots (WASPs) formed in 1943 and made more than 12,000 deliveries of planes over the next year.

Section Wrap-up

Answer these questions to check your understanding of the entire section.

1. How did the United States change to a wartime economy?

_____

_____

_____

2. What were the issues involved in raising an army for the United States?

_____

_____

_____

In the space provided, write a letter to the editor arguing for or against peacetime recruitment for the military.

_____

_____

_____

_____

_____

_____

_____

_____

_____

_____

The Early Battles

Big Idea

As you read pages 494–499 in your textbook, complete the time line below
by listing some of the major battles discussed and the victor in each.

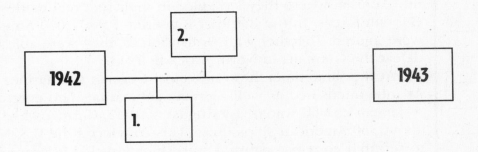

1942   2.   1943

1.

 **Notes** | **Read to Learn**

Holding the Line Against Japan *(page 494)*

Making Inferences

*Make an inference
about how poor con-
ditions affected the
outcome at Bataan.*

_____

_____

_____

_____

_____

_____

The Japanese continued to win victories in the Pacific until
the Battle of Midway. Two days after their attack on Pearl
Harbor, Japanese troops landed on the Philippine Islands,
strongly outnumbering American and Filipino forces. General
Douglas MacArthur decided to retreat to the Bataan Peninsula.

Conditions were horrible. Soldiers starved, and malaria,
scurvy, and dysentery ran rampant. Eventually the defenders of
Bataan surrendered. They were forced to march 65 miles to a
Japanese prison camp. Almost 10,000 troops died on the way.
The march was later called the Bataan Death March.

By early 1942, the United States was preparing to drop
bombs on Tokyo. President Roosevelt ordered Lieutenant
Colonel James Doolittle to command the mission. America
bombed Japan for the first time in April of that year. Doolittle's
raid sent Japanese strategy into a tailspin. Thanks to the work
of code breakers, American forces were able to decode Japan's
plan to attack both New Guinea and Midway. This allowed
Admiral Chester Nimitz to ambush the Japanese fleet at Midway
and win the battle. The Battle of Midway was a turning point.

 **Notes** | # Read to Learn

Stopping the Germans (page 497)

Analyzing Information

Complete the sentence.

The Battle of Stalingrad was a turning point in the war because

_____

_____

_____

_____

_____

Predicting

Based on the passage, make two predictions about World War II.

1. _____

_____

_____

_____

2. _____

_____

_____

_____

_____

In 1942, Joseph Stalin wanted President Roosevelt to directly attack Germany in Europe. Winston Churchill, however, wanted to attack the **periphery,** or edges, of the German empire. Roosevelt agreed and ordered troops to invade Morocco and Algeria in North Africa. These were French territories under German control.

General Patton led the American forces in Morocco. They quickly captured the city of Casablanca. Then they headed east into Tunisia, where they struggled in their first real battle with German forces. In the Battle of Kasserine Pass, 7,000 Americans were injured. Together with British forces, they were able to defeat the Germans in North Africa in 1943.

At the same time, the war against German submarines in the Atlantic intensified as well. German submarines had entered American coastal waters. By August of 1942, Germans had sunk about 360 American ships there. This convinced the U.S. Navy to set up a **convoy system.** Cargo ships traveled in groups escorted by navy warships. American and British shipyards also upped production of cargo ships. Soon they were producing more ships than the German submarines were sinking. The United States was also using new technology such as radar, sonar, and depth charges against the submarines. The war slowly turned in favor of the Allies.

In the spring of 1942, Hitler was confident he could beat the Soviets by wrecking the Soviet economy. He considered the city of Stalingrad central to his efforts. Hitler ordered his troops to capture and hold the city at all costs. In September of that year, German troops entered Stalingrad, but they were not equipped for the cold in ways the Soviet army was. The Germans lost thousands of soldiers. In November, Soviet reinforcements arrived and trapped almost 250,000 German troops within the city. The Germans surrendered the city in February of 1943. Germany was now on the defensive.

Answer these questions to check your understanding of the entire section.

1. How were the Allies able to fight a war on two fronts and turn the war against the Axis Powers in the Pacific, Russia, and the North Atlantic?

   _____

   _____

   _____

2. How did generals MacArthur and Patton and Lieutenant Colonel James Doolittle contribute to the war effort?

   _____

   _____

   _____

In the space provided, write a news account of the Battle of Stalingrad.

_____

_____

_____

_____

_____

_____

_____

_____

_____

_____

Life on the Home Front

Big Idea

As you read pages 500–507 in your textbook, complete this graphic organizer by listing opportunities for women and African Americans before and after the war. Evaluate what progress was still needed after the war.

Opportunities

	Before War	After War	Still Needed
Women	1.	2.	3.
African Americans	4.	5.	6.

 **Notes**

Read to Learn

Women and Minorities Gain Ground (page 500)

Evaluating Information

Does the passage do a good job explaining how women and minorities gained ground? Circle your answer. Then explain it.

Yes   No

_____

_____

_____

_____

_____

Before the war, most Americans believed married women should not work outside the home. However, the labor shortage during the war forced factories to hire married women. "Rosie the Riveter" was the symbol of the campaign to hire women. Images of Rosie appeared on posters and in newspaper ads. Although most women left the factories after the war, their work permanently changed American attitudes about women in the workplace.

Many factories did not want to hire African Americans. A. Philip Randolph was the head of the Brotherhood of Sleeping Car Porters—a major union for African American railroad workers. He told President Roosevelt that he was going to organize a march on Washington. Roosevelt responded by issuing an order saying that discrimination in hiring workers in defense industries would not be tolerated. He created the Fair Employment Practices Commission to enforce the order.

To help farmers in the Southwest overcome the labor shortage, the government started the Bracero Program in 1942. It arranged for Mexican farm workers to help in the harvest.

A Nation on the Move (page 502)

Making Generalizations

How were minorities treated during the war?

_____

_____

_____

_____

_____

Underline three facts that support your generalization.

The wartime economy created millions of new jobs. However, people who wanted them did not always live near the factories. Many workers moved to the **Sunbelt,** a region including southern California and the Deep South. Many African Americans moved north in the Great Migration. They were often met with suspicion and intolerance.

In California, **zoot-suit** wearers—often Mexican American teenagers—faced prejudice. The baggy zoot suit used more material than the **victory suit.** Some thought that wearing it was unpatriotic. In June of 1943, 2,500 soldiers and sailors stormed Mexican American neighborhoods in Los Angeles. They attacked Mexican American teenagers. Police did not intervene.

After Japan attacked Pearl Harbor, all people of Japanese ancestry on the West Coast were ordered to move to internment camps. In *Korematsu* v. *the United States,* Fred Korematsu argued that his civil rights had been violated. He took his case to the Supreme Court, but he lost. After the war, the Japanese American Citizens League (JACL) tried to help Japanese Americans who had lost property during the relocation.

Daily Life in Wartime (page 506)

Problems and Solutions

Identify one problem in the passage. List one solution to it.

Problem:

_____

_____

_____

_____

Solution:

_____

_____

_____

_____

Wages and prices rose quickly during the war. To stabilize prices, President Roosevelt created the Office of Price Administration (OPA) and the Office of Economic Stabilization (OES). They regulated prices and controlled inflation. The demand for raw materials and supplies created shortages. To keep products available for military use, the OPA **rationed** them, or limited their availability. Meat, oil, sugar—even gasoline—were all rationed. Households received ration coupons each month that limited the amounts of rationed goods they could purchase. Americans also planted **victory gardens** to produce more food. The government ran scrap drives to collect the spare rubber, tin, aluminum, and steel the military needed.

The United States raised taxes to help pay for the war. Because most Americans opposed a high tax increase, the taxes raised during World War II paid for only 45 percent of the war's cost. People bought bonds issued by the government as a way to make up the difference. The government promised to pay back the money, plus interest, at a later date. Individuals bought nearly $50 billion worth of war bonds. Banks, insurance companies, and other financial institutions bought the rest—more than $100 billion worth of bonds.

Answer these questions to check your understanding of the entire section.

1. How did the wartime economy create opportunities for women and minorities?

_____

_____

_____

2. How did Americans cope with shortages and rapidly rising prices?

_____

_____

_____

Suppose you are a woman living during the war. Write a journal entry describing a typical day in your life.

_____

_____

_____

_____

_____

_____

_____

_____

_____

_____

Pushing Back the Axis

Big Idea

As you read pages 508–515 in your textbook, complete this graphic organizer by filling in the names of some of the battles fought. Indicate whether Allied or Axis forces won the battle.

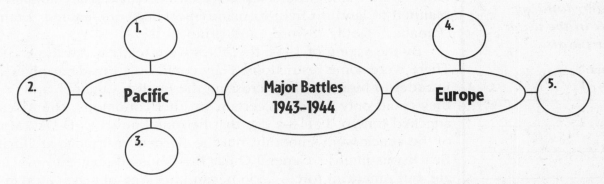

1.
2.
Pacific
3.

Major Battles
1943–1944

Europe
4.
5.

 **Notes**   **Read to Learn**

Striking Germany and Italy *(page 508)*

Predicting

Skim the passage. Make two predictions about what the section will be about.

1. _____

_____

_____

_____

2. _____

_____

_____

_____

In January 1943, President Roosevelt met with Prime Minister Winston Churchill at the Casablanca Conference in Morocco. The two leaders agreed to step up the bombing of Germany. The Allies also agreed to attack the Axis forces in Sicily.

Between 1943 and 1945, the air forces of Britain and the United States dropped about 53,000 tons of explosives on Germany every month. The bombing created an oil shortage and destroyed the railroad system as well as many German aircraft factories. Germany's air force could not replace the planes they lost. The Allies now had total control of the air.

General Eisenhower was in charge of the Sicily invasion. Allied troops captured the western half of the island. The Germans were defeated in Sicily. Italy's king arrested Mussolini and began to negotiate a surrender to the Allies. But German troops seized northern Italy and returned Mussolini to power.

Roosevelt and Churchill met with Stalin in late 1943. They reached several agreements—one being that Germany would be broken up after the war. Stalin also agreed to attack Germany once the Allies landed in France.

Landing in France (page 511)

Determining Cause and Effect

Fill in the effect.

Cause: The Allies placed inflated rubber tanks and dummy landing craft in the water near Calais.

Effect: _____

_____

_____

_____

_____

Roosevelt and Churchill met in Egypt to continue planning the invasion of France—otherwise known as Operation Overlord. Roosevelt selected General Eisenhower to command the invasion. The Germans knew the Allies were planning to invade France, so Hitler fortified the coast. The Germans guessed that the Allies would land in Pas-de-Calais. To fuel this misconception, the Allies placed inflated rubber tanks and dummy landing craft along the coast across from Calais. They actually planned to land on five Normandy beaches code-named "Utah," "Omaha," "Gold," "Sword," and "Juno."

By the spring of 1944, the Allies were ready to invade France. There were some restrictions. They could only invade at night in order to hide the ships crossing the English Channel, and they could only invade in certain weather conditions. The Allies attacked June 6, 1944—a day that became known as D-Day. Most of the attack went smoothly, but the German resistance at Omaha Beach was intense. General Omar Bradley made plans to evacuate, but American forces soon began knocking out the German defenses. By the end of the day, the invasion was successful.

Driving Japan Back (page 513)

Identifying the Main Idea

Write the main idea of this passage.

_____

_____

_____

_____

_____

_____

_____

The United States also developed a strategy to defeat Japan. It had two parts. In the first, Admiral Nimitz commanded the Pacific Fleet as it hopped from one central Pacific island to the next. This campaign started in the fall of 1943, but the Pacific's geography posed a problem. Many of the islands were coral reef atolls, and the water over the reefs was often shallow. U.S. ships ran aground before reaching the shore, forcing troops to wade to shore. Many died from Japanese gunfire before reaching the shore. One vehicle, called an **amphtrac,** successfully crossed the reefs to deliver troops.

In the second part of the plan, General MacArthur's troops invaded Guadalcanal, in the southwest Pacific, in 1942. By early 1944, MacArthur's troops had captured enough islands to surround Japan's main military base in the region. U.S. troops turned their focus to recapturing the Philippines. In response, Japan attacked from the north and west. Some Japanese fighters were **kamikaze** pilots—those who deliberately flew their planes into American ships. The pilots died, but also inflicted severe damage. The Japanese eventually retreated, but the battle to recapture the Philippines was long. It was still going on when word came in August 1945 that Japan had surrendered.

Answer these questions to check your understanding of the entire section.

1. What were the goals of the two major offensives the Allies launched in Europe in 1943?

_____

_____

_____

2. What was the American strategy for pushing back the Japanese in the Pacific?

_____

_____

_____

Suppose you will debate the effectiveness of the Allies' strategies for defeating the Axis Powers. Summarize the arguments you would make in a brief paragraph.

_____

_____

_____

_____

_____

_____

_____

_____

_____

_____

_____

The War Ends

Big Idea

As you read pages 518–525 in your textbook, complete the outline below using the major headings of the section.

The War Ends

I. **The Third Reich Collapses**
   A. _____
   B. _____
II. _____
   A. _____
   B. _____
   C. _____
   D. _____
   E. _____
   F. _____
III. _____
   A. _____
   B. _____

Notes | Read to Learn

The Third Reich Collapses (page 518)

Formulating Questions

Write two questions you have based on the passage.

1. _____
_____
_____
_____

2. _____
_____
_____
_____

Hedgerows, or dirt walls covered in shrubbery, surrounded many fields in Normandy, enabling the Germans to defend their positions. On July 25, 1944, American bombers blew a hole in German lines and America tanks raced through the gap. Then, on August 25, the Allies liberated Paris.

Hitler staged one last desperate offensive by cutting off Allied supplies coming through the port of Antwerp, Belgium. His attack, known as the Battle of the Bulge, caught the Americans by surprise. Three days later, however, General Patton and his troops slammed into German lines. Allied aircraft bombed German fuel depots. Patton's troops soon broke through the German lines. The United States won the battle.

By the time the Battle of the Bulge ended, the Soviets had pushed Hitler's troops out of Russia and across Poland. As Soviets drove toward Berlin from the east, American forces pushed toward it from the west. Soviet troops arrived in Berlin on April 21, 1945, and by April 30, Hitler had killed himself. His successor, Karl Doenitz, surrendered unconditionally to the Allies on May 7.

 **Notes** | # Read to Learn

Japan Is Defeated *(page 520)*

Distinguishing Fact from Opinion

List one fact and one opinion from the passage about the atomic bomb.

Fact:

_____

_____

_____

_____

Opinion:

_____

_____

_____

_____

President Roosevelt died on April 12, 1945, after suffering a stroke. Harry S. Truman became president and had to end the war in Japan. The United States tried sending B-29s to bomb Japan, but they ran out of fuel by the time they reached Japan and could not hit their targets. U.S. troops invaded Iwo Jima so they could establish a place for the bombers to refuel. Iwo Jima's geography was difficult. American troops succeeded in capturing the island, but more than 6,800 marines died in the process.

While American engineers prepared airfields on Iwo Jima, General Curtis LeMay decided to change plans. He ordered B-29s to drop bombs filled with **napalm,** which exploded and ignited fires. The firebombs killed many civilians. Japan still refused to surrender. American troops invaded Okinawa in April of 1945 and captured it in late June.

President Truman knew the United States had a new weapon that could force Japan's unconditional surrender—the atomic bomb. The American program to build it, code-named the Manhattan Project, had started under Roosevelt. After much debate, President Truman ordered the bomb dropped. He believed doing so was justified because it would save American lives. On August 6, 1945, an atomic bomb was dropped on Hiroshima. Three days later, another was dropped on Nagasaki. The bombs killed tens of thousands of people. Japan surrendered on August 15, V-J Day. World War II was over.

Building a New World *(page 524)*

Analyzing Information

Circle the names of the five permanent members of the Security Council. How were these members probably chosen?

_____

_____

_____

_____

In 1944, delegates from 39 countries met in Washington, D.C. They discussed forming a new organization, the United Nations. It would have a General Assembly in which every member nation would have one vote. It would also have an eleven-member Security Council. Britain, France, China, the Soviet Union, and the United States would be the council's permanent members. They would have veto power. In 1945, representatives from 50 countries came to San Francisco to officially organize the United Nations. They designed its **charter,** or constitution. The General Assembly would vote on resolutions and choose the nonpermanent security group's members. The Security Council attended to international peace and security.

In August 1945, the United States, Britain, France, and the Soviet Union created the International Military Tribunal (IMT). At the Nuremberg trials, the IMT tried German leaders for war crimes. Many of these leaders were executed. Several Japanese leaders were also tried and executed.

Copyright © Glencoe/McGraw-Hill, a division of The McGraw-Hill Companies, Inc.

Section Wrap-up

Answer these questions to check your understanding of the entire section.

1. What tactics did the Allies use to defeat Japan?

_____

_____

_____

2. Why did the Allies create the United Nations and hold war crimes trials?

_____

_____

_____

In the space provided, write a brief newspaper article about the formation of the United Nations. Include details about its members and its purpose.

_____

_____

_____

_____

_____

_____

_____

_____

_____

_____

_____

_____

The Origins of the Cold War

Big Idea

As you read pages 532–537 in your textbook, complete the graphic organizer by filling in the names of the conferences held among the "Big Three" Allies and the outcomes of each.

Conferences	Outcomes
1.	2.
3.	4.

 **Notes** | **Read to Learn**

The Yalta Conference *(page 532)*

Making Generalizations

Read the passage. Underline two statements that support this generalization:

The Soviet Union was against spreading democracy in Europe.

In February 1945, Roosevelt, Churchill, and Stalin met at Yalta. There, they discussed Poland. Churchill and Roosevelt wanted the Poles to choose their own government. Stalin supported the Communist government it had set up during the war. They compromised. The Communist government stayed, but Stalin agreed to hold free elections quickly. They also divided Germany into four zones. Great Britain, the United States, the Soviet Union, and France each controlled a zone. Just two weeks after Yalta, the Soviet Union forced Romania to form a Communist government. They also refused to allow elections in Poland.

Relations between the United States and the Soviet Union were strained from 1946 to 1990, an era known as the Cold War. The conflict arose because the countries had different goals. The Soviet Union was worried about its security and wanted to keep Germany weak. The Soviets also wanted to spread communism to other nations. The United States focused on economic problems. Americans believed economic growth and democracy were important in order to keep world peace.

Truman Takes Control *(page 535)*

Analyzing Information

Read the statements. Write T by the one Truman might have said. Write S by the one Stalin might have said.

1. _____ *Poland and Czechoslovakia can have their own governments, but they must remain friendly to the Soviet Union.*

2. _____ *The people of Poland and Eastern Europe must be allowed to elect their own governments.*

Problems and Solutions

Write Truman's solution.

Problem: Stalin wanted reparations from Germany.

Solution:

_____

_____

_____

_____

_____

_____

_____

Vice President Harry S. Truman became the president after Roosevelt died in 1945. Truman was anticommunist and did not trust Stalin. He also did not want to appease Stalin. He demanded that Stalin hold free elections as promised. Truman finally met Stalin in July 1945 at the Potsdam Conference, where they worked out a deal on Germany. Truman believed that Germany's industrial economy had to be revived. He thought this was necessary for all of Europe's recovery. Truman also thought that if its economy stayed weak, Germany might turn to communism. Stalin wanted reparations from Germany. He felt that the Germans should pay for the damage they caused to the Soviet Union.

Truman suggested that the Soviet Union take reparations from the zone under its own control. He also offered small amounts of industrial equipment from other zones, which the Soviets could pay for with agricultural goods from their zone. Stalin did not like Truman's proposal. However, Truman hinted that he had an atomic bomb. Stalin accepted.

The Soviets refused to uphold the Declaration of Liberated Europe. They set up pro-Soviet Communist governments in Eastern Europe. These countries were called **satellite nations.** They had their own governments, but remained Communist and friendly to the Soviet Union. Churchill later called the Communist takeover of Eastern Europe an **iron curtain** that separated Eastern Europe from the West.

Answer these questions to check your understanding of the entire section.

1. How did Stalin support the spread of communism in Europe?

_____

_____

_____

2. Why did President Truman disagree with Stalin about German reparations?

_____

_____

_____

Suppose you are living in the Soviet Union after World War II. Write a letter to American President Truman. Explain why the Germans should pay high reparations to your country. Include examples to support your position.

_____

_____

_____

_____

_____

_____

_____

_____

_____

_____

_____

_____

_____

The Early Cold War Years

Big Idea

As you read pages 538–545 in your textbook, complete the time line by recording some major events related to the Korean War.

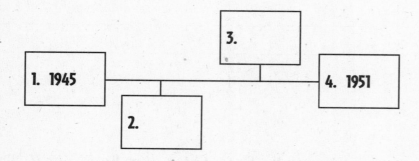

1. 1945

2.

3.

4. 1951

 **Notes** | **Read to Learn**

Containing Communism *(page 538)*

Determining Cause and Effect

Write the cause.

Cause:

_____

_____

_____

_____

Effect: The Soviets blockaded Berlin in anger.

In 1945 Britain and the United States pushed the Soviets to hold free elections in Eastern Europe, but they refused. One diplomat suggested the use of diplomacy, economics, and military action to stop Soviet expansion. This policy became known as **containment.** Soon after, Soviet-related crises erupted Iran and in Turkey. The Soviets backed down only under threats of force from the United States. In 1947 Truman asked Congress for money to help Greece and Turkey fight communism. To weaken the appeal of communism, the United States also created the Marshall Plan. It gave Europe aid to rebuild its economies.

In 1948 the United States, France, and Britain combined their zones with West Berlin to create West Germany. The Soviets blockaded Berlin in anger. Truman ordered the Berlin airlift, in which cargo planes brought food and other supplies to the city. Stalin finally lifted the blockade, but Americans and Western Europe were moved to form NATO, the North Atlantic Treaty Organization. Twelve nations agreed to help each other if attacked. The Soviets set up the Warsaw Pact alliance.

The Korean War (page 542)

Detecting Bias

Reread the passage. Place an X next to the statement or statements that show how MacArthur may have felt about Truman's leadership.

Identifying the Main Idea

Reread the passage. Which best states the main idea of the passage? Circle it.

1. The Korean War made the UN focus on the containment policy.

2. The spread of the Cold War to Asia forced a change in American foreign policy.

The Cold War spread to Asia. In China, Mao Zedong led Communist forces in a revolt against Chiang Kai-shek's Nationalist government. Their fight began in the 1920s. However, the two sides stopped fighting during World War II and joined forces to stop the Japanese invasion. After the war ended, the two groups began fighting again. The United States wanted to stop the spread of communism in Asia. It sent Chiang Kai-shek $2 billion in aid. However, the Communists captured the capital Beijing and moved south. The Nationalists left the mainland and fled to Taiwan. In 1949 the Communists set up the People's Republic of China.

In the same year, the Soviet Union tested its first atomic weapon. In 1950 it signed a treaty of alliance with China. Americans feared that these allies would support Communist revolutions around the world. The United States set up formal relations with the Nationalists on Taiwan. The United States also changed it policy toward Japan. General Douglas MacArthur was put in charge of occupied Japan, where he encouraged democracy and quick economic recovery. Americans saw Japan as a way to defend Asia against communism.

After World War II, the Allies divided Korea at the 38th parallel. The Soviet-controlled north became Communist. In the U.S.-controlled south, an American-backed government was set up. The Soviets gave military aid to North Korea, which built a huge army and invaded South Korea on June 25, 1950. President Truman saw this as a test of the containment policy. He sent MacArthur and the American military to Korea. Truman also asked the United Nations for troops to help. In September 1950, MacArthur ordered an invasion. The North Koreans were taken by surprise, and they retreated across the 38th parallel. MacArthur pushed the North Koreans toward the Chinese border. The Chinese were afraid of a UN invasion and warned the UN troops to retreat. Then the Chinese invaded Korea and pushed UN troops south.

General MacArthur wanted to expand the war into China. He criticized Truman for wanting a **limited war,** a war fought to achieve limited goals. In response, Truman fired MacArthur. By 1951 the UN forces drove the Chinese and North Koreans back over the 38th parallel. An armistice was signed in July 1953. By then more than 35,000 Americans had died in the war. During the Korean War, the United States began a military buildup. In the past, the United States focused on Europe to contain communism. Now it had to focus its military on Asia. Defense agreements were signed and aid was given to those fighting communism in Asia.

Section Wrap-up

Answer these questions to check your understanding of the entire section.

1. How did the Korean War change the American view of containment?

_____

_____

_____

2. What steps did the United States take toward containing communism after World War II?

_____

_____

_____

Descriptive Writing

In the space provided, write a report to President Truman summarizing the crises that involved Communist forces from 1945 to 1953. Include American responses to each crisis into your report.

_____

_____

_____

_____

_____

_____

_____

_____

_____

_____

_____

_____

The Cold War and American Society

Big Idea

As you read pages 546–553 in your textbook, use the major headings of the section to complete the outline.

The Cold War and American Society

I. A New Red Scare
   B. _____
   C. _____
II. _____
   A. _____
   B. _____
   C. _____
III. _____
   A. _____
   B. _____

Notes

Read to Learn

A New Red Scare (page 546)

Formulating Questions

Read the questions below. Circle the question that is answered in the passage. Underline the question that requires further study.

1. How did the loyalty review program impact federal employees?

2. How did Chambers know that Hiss was a spy?

During the 1950s, Americans were caught up in the Red Scare. It began in September 1945 with a Soviet defector who reported that Soviet spies were inside the United States looking for information about the atomic bomb. This led to fear of a Communist **subversion,** or a plot to overthrow the government.

In 1947 Truman set up a **loyalty review program** to screen federal employees to test their loyalty. Over 2,000 people lost their jobs. The FBI infiltrated groups and wiretapped telephones. FBI Director J. Edgar Hoover also urged the House Un-American Activities Committee to hold public hearings on subversion. One of the hearings focused on the film industry. Many in Hollywood refused to testify and were blacklisted.

In 1948 Whittaker Chambers, a magazine editor, testified that several government officials were spies. One the spies was Alger Hiss of the State Department. Hiss denied this charge, but was later found guilty. Hiss was also convicted of **perjury,** or lying under oath. In another case, Ethel and Julius Rosenberg were found guilty of passing along atomic secrets to the Soviets and they were executed.

 **Notes** | # Read to Learn

McCarthyism *(page 549)*

Copyright © Glencoe/McGraw-Hill, a division of The McGraw-Hill Companies, Inc.

Drawing Conclusions

Place an X next to the statements in the passage that support this conclusion:

McCarthy's investigative methods ruined the careers of many government employees.

In 1949 the Red Scare grew worse. The Soviet Union tested an atomic bomb, and China fell to the Communists. Many Americans believed that they were losing the Cold War and that Communists had infiltrated the government. In February of 1950, Senator Joseph McCarthy claimed that he had a list of 205 Communists working in the State Department. He accused many politicians and others of being Communists. He never produced the list as proof.

The McCarran Act was passed in 1950. This law required all Communist organizations to register with the government. The groups were also forced to share their records with the government. The law stopped Communists from getting passports or traveling abroad. It stated that they could be arrested during emergencies. Truman tried to veto the bill, but Congress overrode the veto. The bill became law.

In 1952 McCarthy became chairman of the Senate subcommittee on investigations. Then he forced government officials to testify about Communist influences. McCarthy turned the investigations into witch hunts based on weak evidence and fear. He destroyed reputations with unfounded charges. This became known as McCarthyism. McCarthy would badger witnesses and refuse to accept their answers. His methods left a sense of suspicion and guilt about the witnesses.

In 1954 McCarthy began to question members of the United States Army. McCarthy's investigation was aired on television, and millions of Americans watched. McCarthy's popularity decreased as people finally challenged him and his methods. In 1954 the Senate passed a vote of **censure,** or formal disapproval, against McCarthy. His influence was gone. He faded from public view.

Life During the Early Cold War *(page 550)*

Predicting

Read this section's title. What do you think this passage will cover?

_____

_____

_____

_____

The Red Scare and the spread of nuclear weapons shaped everyday life in the United States during the 1950s. Americans were upset when the Soviet Union tested the powerful hydrogen, or H-bomb. They began to prepare for a surprise Soviet attack. They set up special areas as bomb shelters. Students also practiced bomb drills called "duck-and-cover" drills. Experts warned that these measures would not protect people from the initial blast or the **fallout**—the radiation left after the blast. For each person killed by the blast, four more would die from fallout.

The fear of communism influenced American movies and fiction. Many movies focused on FBI activities in spy cases. Novels described the effects of nuclear war.

Section Wrap-up

Answer these questions to check your understanding of the entire section.

1. Why did President Truman set up the loyalty review program?

   _____

   _____

   _____

2. Why were American preparations for a Soviet attack unlikely to be successful?

   _____

   _____

   _____

In the space provided, write a newspaper editorial that includes the disadvantages of the government's loyalty review program and the McCarren Act.

_____

_____

_____

_____

_____

_____

_____

_____

_____

_____

_____

_____

Chapter 15, Section 4 (Pages 554–559)
Eisenhower's Cold War Policies

Big Idea

As you read pages 554–559 in your textbook, complete the graphic organizer by filling in aspects of Eisenhower's "New Look."

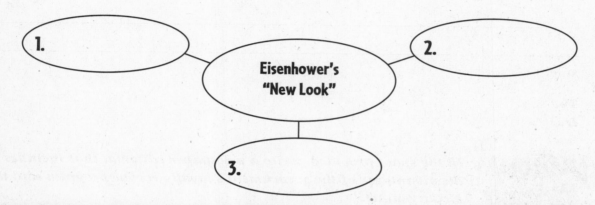

1.

Eisenhower's "New Look"

2.

3.

 **Notes** | **Read to Learn**

Massive Retaliation *(page 554)*

Problems and Solutions

Write one problem addressed by the massive retaliation policy.

_____

_____

_____

_____

_____

_____

_____

Republican Dwight D. Eisenhower won the 1952 presidential election in a landslide. He believed a strong military and economy were essential to win the Cold War. He also thought that conventional wars cost too much money. Eisenhower believed the United States had to prevent wars by threatening nuclear war. This policy became known as **massive retaliation.** It allowed him to cut military spending by billions of dollars. Eisenhower shrunk the army but invested in nuclear weapons and new technology to deliver them.

Eisenhower supported **brinkmanship**—the willingness to go to brink of war to force another nation to back down. Some thought this policy was dangerous, but Eisenhower used the threat to end the Korean War and protect Taiwan.

In 1955 Egypt seized the Suez Canal from an Anglo-French company that controlled it. Egypt wanted to use the profits from the canal to pay for a dam. In response, Britain and France invaded Egypt. The Soviet Union offered to help Egypt by attacking Britain and France. Eisenhower threatened a nuclear war with the Soviets. Britain and France retreated.

Covert Operations *(page 557)*

Synthesizing Information

Number the events below in the order in which they occurred.

____ *An uprising in Hungary was crushed by the Soviet Union.*

____ *The Shah of Iran was put back in power by a CIA coup.*

____ *Khrushchev cancelled the Paris Summit.*

Making Generalizations

Reread the paragraph about Guatemala. What do you think the CIA feared would happen if they did not launch a covert operation?

_____

_____

_____

_____

_____

_____

Eisenhower knew that brinkmanship would not work all the time. He knew it would not stop Communists from starting revolutions within countries. Eisenhower used **covert**—or hidden—operations to prevent revolutions. These were run by the Central Intelligence Agency, or CIA. Many of these operations took place in **developing nations,** or nations with mostly agricultural economies. Many of these nations blamed American capitalism for their problems. They looked to the Soviet Union as a model for industrialization. Americans feared that these nations would stage Communist revolutions, so Eisenhower offered financial aid to many of these nations. In places where the Communists were stronger, the CIA used covert operations. The CIA overthrew anti-American leaders. They replaced them with pro-American leaders.

Covert operations worked in Iran. There the prime minister overthrew the Shah of Iran and then wanted to make an oil deal with the Soviet Union. The CIA organized riots and a coup, and the prime minister was overthrown. The Shah returned to power.

In Guatemala, the president won his office with Soviet support. His programs took over large estates. Some of the estates were owned by Americans. Then Guatemala received weapons from Czechoslovakia. The CIA armed and trained rebels to overthrow the pro-Communist president.

Sometimes covert operations did not work. Nikita Krushchev took over the Soviet Union after Stalin died. The CIA got a copy of a speech Krushchev made in which he attacked Stalin's policies. The CIA broadcast the speech in Eastern Europe. In 1956 a revolt in Hungary began. The Soviets moved troops into Hungary and stopped the revolt.

In 1957 Eisenhower asked Congress to allow the use of the military to stop communism in the Middle East. This became known as the Eisenhower Doctrine. American troops went to Lebanon to protect its government. In 1958 Khrushchev demanded that the United States and its allies take their troops out of West Berlin. The United States threatened to use military force to protect Berlin. The Soviet Union backed down again.

Khrushchev visited Eisenhower in the United States in late 1959. They planned to hold a summit in Paris in 1960. Before the summit began, an American U-2 spy plane was shot down over the Soviet Union. Eisenhower refused to apologize. Khrushchev cancelled the summit. As Eisenhower prepared to leave office, he delivered a farewell address. In his speech, he pointed out a new relationship between the military and defense industries. He warned Americans to guard against the influence of this **military-industrial complex** in a democracy.

Section Wrap-up

Answer these questions to check your understanding of the entire section.

1. What did Eisenhower think was necessary to win the Cold War?

_____

_____

_____

2. What was one example of how covert operations did not work?

_____

_____

_____

In the space provided, write an essay that compares the advantages of covert operations with those of brinkmanship.

_____

_____

_____

_____

_____

_____

_____

_____

_____

_____

_____

_____

Truman and Eisenhower

Big Idea

As you read pages 566–571 in your textbook, complete the graphic organizer by listing the characteristics of the U.S. postwar economy.

```
          Characteristics
        of a Postwar Economy

  ┌──────┬──────┬──────┬──────┐
  │  1.  │  2.  │  3.  │  4.  │
  └──────┴──────┴──────┴──────┘
```

Notes

Read to Learn

Return to a Peacetime Economy (page 566)

Predicting

Read the first paragraph. Then predict what happened next.

_____

_____

_____

_____

_____

_____

_____

Americans feared that the end of military production and the return of soldiers would bring unemployment and recession. Instead, Americans who had lived with shortages during the war helped to grow the economy after the war by buying consumer goods. Demand for goods led to inflation and labor unrest. Strikes occurred in the automobile, steel, and mining industries. President Truman tried to prevent energy shortages and railroad strikes by forcing miners and others back to work.

Labor unrest and inflation led to a change in leadership. In the 1946 elections, the Republicans took control of both houses of Congress. To decrease the power of unions, the new Congress proposed the Taft-Hartley Act. The act outlawed the **closed shop,** or the practice of forcing business owners to hire only union members. It allowed states to pass **right-to-work laws** to outlaw **union shops** in which workers were forced to join unions. The law also prohibited featherbedding, or limiting output in order to create more jobs. President Truman vetoed the bill, but Congress passed the act in 1947 over his veto. Labor leaders claimed the law ended many of the gains unions made since 1933.

Truman's Program (page 568)

Determining Cause and Effect

List two reasons why the Democrats took control of the Congress in 1948.

1. _____

   _____

   _____

   _____

   _____

2. _____

   _____

   _____

   _____

   _____

The Republicans controlled Congress, but President Truman pushed for his programs anyway. He tried to increase Social Security benefits and the minimum wage, and to create more government jobs and a national health insurance system. The president planned public works projects such as new public housing. Truman pressed Congress to pass a civil rights bill to protect African Americans' rights. Then he ended segregation in the military and discrimination in hiring for federal jobs. Several of these plans were stopped by the Republicans and Southern Democrats in Congress.

Few people believed that Truman would win the 1948 election. He faced Republican Governor Thomas Dewey and two candidates nominated by former Democrats. Many Americans thought that Dewey would win by a landslide. The president traveled more than 20,000 miles and made over 350 speeches during his campaign. He blamed the Republican Congress for not passing his programs, calling them the "Do-Nothing Congress." Americans soon believed him, and he won by a small margin. The Democrats also won control of Congress.

The president pushed the new Congress to pass his Fair Deal programs, and they responded by passing parts of it. Congress increased the minimum wage and expanded Social Security benefits. It also approved the National Housing Act of 1949. However, Congress did not pass national health insurance and civil rights laws.

The Eisenhower Years (page 570)

Making Inferences

Reread the passage. Underline the examples that support this inference:

Eisenhower wanted to help people in need.

In 1952, the Republicans chose General Dwight Eisenhower as their candidate for president. Eisenhower was very popular and went by the name "Ike." He easily won the election against Democrat Adlai Stevenson.

President Eisenhower believed in **dynamic conservatism.** This was a balance of conservative economics and social activism. The president made many conservative decisions. He chose business leaders for his cabinet and stopped government price controls. Furthermore, he halted aid to businesses, schools, and public housing.

However, the president increased Social Security benefits and the minimum wage. Eisenhower's programs also helped farmers and people without jobs. He pushed for public works projects. The Federal Highway Act of 1956 spent $25 billion to build interstate highways. These programs helped him win a second term in 1956.

Section Wrap-up

Answer these questions to check your understanding of the entire section.

1. What were the results of the 1946 election?

_____

_____

_____

2. What changes did President Eisenhower's dynamic conservatism bring to the economy?

_____

_____

_____

Write a letter to your neighbor asking him or her to vote for President Truman in the upcoming 1948 election. Include several reasons why you think that President Truman should be reelected.

_____

_____

_____

_____

_____

_____

_____

_____

_____

_____

_____

Chapter 16, Section 1

The Affluent Society

Big Idea

As you read pages 572–579 in your textbook, complete the time line by recording major events of science, technology, and popular culture during the 1950s.

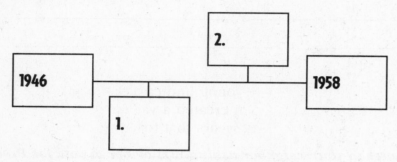

1946	
	2.
1.	**1958**

Notes | Read to Learn

American Abundance *(page 572)*

Identifying the Main Idea

Write the main idea of the passage.

_____

_____

_____

_____

_____

_____

_____

The 1950s was a decade of wealth. New businesses and technology produced many new goods and services. Americans earned more money than ever before, and they spent it on new goods such as refrigerators. Advertising increased as businesses pressed Americans to buy their goods. Much of it was aimed at people living in suburbs that grew around large cities. As people left the crowded cities, the population of the suburbs doubled. The suburbs offered inexpensive homes that people could buy with low-interest loans and money from income tax deductions. Many new homeowners and others started families between 1945 and 1961. This period is called the **baby boom,** and 61 million children were born.

Fewer **blue-collar workers,** or laborers, were needed to work on farms or in factories. More Americans took **white-collar jobs,** or office jobs, in large corporations. Many corporations became **multinational corporations** by moving overseas, often near important resources. **Franchises** also sprung up across the nation. In a franchise, a person owns and runs one of several stores of a chain operation.

Read to Learn

Scientific Advances *(page 574)*

Making Generalizations

Read the summary and then complete the statement below.

Advances in electronics and medicine helped to make people's lives _____ and _____.

The United States witnessed many advances in electronics and medicine after World War II. In 1947, American scientists developed a small tool called a transistor. This led to the invention of small portable radios and calculators. Scientists created one of the earliest computers in 1946. Soon after, newer models were being used by businesses. The computers and other changes helped people work quickly and efficiently. Americans began to enjoy more free time for leisure activities.

Advances in medicine ended or reduced the threat of many diseases. New treatments for cancer and heart disease, such as chemotherapy and CPR, helped patients survive. New antibiotics cured deadly diseases. Polio, however, was still a large problem. The disease attacked the young and caused death. Then Jonas Salk and later Albert Sabin created a vaccine. The threat of polio almost disappeared in the years that followed.

The New Mass Media *(page 576)*

Problems and Solutions

*The rise of television led to problems in other industries. Read the summary. Write the letter **P** next to the sentences that describe these problems. Write the letter **S** next to the sentences that describe the solutions.*

Televisions were popular household fixtures by the end of the 1950s. Approximately 40 million television sets were in use by 1957. Television programs included comedy, action and adventure, and variety shows. In 1953, Lucille Ball starred in the popular show *I Love Lucy*. Americans enjoyed the action show The *Lone Ranger* and the police show *Dragnet*. Television news became an important source of information. Variety shows, quiz shows, and televised sports were also popular. However, as people watched more television, they stopped watching movies.

One-fifth of the nation's movie theaters had closed by 1960. Hollywood tried to make films more exciting. They tried contests, prizes, and even 3-D films. These plans did not bring people back to the theaters. Full-colored movies shown on large, wide screens brought people back. These kinds of movies were expensive to make, but they drew in audiences and made large profits.

Television also took away radio listeners. The radio industry looked for new ways to draw listeners. Many radio stations began to broadcast music, news, and talk shows for people in their cars. Radio stations survived and the industry grew. The number of radio stations more than doubled to more than 3,600 between 1948 and 1957.

New Music and Poetry (page 577)

Detecting Bias

Circle the group that may not have appreciated rock 'n' roll music. Explain why.

teens

beats

African Americans

_____

_____

_____

In the 1950s, the sounds of African American rhythm and blues music was the basis for a new type of music called **rock 'n' roll**. American teens loved the music and its themes. They rushed to buy records from Buddy Holly, Elvis Presley, and other artists. Many parents thought rock 'n' roll was loud, mindless, and dangerous. This music, along with new types of clothing and literature, united teens. The result was a **generation gap**, or a cultural separation between children and their parents.

During the 1950s, white artists who called themselves **beats** criticized American life. The beats used poetry and literature to attack American popular culture and values. African American artists looked for acceptance in the nation. Instead, they were mostly rejected by television and mass media while finding some acceptance through their music.

Section Wrap-up

Answer these questions to check your understanding of the entire section.

1. What led to the growth of suburbs?

_____

_____

2. What types of programs did television show in the 1950s?

_____

_____

Descriptive Writing

In the space provided, write a short poem about the economy or society of the United States in the 1950s. You might write your poem from a beat's perspective.

_____

_____

_____

_____

_____

_____

The Other Side of American Life

Big Idea

As you read pages 582–587 in your textbook, complete the outline using the major headings of the section.

The Other Side of American Life

I. **Poverty Amidst Prosperity**

   A. _____

   B. _____

   C. _____

   D. _____

   E. _____

II. _____

Notes   Read to Learn

Poverty Amidst Prosperity *(page 582)*

Formulating Questions

Place an X next to the question best answered by the passage.

____ *What were urban renewal projects?*

____ *What groups of Americans suffered from poverty in the 1950s?*

Many Americans prospered during the 1950s. However, more than 30 million Americans lived below the **poverty line,** the lowest income needed to support a family. Many were African Americans, some of the approximately 3 million who had moved north after 1940. They came to find work and better lives but found racial discrimination, few jobs, and low pay. The cities failed to offer adequate housing, schools, or medical care. Government **urban renewal** programs built new public housing but often increased crime and poverty and destroyed more homes than they built.

Hispanics in the United States also faced poverty. Nearly 5 million Mexicans came to work on farms and ranches during the 1950s and 1960s. Called braceros, these people worked long hours for low pay. Native Americans were the poorest group in the nation. The government's **termination policy** forced many to move off of reservations and into cities and made them subject to the same laws and conditions as other Americans. Many white families in Appalachia also faced difficulties. Work, doctors, and nutritious foods were all scarce there.

Read to Learn

Juvenile Delinquency (page 587)

(page 587)

Distinguishing Fact from Opinion

Read the second paragraph of the passage. Circle three sentences that describe opinions.

Drawing Conclusions

Write a conclusion you can draw based on the passage.

_____
_____
_____
_____
_____
_____
_____
_____
_____

Another problem facing the nation was **juvenile delinquency,** or the antisocial and criminal behavior of young people. Juvenile crime rose by 45 percent between 1948 and 1953. A 1954 book titled *1,000,000 Delinquents* claimed that by 1955 one million young people would get into trouble. The book was correct. Americans searched for the causes.

Experts blamed juvenile delinquency on several causes. They blamed it on a lack of religion and discipline. Others claimed that television, movies, and comic books were the causes. A number of experts pointed the finger at the rising divorce rate and fears of the military draft. Some critics said that young people were just acting out against tradition. Bishop Fulton J. Sheen stated that Americans were raising bored children. He claimed children were looking for new ways to have fun. Many tried to link delinquency with poverty. However, delinquency involved children from all classes and races in American society. Most teens were not involved in crime or drugs, but the public came to think of all young people as juvenile delinquents. Many parents thought that improving the nation's schools was the solution to delinquency.

In the 1950s, the baby boomers began entering the school system. The number of school children increased by 13 million. School districts struggled to pay for new schools and new teachers. Americans became even more concerned about education after 1957. In that year, the Soviet Union launched the world's first satellites. Americans were afraid of falling behind their Cold War enemy. They believed that schools lacked technical education. New efforts were made to improve math and science education in the schools.

Answer these questions to check your understanding of the entire section.

1. What was the result of urban renewal programs?

_____

_____

_____

2. What were some concerns about the educational system in the United States during the 1950s?

_____

_____

_____

 *Compare the experiences of African Americans in the inner cities with Hispanics and Native Americans. What did these groups have in common?*

_____

_____

_____

_____

_____

_____

_____

_____

_____

_____

_____

The New Frontier

Big Idea

As you read pages 596–601 in your textbook, complete the graphic organizer by listing some domestic successes and setbacks of Kennedy's administration.

Successes	Setbacks
1.	4.
2.	5.
3.	6.

Notes | Read to Learn

The Election of 1960 (page 596)

Making Inferences

Read the passage to answer the question below.

Americans saw Kennedy as youthful and optimistic. How do you think they viewed Nixon?

_____

_____

_____

_____

_____

The presidential election of 1960 centered on the economy and the Cold War. Television played an important part in the election. The Democrats nominated John F. Kennedy, a Catholic from a wealthy Massachusetts family. The Republicans nominated Vice President Richard M. Nixon, a Quaker from California who had simple beginnings.

The candidates' opinions on the economy and the Cold War were similar. Kennedy believed that the Soviets were a serious threat. He was concerned about a **"missile gap."** He believed that the United States had fallen behind the Soviet Union in the number of weapons it had. Nixon felt that the Democrats' plans would boost inflation. He also believed that he had the foreign policy experience needed to lead the nation.

Kennedy's religion became an issue in the campaign. The United States had never had a Catholic president and many Protestants were concerned about Kennedy's loyalties. Kennedy emphasized his belief in the separation of church and state. Four televised presidential debates also influenced voters. Kennedy's youth and optimism made him popular. He narrowly won the popular vote and the Electoral College to become president.

Kennedy Takes Office (page 597)

Identifying the Main Idea

Reread the passage. Fill in the missing words of the main idea.

Although _____ refused to pass many of Kennedy's programs, the president was able to enact legislation helping groups such as _____ and the disabled.

After Kennedy was elected, he sent his New Frontier legislation to Congress. Kennedy had little support in Congress and found it difficult to get his programs passed. The Democrats in Congress followed their own interests instead of the president's. Southern Democrats and Republicans also viewed the New Frontier as too expensive.

However, some of Kennedy's economic programs were passed. In the late 1950s, unemployment was high and the economic growth rate was low. Kennedy suggested deficit spending to boost the economy. He convinced Congress to spend more on defense and space exploration. This created more jobs and grew the economy. He also asked business leaders to keep prices and pay increases down. Kennedy pushed for tax cuts as well, but was unsuccessful. However, Kennedy increased the minimum wage and passed public works projects.

Many women held important positions in Kennedy's administration. He even issued an executive order to end gender discrimination in the federal civil service. In 1963, he signed the Equal Pay Act for women.

Warren Court Reforms (page 600)

Problems and Solutions

In the passage, underline the solution to the problem described below.

Problem: By 1960 more people lived in urban areas, but rural districts had more representation.

In 1953 Earl Warren became the chief justice of the United States. The Warren Court issued several rulings that reshaped American society. It made important decisions about **reapportionment**, which is the way states drew up political districts based on changes in population. By 1960 more people lived in urban areas than rural areas. However, many states had not changed their electoral districts to match. The Court ruled that the system was unconstitutional. The ruling forced states to reapportion electoral districts. It gave people's votes equal weight.

The Supreme Court also began to use the Fourteenth Amendment to apply the Bill of Rights to the states. This amendment ruled that states could not deprive individuals of the right to **due process.** This meant that the law could not treat individuals unfairly or unreasonably. It also meant that the courts had to follow correct procedures and rules to try cases. Using due process applied the federal Bill of Rights to the states. In other rulings, the Court did not allow states to use evidence found illegally. It also stated that defendants had the right to lawyers and to be told they could stay silent before questioning. It also bolstered the separation of church and state.

Section Wrap-up

Answer these questions to check your understanding of the entire section.

1. Why was John F. Kennedy's religion an issue in the 1960 election, and how did Kennedy deal with this issue?

_____

_____

_____

2. How did Kennedy help the economy of the United States in the early 1960s?

_____

_____

_____

You just watched one of the televised presidential debates between John F. Kennedy and Vice President Nixon. Write a summary for a friend who missed it. Describe the two men and their political views.

_____

_____

_____

_____

_____

_____

_____

_____

_____

_____

JFK and the Cold War

Big Idea

As you read pages 602–607 in your textbook, complete the time line to record some major events of the Cold War in the 1950s and early 1960s.

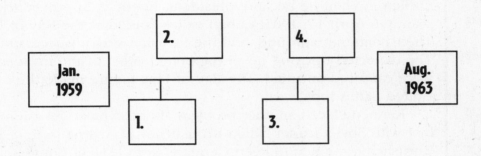

| Jan. 1959 | 2. | 4. | Aug. 1963 |

1.

3.

Notes

Read to Learn

Containing Communism (page 602)

Analyzing Information

Read the passage to answer the question below.

What two things did Kennedy do to help fight the spread of communism in Latin America?

1. _____

_____

2. _____

_____

Kennedy tried to reduce the threat of nuclear war and contain communism. He wanted the option of a **flexible response,** in which conventional troops and weapons could be used to contain communism. He expanded the Special Forces. This army unit used guerilla warfare in limited conflicts.

Kennedy also tried to improve relations with Latin America. Many governments there were controlled by the wealthy few. Most of the people lived in poverty. In some countries, leftist groups tried to overthrow their governments. To improve conditions in Latin America, Kennedy proposed an Alliance for Progress. This was a series of aid projects in which the United States promised $20 billion to help these countries. The projects set up better schools, housing, and health care.

The United States and the Soviet Union also competed in a **space race** in which both superpowers attempted to dominate space technology. In 1961 the Soviets launched the first person into space. A few weeks later, Kennedy made a speech in which he announced the goal of landing a man on the moon before the end of the decade. In 1969 the United States achieved this goal.

Notes | Read to Learn

Crises of the Cold War (page 605)

Drawing Conclusions

Review the summary. Circle the sentences that support the following conclusion.

The United States feared a Communist Cuba and tried to eliminate this threat by any means.

Distinguishing Fact from Opinion

Underline the sentence that describes Kennedy's opinion about Soviet missiles in Cuba.

President Kennedy faced several crises in the Cold War. The first one started when Fidel Castro seized power in Cuba in 1959. Castro established ties with the Soviet Union. He also took over American and other foreign-owned businesses located in Cuba. Americans believed that the Soviets wanted to use Cuba as a base to spread communism in the Western Hemisphere. Eisenhower authorized the CIA to arm Cuban exiles and train them to invade Cuba, hoping that the invasion would start an uprising. When he became president, Kennedy approved the plan. On April 17, 1961, Cuban exiles landed at the Bay of Pigs. Their boats ran aground, and the invasion was unsuccessful. The expected uprising never happened. Most of the invaders were captured or killed. The Bay of Pigs failure made the United States look weak.

Kennedy faced another problem after the failed invasion. He met with Soviet leader Nikita Khrushchev in Austria in June 1961. Khrushchev wanted to keep Germans from leaving Communist East Germany and fleeing to West Berlin. He demanded that Western powers leave Berlin. When Kennedy refused, the Soviets built the Berlin Wall. It was guarded by armed soldiers who shot at people attempting to escape. The wall separated East Berlin from West Berlin for nearly 30 years.

In 1962 the United States learned that Soviet workers and equipment had arrived in Cuba. On October 22, 1962, Kennedy told Americans that photos taken by spy planes showed that the Soviets had placed missiles in Cuba. He believed that the weapons threatened the United States. He then ordered a naval blockade to stop more missiles from being delivered to Cuba. However, the Soviets continued to work on the missile sites.

The leaders of the two countries began secret talks. Both nations reached an agreement on October 28. The United States publicly agreed not to attack Cuba and privately agreed to remove its own missiles from Turkey. The Soviet Union agreed to remove the missiles from Cuba. The Cuban missile crisis brought the world close to nuclear war. It made the Soviet Union and United States see the dangers of nuclear war. They agreed to a treaty that banned testing of nuclear weapons in the atmosphere.

On November 22, 1963, President Kennedy was shot and killed while visiting Dallas, Texas. Lee Harvey Oswald, the man accused of killing the president, was then shot and killed while in police custody. In 1964 a commission headed by Chief Justice Warren stated that Oswald acted alone. The United States and the world mourned the loss of President Kennedy.

Section Wrap-up

Answer these questions to check your understanding of the entire section.

1. How was Kennedy's military policy different from Eisenhower's?

   _____

   _____

   _____

2. What were the results of the Cuban missile crisis?

   _____

   _____

   _____

Some people think that the Alliance for Progress is not a good use of money. Use a television ad to help change their minds. Write a script for a short television commercial that supports President Kennedy's program.

_____

_____

_____

_____

_____

_____

_____

_____

_____

_____

_____

The Great Society

Big Idea

As you read pages 610–615 in your textbook, complete the graphic organizer to list some social and economic programs started during Johnson's administration.

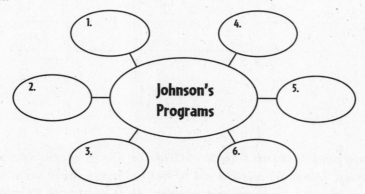

1.

2.

3.

Johnson's Programs

4.

5.

6.

 **Notes** | **Read to Learn**

Johnson Takes the Reins *(page 610)*

Formulating Questions

Write a question that might help you learn more about the "War on Poverty."

_____

_____

_____

_____

_____

_____

_____

_____

Vice President Lyndon Johnson was sworn in as president hours after Kennedy's death. Johnson had served in Congress for 26 years, developing a reputation as someone who got things done. Johnson always tried to build **consensus,** or general agreement. Unlike Kennedy, Johnson was not an elegant society man. His image was that of a plainspoken Texan.

Johnson wanted to push Kennedy's antipoverty and civil rights programs through Congress. He believed that governments should improve their citizens' lives. In his State of the Union address in 1964, Johnson declared a "War on Poverty in America." By the summer of 1964, he persuaded Congress to pass the Economic Opportunity Act. The act created new jobs. It established the Office of Economic Opportunity to coordinate new programs. Many of these programs were aimed at inner-city youth. The Neighborhood Youth Corps provided a work-study program. The Job Corps helped unemployed young people learn job skills. The VISTA program operated like a domestic Peace Corps for poor neighborhoods and rural areas. Johnson was reelected in 1964.

The Great Society (page 613)

Synthesizing Information

Review the second and third paragraph of the summary. Place an X next to the sentence below that is true.

____ *The Great Society targeted the health, education, and housing of the poor.*

____ *The Great Society's main focus was on immigration reform.*

____ *Medicare and Medicaid were the only successful Great Society programs.*

Determining Cause and Effect

Write the effect that goes with the cause below.

Cause: Money was needed for the war in Vietnam.

Effect:

_____

_____

_____

_____

President Johnson began his domestic programs soon after the election. He called them the "Great Society." The Civil Rights Act of 1964 was passed during his administration. This met many of the goals of the civil rights movement. The Voting Rights Act of 1965 also ensured that African Americans had the right to vote. Johnson's programs were passed for many reasons. The civil rights movement brought many of the problems of African Americans to light. Also, the economy was strong, so Americans thought that poverty could be reduced.

More than 60 of Johnson's programs were passed between 1965 and 1968. Among these were Medicare and Medicaid. Medicare is a health insurance program for the elderly. Medicaid provides health care for people on welfare. Other programs supported education. The Elementary and Secondary Education Act of 1965 gave millions of dollars to public and private schools. This paid for books and other educational materials. Project Head Start is an education program for poor preschool children. College preparation for low-income teenagers was offered through the Upward Bound program.

Johnson also urged Congress to pass laws that would help inner-city neighborhoods. One law created a new agency called the Department of Housing and Urban Development. It was led by Robert Weaver. He was the first African American to serve in a president's cabinet. Other laws gave federal funding to many city programs. These programs spent billions of dollars on transportation, healthcare, and housing.

One law changed the makeup of the American population. The Immigration Reform Act of 1965 continued to limit the number of immigrants allowed in the United States each year. However, it ended the national origin system. That system gave preference to immigrants from Northern Europe. The new law allowed immigration from all of Europe, Asia, and Africa.

The Great Society programs improved the lives of many Americans. However, people debated the programs' success. Many of these programs had been created quickly and did not work well. Some people believed that the federal government had become too involved in people's lives. The programs were also expensive. When money was needed for the war in Vietnam, the programs lost funding. However, some programs and agencies still exist today. They include Medicare, Medicaid, and Project Head Start. The Department of Housing and Urban Development and the Department of Transportation are two agencies that also exist today.

Section Wrap-up

Answer these questions to check your understanding of the entire section.

1. What was the purpose of the Office of Economic Opportunity?

_____

_____

_____

2. What are Medicare and Medicaid?

_____

_____

_____

Suppose you are visiting the United States from another country. You want to share the benefits of the Great Society with people in your home country. Write a letter to a friend that lists the advantages of the Great Society's programs.

_____

_____

_____

_____

_____

_____

_____

_____

_____

_____

The Movement Begins

Big Idea

As you read pages 622–629 in your textbook, complete the graphic organizer
by listing the causes of the civil rights movement.

1. _____

2. _____

3. _____

Civil Rights Movement

 **Notes**

Read to Learn

The Origins of the Movement *(page 622)*

Determining Cause and Effect

List one effect of the **Brown *v*. Board of Education** *decision.*

_____

_____

_____

_____

_____

_____

_____

The Supreme Court's 1896 decision in *Plessy* v. *Ferguson* set up a **separate but equal** policy. Laws that segregated African Americans were allowed as long as African Americans had equal places. Areas that did not have segregation laws often had **de facto segregation.** This was segregation by custom and tradition. In the 1940s members of the CORE organization began using **sit-ins,** a form of protest. CORE integrated many restaurants and public places in Northern cities.

In May 1954 the Supreme Court ruled in *Brown* v. *Board of Education* that segregation violated the Fourteenth Amendment. The ruling signaled to African Americans that it was time to challenge other forms of segregation. The *Brown* decision also upset many white Southerners. Many ignored the Supreme Court's ruling and kept schools segregated for years.

On December 1, 1955, Rosa Parks was arrested in Montgomery, Alabama, for refusing to give up her bus seat to a white person. She challenged bus segregation in court. African Americans in Montgomery quickly started a boycott of the bus system. In the next few years, boycotts and protests spread across the nation.

 | **Read to Learn**

The Civil Rights Movement Begins (page 626)

Making Generalizations

Read the passage above and then complete the statement below.

Martin Luther King, Jr., became an influential civil rights leader because

_____

_____

_____

_____

_____

The Montgomery bus boycott marked the beginning of the civil rights movement among African Americans. The boycott was a success. Some African American leaders formed the Montgomery Improvement Association, which worked with city leaders to end segregation. The MIA chose the young minister Martin Luther King, Jr., to lead the group. King believed the way to end segregation was through nonviolent methods. This approach was based on the ideas of Mohandas Gandhi. A powerful speaker, King encouraged his listeners to disobey unjust laws. The Supreme Court decided Rosa Parks' case in 1956. It said that Alabama's bus segregation laws were unconstitutional.

African American churches and ministers played an important part in the success of the boycott. People met at churches to plan and organize protest meetings. African American ministers set up the Southern Christian Leadership Conference in 1957. King was the SCLC's first president. The SCLC set out to end segregation in America. It also pushed African Americans to register to vote. The group challenged segregation of public transportation and other public places.

Eisenhower Responds (page 629)

Making Inferences

Underline the parts of the summary that support the following inference:

Inference: President Eisenhower believed in putting the law above his personal beliefs.

_____

_____

_____

_____

_____

_____

President Eisenhower personally opposed segregation. But he disagreed with those who wanted to end it through protests and court rulings. He believed that segregation should end gradually. Eisenhower thought that the Supreme Court's decision in *Brown* v. *Board of Education* was wrong. However, he also thought that the federal government had the duty to uphold the decision.

In September 1957 the Little Rock, Arkansas, school board won a court order to admit nine African American students to Central High School. The governor of Arkansas ordered troops from the Arkansas National Guard to prevent the nine students from entering the school. Eisenhower ordered U.S. Army troops to Little Rock to protect the students and to uphold the law.

In the same year that the Little Rock crisis took place, Congress passed the Civil Rights Act of 1957. It was intended to protect African Americans' right to vote. The law created a civil rights division within the Department of Justice. It also created the United States Commission on Civil Rights to investigate instances in which the right to vote was denied.

Section Wrap-up

Answer these questions to check your understanding of the entire section.

1. How did the Southern Christian Leadership Conference originate?

_____

_____

_____

2. Describe the role of the federal government in enforcing civil rights laws.

_____

_____

_____

In the space provided, write a short poem about the nine African American students trying to attend Central High School in Little Rock, Arkansas. You might write your poem from the perspective of one of the students.

_____

_____

_____

_____

_____

_____

_____

_____

_____

_____

_____

Challenging Segregation

Big Idea

As you read pages 630–639 in your textbook, complete the graphic organizer about the challenges to segregation in the South.

Cause	Effect
Sit-In Movement	3.
Freedom Riders	4.
1.	African American support of Kennedy
2.	African American voter registration

 **Notes** | **Read to Learn**

The Sit-In Movement (page 630)

Distinguishing Fact from Opinion

Read the first paragraph. Underline the sentences that express or explain a person's opinion.

In 1959 four college students in Greensboro, North Carolina, staged a sit-in that touched off a new mass movement for civil rights. By 1961 sit-ins were held in more than 100 cities. Many African American college students joined the sit-in movement. Students like Jesse Jackson thought sit-ins were a way to take things into their own hands. At first, the leaders of the NAACP and the SCLC were concerned about the sit-ins. They feared that the students might fight back if attacked. The students remained peaceful, despite being punched, kicked, and beaten.

As the sit-ins spread, student leaders realized that they needed to create an organization of their own. Ella Baker, the executive director of the SCLC, invited student leaders to a convention in Raleigh, North Carolina, where she urged them to start their own organization instead of joining SCLC or the NAACP. The students established the Student Nonviolent Coordinating Committee (SNCC). SNCC was instrumental in desegregating public places in many communities. Members of SNCC began working in the rural areas of the Deep South.

The Freedom Riders (page 632)

Synthesizing Information

How was the reaction of segregation supporters to the early sit-ins, the Freedom Rider turn-outs, and demonstrations in Birmingham similar?

_____

_____

_____

_____

_____

_____

_____

In 1961 civil rights volunteers began traveling to the South. They hoped to draw attention to the South's segregation of bus terminals. These groups became known as Freedom Riders. White mobs often attacked the Freedom Riders when they arrived in Southern cities. President John F. Kennedy decided he had to do something to stop the violence. At first Kennedy seemed as cautious as Eisenhower on civil rights. Kennedy needed the support of Southern senators to get his legislation passed. He did not want to challenge these senators on the subject of civil rights.

However, Kennedy did name about 40 African Americans to high-level government jobs. He also allowed the Justice Department to actively support the civil rights movement. In addition, he ordered the Interstate Commerce Commission to tighten regulations against segregated bus terminals.

Meanwhile, activists worked to integrate public schools. African American James Meredith applied to the University of Mississippi but was denied admittance. President Kennedy ordered army troops to protect Meredith.

To force Kennedy to support civil rights, Martin Luther King, Jr., ordered demonstrations in Birmingham, Alabama. The demonstrations turned violent and were broadcast on national television. Kennedy then prepared a new civil rights bill.

The Civil Rights Act of 1964 (page 636)

Problems and Solutions

What did Dr. King do to help get Kennedy's civil rights bill through Congress?

_____

_____

_____

_____

_____

_____

In June 1963, Alabama governor George Wallace stood in front of the University of Alabama's admissions office. He was trying to stop two African Americans from enrolling. Federal marshals ordered him to move. President Kennedy used this event to present his civil rights bill.

To build support for the bill, Martin Luther King, Jr., took part in a large march in Washington, D.C. On August 28, 1963, more than 200,000 demonstrators gathered peacefully at the nation's capital. Dr. King delivered his powerful "I Have a Dream" speech. The march built support for Kennedy's civil rights bill.

In November 1963, Kennedy was assassinated. Vice President Lyndon Johnson became president. The civil rights bill passed the House of Representatives in February 1964. In the Senate, Southern Democrats participated in a **filibuster.** This means that they kept speaking and refused to allow **cloture,** or ending debate. The bill finally passed. It was the largest civil rights law Congress had ever enacted. It gave the federal government broad power to prevent racial discrimination.

The Struggle for Voting Rights (page 639)

Formulating Questions

Place an X next to the question best answered by the passage.

____ **Where were literacy tests most common?**

____ **What events led to the passing of the Voting Rights Act of 1965?**

To keep the pressure on the president and Congress to act on voting rights, Dr. King and others organized an Alabama march from Selma to Montgomery. It began on March 7, 1965. At one point in the march, state troopers and deputized citizens rushed the demonstrators. The attack left more than 70 African Americans hospitalized. The nation was shocked at the brutality it saw on television. President Johnson was furious. He went before Congress to present a new voting rights law.

In August 1965, Congress passed the Voting Rights Act of 1965. It ordered federal examiners to register qualified voters. It ended discriminatory practices such as literacy tests. The civil rights movement had achieved its two goals. Segregation had been outlawed, and laws were in place to protect voting rights.

Section Wrap-up

Answer these questions to check your understanding of the entire section.

1. Why was Kennedy cautious about supporting civil rights when he first took office?

_____

_____

2. By the end of 1965, what two major goals had the civil rights movement achieved?

_____

_____

Persuasive Writing

Suppose it is February of 1965 and Martin Luther King, Jr., has asked you whether he should organize a march from Selma to Montgomery. King is worried the march may turn violent. Write a letter to Dr. King giving your opinion.

_____

_____

_____

_____

_____

_____

New Civil Rights Issues

Big Idea

As you read pages 642–647 in your textbook, complete the chart by filling in three major violent events in the civil rights movement and their results.

Event	Result
1.	
2.	
3.	

 **Notes**

Read to Learn

Urban Problems *(page 642)*

Identifying the Main Idea

Write the main idea of the passage.

_____

_____

_____

_____

_____

_____

_____

In the 1960s, **racism,** discrimination toward someone because of his or her race, was still common. In 1965 about 70 percent of African Americans lived in large cities. They were often trapped by poverty in the inner city. They were aware of the gains made by the civil rights movement, but knew the gains did not address their social and economic problems. Their anger at the situation erupted into violence. Race riots broke out around the country. Thirty-four people were killed during a six-day riot in Watts, a neighborhood in Los Angeles. The worst riot occurred in Detroit in 1967. The U.S. Army was called in to control the situation.

President Johnson picked Otto Kerner to head a commission to look at the causes of the riots. It blamed racism for most of the problems in the inner city and recommended more jobs and housing for African Americans. In 1965 Dr. King decided to focus on improving the economic conditions of African Americans. He and his wife moved into a slum apartment in Chicago to call attention to the problems there. The Chicago Movement was largely unsuccessful in ending urban poverty.

Black Power (page 644)

Comparing and Contrasting

How did Black Panthers' view of violence differ from that of Dr. Martin Luther King, Jr.?

_____

_____

_____

_____

_____

_____

_____

_____

_____

Dr. King's failure in Chicago convinced some African Americans that nonviolence was not the solution to their problems. Many poor, young African Americans turned away from King's movement. They turned to more aggressive forms of protest. Many called for **black power.** A few believed that the term meant that self-defense and violence were acceptable when defending one's freedom. Others thought that black power meant that African Americans should control the social, political, and economic direction of their struggle for equality. Black power stressed pride in African American culture. It rejected the idea that African Americans should try to imitate white society. Black power was very popular in the poor urban neighborhoods where many African Americans lived.

By the early 1960s, Malcolm X had become the symbol of black power. He gained fame as part of the Nation of Islam, or the Black Muslims, but by 1964 he had broken with the group. He started to believe, unlike the Black Muslims, that an integrated society was possible. In February 1965 members of the Nation of Islam killed Malcolm X in New York. Malcolm X is remembered for encouraging African Americans to believe in their abilities to make their own way in the world.

Malcolm X's ideas affected a new generation of militant African American leaders. One group, the Black Panthers, preached black power, black nationalism, and economic self-sufficiency. The Black Panthers believed a revolution was necessary. They urged African Americans to arm themselves and confront white society to force whites to grant them equal rights.

Martin Luther King, Jr., Is Killed (page 647)

Determining Cause and Effect

Write one effect.

Cause: Dr. King is assassinated.

Effect: _____

_____

_____

By the late 1960s, the civil rights movement was divided. Some African Americans called for violent action. This angered many white supporters of the civil rights movement.

In 1968 Dr. Martin Luther King, Jr., went to Memphis, Tennessee, to support a strike of African American sanitation workers. On April 4 he was shot to death as he stood on his hotel balcony. King's death touched off riots in more than 100 cities. After Dr. King's death, Congress passed the Civil Rights Act of 1968. The law banned discrimination in the sale and rental of housing. The civil rights movement continued, but it lacked the vision that Dr. King had given it. Still, the civil rights movement of the 1950s and 1960s had created many new opportunities for African Americans.

Section Wrap-up

Answer these questions to check your understanding of the entire section.

1. What division arose between Dr. King and the black power movement?

   _____

   _____

   _____

2. Why did the civil rights movement lose its focus after 1968?

   _____

   _____

   _____

In the space provided, write a brief history of the black power movement. Be sure to include any important dates, events, and key figures from the passages.

_____

_____

_____

_____

_____

_____

_____

_____

_____

_____

Going to War in Vietnam

Big Idea

As you read pages 654–661 in your textbook, complete the graphic organizer by providing reasons why the United States aided France in Vietnam.

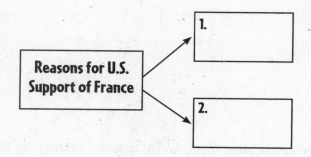

Reasons for U.S. Support of France

1.

2.

 **Notes** | **Read to Learn**

American Involvement in Vietnam (page 654)

Making Inferences

Why do you think guerrilla troops try to look like civilians?

_____

_____

_____

_____

_____

_____

_____

From the late 1800s, France ruled Vietnam. By the early 1900s, several political parties wanted independence from France. One of the leaders of the movement was Ho Chi Minh. In 1941, after Japan had taken control of Vietnam, Ho Chi Minh organized a group called the Vietminh to try to get rid of the Japanese. When Japan was defeated in 1945, it gave up control of Vietnam. France asked the United States to regain control of Vietnam. The United States did not want Vietnam to be communist, so it agreed. President Eisenhower continued to support the French because he believed in the **domino theory,** which said that if Vietnam fell to communism, other Southeast Asian nations would also.

The Vietminh used **guerrillas,** or irregular troops who look like civilians and are difficult to fight. In 1954 the Vietminh defeated the French at Dien Bien Phu. Negotiations to end the conflict took place in Geneva, Switzerland. Vietnam was divided into North Vietnam and South Vietnam. Ho Chi Minh and the Vietminh controlled North Vietnam. A pro-Western regime controlled South Vietnam.

Notes | Read to Learn

America Becomes Involved in Vietnam *(page 657)*

Analyzing Information

How did the Gulf of Tonkin Resolution benefit President Johnson?

_____

_____

_____

_____

_____

_____

_____

_____

Ho Chi Minh tried to reunify Vietnam by force. He started a new guerrilla army called the Vietcong. Eisenhower sent military advisers to help South Vietnam, but the Vietcong's power increased. President Kennedy continued to support South Vietnam. The United States believed that the Vietcong were popular because South Vietnam's government, led by Ngo Dinh Diem, was corrupt. Several Vietnamese generals overthrew Diem and executed him. After his death, the government became even more unstable. The United States became even more involved as it tried to support the weak South Vietnamese government. Shortly after Diem's death, Kennedy was assassinated. The conflict in Vietnam fell to President Johnson.

President Johnson was determined to stop Vietnam from becoming communist. Johnson asked Congress for authorization to use force to defend American forces. Congress passed the Gulf of Tonkin Resolution. It essentially handed over war powers to the president. Shortly afterward, the Vietcong began to attack American bases. Johnson ordered American aircraft to strike North Vietnam. In March 1965 Johnson began a bombing campaign against North Vietnam and ordered the first American combat troops into Vietnam.

A Bloody Stalemate *(page 660)*

Synthesizing Information

Reread the passage. Underline the reasons that American troops could not defeat the Vietcong.

The Vietcong used ambushes and booby traps. They blended into the civilian population and vanished. American troops tried to find the enemy and bomb their positions, destroy their supply lines, and force them into the open. To prevent the Vietcong from hiding in the jungles, American planes dropped **napalm,** a jellied gasoline that explodes on contact. They also used **Agent Orange,** a chemical that strips leaves from trees.

American military leaders believed that continuous bombing and the killing of many Vietcong would make them surrender. However, the guerrillas did not surrender. North Vietnam received supplies from the Soviet Union and China, and then sent supplies to South Vietnam through a network known as the Ho Chi Minh trail. President Johnson did not order an invasion of North Vietnam because he feared this would bring China into the war. Instead of conquering enemy territory, American troops tried to defeat the enemy by slowly wearing them down. As casualties on both sides mounted through 1967, the Vietcong still showed no sign of surrendering.

Section Wrap-up

Answer these questions to check your understanding of the entire section.

1. Why did Ho Chi Minh organize the Vietminh?

_____

_____

_____

2. Why did the United States want to prevent Vietnam from becoming communist?

_____

_____

_____

In the space provided, write a short essay describing the military tactics of the Vietcong and explain how American military forces tried to counter these tactics.

_____

_____

_____

_____

_____

_____

_____

_____

_____

_____

_____

Chapter 19, Section 2 (Pages 664–669)
Vietnam Divides the Nation

Big Idea

As you read pages 664–669 in your textbook, complete the graphic organizer by listing the reasons for opposition to the Vietnam War.

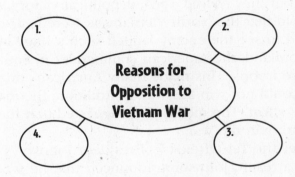

1.

2.

Reasons for Opposition to Vietnam War

4.

3.

 **Notes** | **Read to Learn**

An Antiwar Movement Emerges *(page 664)*

Determining Cause and Effect

Write the effect that goes with the cause.

Cause: People saw images of wounded and dead American soldiers in the media.

Effect:

_____

_____

_____

_____

_____

Opposition to the Vietnam War grew in the late 1960s. Many Americans believed a **credibility gap** had developed. Images of wounded and dead American soldiers in the media made Americans doubt the government's truthfulness about the war. Many college students protested the war. Some held **teach-ins,** or informal discussions about the war.

People opposed the war for different reasons. Some believed it was a civil war that did not involve the United States. Others believed South Vietnam was a corrupt dictatorship, and supporting it was immoral. Some were against the draft system. At the beginning of the war, college students were able to postpone military service until after they graduated. Minorities and young people from low-income families were more likely to serve in the military because they could not afford college. In 1969 the government issued a lottery system for the draft. Despite the antiwar protests, a majority of people in early 1968 supported the war. Those who wanted to withdraw from Vietnam were called **doves.** Those who wanted to stay and fight were called **hawks.**

Copyright © Glencoe/McGraw-Hill, a division of The McGraw-Hill Companies, Inc.

 **Notes** | **Read to Learn**

1968: The Pivotal Year (page 667)

Predicting

Reread the passage. Underline the sentences that help you predict what Nixon will do as president.

Making Generalizations

Place an X next to the generalization that the passage supports.

_____ **1968 was a difficult year for the United States.**

_____ **In 1968, most Americans supported the Vietnam War.**

On January 30, 1968, the Vietcong and North Vietnamese launched a surprise attack during Tet, the Vietnamese New Year. It was called the Tet Offensive. Guerrillas attacked American airbases in South Vietnam and most of the South's major cities. After about a month of fighting, the American and South Vietnamese soldiers fended off the enemy troops.

In the Tet Offensive, the North Vietnamese suffered heavy losses, but they scored a major political victory. Americans had been told that the North Vietnamese were near defeat. They were shocked to see the enemy launch such a huge attack. General Westmoreland, the American commander in South Vietnam, called for more troops. This made many Americans think that the United States could not win the war. In addition, the media criticized the military effort. The media also suggested that the United States could not win the war.

After the Tet Offensive, President Johnson's approval rating fell. As a result, Johnson announced that he would not run for reelection in 1968. Even before his announcement, Democrats began looking for a different candidate. Eugene McCarthy, a dove, announced his candidacy in November 1967. Senator Robert Kennedy also declared that he would run.

In April 1968 Dr. Martin Luther King, Jr., was killed. This led to riots in several cities. In June 1968, Senator Robert Kennedy was shot and killed after winning California's Democratic primary. Violence continued in 1968 with a clash between police and protesters at the Democratic National Convention in Chicago. Protesters demanded that the Democrats adopt an antiwar platform.

The delegates to the convention chose Johnson's vice president, Hubert Humphrey, as their presidential nominee. At the same time, protesters and police began fighting near the convention hall. A riot broke out on the streets of downtown Chicago.

Richard Nixon was the Republican presidential candidate. He benefited from the violence associated with the Democratic Party. Nixon promised to restore law and order. He also announced that he had a plan to end the Vietnam War. Nixon defeated Humphrey.

Section Wrap-up

Answer these questions to check your understanding of the entire section.

1. Why did some Americans consider the draft system unfair?

_____

_____

_____

2. What was the Tet Offensive, and how did it affect American perceptions of the war?

_____

_____

_____

In the space provided, write about an antiwar demonstration in the late 1960s as if you were actually there. What position on the war would you take? What might you see and hear?

_____

_____

_____

_____

_____

_____

_____

_____

_____

_____

_____

The War Winds Down

Big Idea

As you read pages 670–675 in your textbook, complete the graphic organizer by listing some steps that President Nixon took to end American involvement in Vietnam.

Steps Nixon Took
1.
2.
3.
4.

 **Notes**   **Read to Learn**

Nixon Moves to End the War *(page 670)*

Problems and Solutions

In the passage, underline President Nixon's solution to the following problem:

Problem: After the 1972 election, peace talks with North Vietnam broke down.

President Nixon appointed Henry Kissinger to use diplomacy to end the war. Kissinger started a policy called **linkage**, in which the United States tried to persuade the Soviet Union and China to reduce aid to North Vietnam. Kissinger also began talks with a North Vietnamese negotiator. Nixon set up a plan called **Vietnamization**, which called for a gradual withdrawal of American troops. He still kept some troops in Vietnam to preserve America's strength during negotiations. In April 1970 Nixon announced that American troops had invaded Cambodia to destroy Vietcong bases there. Members of Congress were upset with the president for not notifying them of this plan and repealed the Gulf of Tonkin Resolution.

By 1971 most Americans wanted to end the war. In October 1972 Kissinger announced that peace was near. Nixon won the 1972 election. Soon after, peace talks broke down. Nixon began bombing raids to force North Vietnam to resume talks. In January 1973 an agreement was signed to end the war. The United States began to withdraw. In March 1975 North Vietnam invaded South Vietnam and reunited the country under communist rule.

The Legacy of Vietnam *(page 674)*

Identifying the Main Idea

Reread the passage and circle details that support the following main idea:

Main idea: The Vietnam War left lasting effects on the United States.

Drawing Conclusions

Reread the second paragraph of the passage. What is one conclusion you can draw about veterans of the Vietnam War?

_____

_____

_____

_____

_____

Americans hoped to put the Vietnam War behind them. Still, the war had lasting effects on the United States. It had cost more than $170 billion. It resulted in the deaths of about 58,000 Americans. More than 300,000 were injured. About one million North and South Vietnamese soldiers died. Countless Vietnamese civilians lost their lives as well.

The war had a psychological impact on American soldiers. Many Americans considered Vietnam a defeat. They wanted to forget the war. As a result, the sacrifices made by many veterans often went unrecognized. There were few welcome-home parades for American soldiers. The war continued for many American families whose relatives were prisoners of war (POWs) or missing in action (MIA). In spite of many official investigations, some families continued to believe that the government lied about its POW/MIA policies. In 1982 the Vietnam Veterans Memorial in Washington, D.C., was dedicated to help Americans come to terms with the war.

In 1973 Congress passed the War Powers Act. The Act attempted to set limits on the power of the president. The law required the president to inform Congress of any commitment of troops within 48 hours. It also required the president to withdraw troops in 60 to 90 days unless Congress approved the troop commitment. No president has ever recognized this law. However, presidents do ask Congress for authorization before sending troops into combat.

After the Vietnam War, many Americans became more reluctant to involve the United States in the affairs of other nations. The Vietnam War also made Americans more cynical about their government. Many believed that the government had misled them.

Answer these questions to check your understanding of the entire section.

1. How did Henry Kissinger try to use diplomacy to end the Vietnam War?

_____

_____

_____

2. How did the Vietnam War change many Americans' feelings about their government?

_____

_____

_____

In the space provided, write an essay detailing the experiences of veterans returning from the Vietnam War to American society.

_____

_____

_____

_____

_____

_____

_____

_____

_____

_____

_____

_____

Students and the Counterculture

Big Idea

As you read pages 682–685 in your textbook, complete the outline using the major headings of the section.

Students and the Counterculture
I. The Rise of the Youth Movement
A. _____
B. _____
C. _____
II. _____
A. _____
B. _____

Notes Read to Learn

The Rise of the Youth Movement *(page 682)*

Identifying the Main Idea

Write an X by the main idea of the passage.

1. _____ The youth protest movement was most active on college campuses.

2. _____ Young people challenged America's political and social systems during the 1960s.

The 1960s saw the rise of a youth movement that challenged American politics and society. Because of the baby boom, the number of young people attending college in the early 1960s increased. College life enabled them to bond and share feelings about society. This led to the youth protest movement, which began and peaked on college campuses across the country.

Young people concerned about the injustices they saw in the nation's political and social systems formed the "New Left." One famous group of activists was the Students for a Democratic Society (SDS). SDS wrote a declaration in 1962 that called for an end to apathy. It focused on protesting the Vietnam War as well as issues such as poverty and racism.

Other activists formed the Free Speech Movement at the University of California at Berkeley in 1964. They were reacting to a restriction of their rights on campus by the University administration. Arrests of 700 protesters led to even larger protests. The administration finally gave in. The Supreme Court upheld the students' rights to freedom of speech and assembly.

Notes | Read to Learn

The Counterculture *(page 684)*

Determining Cause and Effect

List two effects of the counterculture movement on mainstream America.

1. _____

_____

_____

_____

2. _____

_____

_____

_____

Making Generalizations

Write an X by the generalization you can make based on the passage.

____ *Most members of the early counterculture movement were dissatisfied with traditional American values.*

____ *Most members of the early counterculture movement became addicted to drugs.*

Many young people in the 1960s tried to create an alternative lifestyle based on flamboyant clothing, rock music, drug use, and communal living. They became known as the **counterculture** and were commonly called "**hippies.**" The hippies rejected many traditional middle-class values. They wanted to create a utopian society that was free, close to nature, and based on love, empathy, tolerance, and cooperation. In part, their views were a reaction to the 1950s stereotype of the dull, colorless lives of white collar workers. As the counterculture movement grew, however, newcomers did not understand its original ideas. For them, what mattered most were the outward signs such as long hair, shabby jeans, and the use of drugs.

Some hippies left home and lived together with other young people in **communes.** These were group living arrangements in which members shared everything and worked together. Some hippies set up communes in rural areas, while others lived together in parks or in crowded apartments in cities. Thousands flocked to the Haight-Ashbury district in San Francisco, one of the most famous hippie destinations.

After a few years, the counterculture movement began to decline. Some hippie communities in cities became dangerous places in which to live. Drug use lost its appeal as some young people became addicted or died from overdoses. Others grew older and moved on from this lifestyle.

The counterculture did change aspects of American culture. Members often expressed themselves through clothes. By wearing recycled or patched clothing, they showed their rejection of consumerism and social classes. Ethnic clothing also became popular. Beads imitated Native American costumes. Tie-dyed shirts borrowed techniques from India and Africa. Hair became a powerful symbol of protest. Long hair, beards, and mustaches on young men represented defiance against conformity and the military. In time, longer hair on men and more individual clothes for both men and women became part of the mainstream.

Counterculture musicians expressed their views and feelings through folk music and rock and roll. Thousands celebrated the new protest music at rock festivals, such as Woodstock in New York and Altamont in California. Folk singers such as Bob Dylan, Joan Baez, and Pete Seeger became important voices of the movement. Major rock musicians included Jimi Hendrix, Janis Joplin, and The Who. They used electrically amplified instruments that changed the sound of rock music. These changes continue to influence musicians today.

Answer these questions to check your understanding of the entire section.

1. What were the origins of the nation's youth movement?

_____

_____

_____

2. What were the goals of the serious members of the counterculture?

_____

_____

_____

Imagine you're a young person living in the 1960s. Write a brief letter to an older relative explaining your decision to leave home to join a commune. Try to win them over to your way of thinking.

_____

_____

_____

_____

_____

_____

_____

_____

_____

_____

_____

_____

The Feminist Movement

Big Idea

As you read pages 686–691 in your textbook, complete the graphic organizer to compare the ideas of the two organizations that formed when the women's movement split.

Organization	Ideas
1.	2.
3.	4.

Notes | Read to Learn

A Renewed Women's Movement (page 686)

Formulating Questions

Write one question you have based on the passage.

_____

_____

_____

_____

_____

_____

_____

The Feminist movement emerged in the 1960s. **Feminism** is the belief that men and women should be politically, economically, and socially equal. During World War II, many women joined the nation's workforce. After the war, many women returned to their roles as homemakers. However, more women took jobs outside the home during the 1950s. By the mid-1960s, almost half of American women worked outside the home, often in low-paying jobs. Women often faced employment discrimination, and their resentment grew.

In 1961, President Kennedy set up the Presidential Commission on the Status of Women. Its report helped create a network of feminist activists who lobbied Congress for women's laws. Congress passed the Equal Pay Act in 1963. It outlawed paying men more than women for the same job. Congress also added Title VII to the 1964 Civil Rights Act. It outlawed gender discrimination. In 1966 feminists formed the National Organization for Women (NOW). It focused on greater educational opportunities for women and on aiding women in the workplace.

Successes and Failures *(page 689)*

Problems and Solutions

List one problem women faced in the early 1960s and 1970s. List one solution to it.

Problem:

_____

_____

_____

Solution:

_____

_____

_____

Distinguishing Fact from Opinion

Read the third paragraph. Underline one sentence that tells about an opinion on the issue of abortion.

In the late 1960s and early 1970s, the women's movement fought battles on many fronts. It had many successes but also faced strong opposition. In 1972 Congress passed the Equal Rights Amendment (ERA). If 38 states ratified this amendment, protection against gender discrimination would become part of the Constitution. By 1979, 35 states had done so. However, opposition to the ERA had begun to grow. Many people saw it as a threat to traditional values. Some feared it would take away the legal rights of wives and allow women to be drafted into the military. A vocal opponent of the ERA was Phyllis Schlafly. She organized the nationwide Stop-ERA campaign. By the end of 1979, four states had voted to rescind their approval. The ERA failed in 1982, unable to gain ratification by three-fourths of the states.

A major accomplishment of the women's movement was gaining greater equality for women in education. Leaders of the movement pushed lawmakers to pass federal laws banning discrimination in education. In 1972 Congress passed a collection of laws known as the Educational Amendments. One part of these laws was Title IX. It stopped federally funded schools from discriminating against females in nearly all areas, including admissions and sports.

Another important goal for many women was the repeal of laws against abortion. Until 1973, the right to regulate abortion was given to the states. This was in keeping with the original plan of the Constitution. In the mid-1800s, states also had passed laws prohibiting abortion except to save the mother's life. In the late 1960s, some states began adopting more liberal abortion laws. In 1973 the Supreme Court ruled in *Roe* v. *Wade* that state governments could not regulate abortion during the first three months of pregnancy. This was interpreted as being within a woman's constitutional right to privacy. The decision led to the rise of the right-to-life movement. Members of this movement considered abortion an absolute wrong and wanted it to be banned. The heated battle over abortion continues today.

The women's movement has greatly affected society. Many more women have pursued college degrees and careers outside of the home since the 1970s. Many employers now offer ways to help make work life more compatible with family life. Still, there remains a wide income gap between men and women. Most working women still hold lower paying jobs. In professional positions, however, women have made dramatic gains since the 1970s.

Section Wrap-up

Answer these questions to check your understanding of the entire section.

1. What led to the development of a new feminist movement in the 1960s?

_____

_____

_____

2. What was the significance of Title IX?

_____

_____

_____

Write an article for your school newspaper. In it, explain the effects of the women's movement of the 1960s on students in your school today. How would their lives be different if the new women's movement had never occurred?

_____

_____

_____

_____

_____

_____

_____

_____

_____

_____

_____

Latino Americans Organize

Big Idea

As you read pages 692–697 in your textbook, complete the time line by recording major events in the struggle of Latinos for equal civil and political rights.

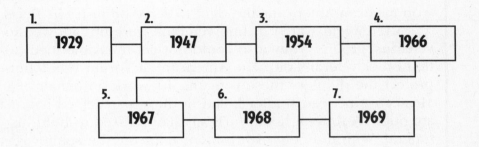

1. 1929 — 2. 1947 — 3. 1954 — 4. 1966
5. 1967 — 6. 1968 — 7. 1969

 **Notes** | **Read to Learn**

Latinos Migrate North *(page 692)*

Drawing Conclusions

Place an X next to two sentences that support this conclusion:

Discrimination had a major impact on the daily lives of Mexican Americans during the 1910s and 1920s.

Many people of Mexican descent lived in Texas, California, Arizona, New Mexico, and Colorado. These areas had once been part of Mexico. In the 1910s and 1920s, some Mexican Americans moved to cities in the Midwest and Northwest. They hoped to find jobs in factories. Most Mexican Americans in the Southwest lived in barrios, partly due to ethnic discrimination. Barrios are poor Hispanic and Latino neighborhoods. Discrimination in employment also kept Mexican Americans from finding well paying jobs. Many worked on farms.

Mexican Americans faced more discrimination during the Great Depression. Federal officials deported many Mexican immigrants in a program known as **"repatriation."** More than 3.7 million Mexicans were also deported while Eisenhower was president. Many of them were legal residents. Some had even been born in this country.

In the 1950s, other Latinos arrived in the country. They included large numbers of Puerto Ricans, and Cubans fleeing a revolution. By the late 1960s, more than 9 million Latinos lived in the United States.

 **Notes** | # Read to Learn

Latinos Organize (page 695)

Making Inferences

What other issues might the American GI Forum have addressed?

1. _____

_____

_____

_____

2. _____

_____

_____

_____

Latinos in the American Southwest were often treated as outsiders whether they were citizens or not. They began to organize to work for equal rights and fair treatment.

In 1929, several Mexican American groups created the League of United Latin American Citizens (LULAC). Its purpose was to fight discrimination against Latino Americans. LULAC helped end segregation in public places in Texas. It also ended the practice of segregating Mexican American children in schools. LULAC openly criticized officials for deporting so many Latinos. It also won Mexican Americans the right to serve on juries in Texas.

After World War II, Latino veterans were not allowed to join veterans' groups. They also could not get the same medical care that other veterans did. The American GI Forum was founded to protect the rights of these veterans. Its work on behalf of a Mexican American soldier killed in the war received national attention. A funeral home in Texas had refused to hold his funeral. With the help of President Johnson, the soldier was buried in Arlington National Cemetery.

Protests and Progress (page 697)

Predicting

Predict two possible outcomes of increased Latino voting.

1. _____

_____

_____

_____

2. _____

_____

_____

_____

Latino Americans still faced prejudice in the 1960s. They did not have the same rights to education, housing, and employment as other Americans. Latinos began campaigns to try to improve their economic status. They also wanted to end discrimination.

In the early 1960s, Latino leaders César Chávez and Dolores Huerta formed two groups to fight for farm workers' rights. The result was a strike against California growers in 1965. The workers demanded union recognition, higher wages, and better benefits. When that effort failed, Chávez organized a national boycott of table grapes. Around 17 million people stopped buying grapes. Profits tumbled. In 1966 Chávez and Huerta merged their two organizations to form the United Farm Workers (UFW). The boycott lasted until 1970. Grape growers agreed to raise wages and improve working conditions.

Latino youths also became involved in civil rights. The Mexican American Youth Organization led school walkouts and demonstrations. Its success led to a new political party, La Raza Unida, in 1969. La Raza worked for Latino causes and encouraged Latinos to vote. Many Mexican Americans began to fight prejudice and celebrate ethnic pride. Leaders began to promote **bilingualism,** or teaching immigrant students in their own language while they learn English.

Answer these questions to check your understanding of the entire section.

1. Why did Latinos in the American Southwest need to organize?

   _____

   _____

   _____

2. How did Latino leaders help farm workers?

   _____

   _____

   _____

In the space provided, write an article about the ways Latinos experienced discrimination in this country. The article is for a Web site devoted to recording the experiences of immigrants.

_____

_____

_____

_____

_____

_____

_____

_____

_____

_____

_____

_____

The Nixon Administration

Big Idea

As you read pages 706–711 in your textbook, complete the graphic organizer by listing Nixon's domestic and foreign policies.

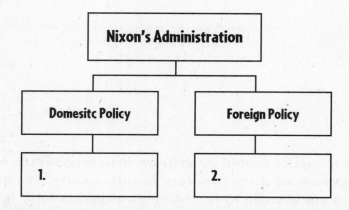

Nixon's Administration

Domesitc Policy

Foreign Policy

1.

2.

Notes | Read to Learn

Appealing to Middle America (page 706)

Making Inferences

Why do you think Nixon targeted antiwar protesters in his attempt to restore law and order?

_____

_____

_____

_____

_____

_____

Richard Nixon was the 1968 Republican presidential candidate. He promised peace in Vietnam, law and order, and a return to conservative values. He won. To restore law and order, Nixon targeted antiwar protesters and opposed Supreme Court rulings that expanded the rights of accused criminals.

Nixon's domestic policy became known as New Federalism. Nixon called for ending several federal programs and giving more control to state and local governments. Congress passed **revenue sharing** bills that gave federal money to state and local agencies. Because states came to depend on federal funds, the federal government could impose conditions on the states. Nixon also tried to increase the power of the executive branch by **impounding,** or refusing to release, funds to Congress for programs he opposed.

Many people argued that the nation's welfare system made it better for poor people to apply for benefits rather than take low-paying jobs. Nixon proposed a plan to give needy families $1,600 per year, which could be supplemented by outside earnings. The plan was defeated in the Senate.

Nixon's Foreign Policy *(page 709)*

Synthesizing Information

Reread the passage. Underline two examples of Nixon's attempts at détente with the Soviet Union and China.

Identifying the Main Idea

Reread the fifth paragraph of the summary. What is the main idea of the paragraph?

Main idea:

_____

_____

_____

_____

_____

_____

_____

_____

President Nixon was more interested in foreign affairs than in domestic issues. He chose Henry Kissinger as his national security adviser. Kissinger was a former Harvard professor. He played a large part in helping Nixon shape his foreign policy.

Both Nixon and Kissinger wanted the United States to gradually withdraw from Vietnam. They wanted to continue to help train the South Vietnamese to defend themselves. This policy was called Vietnamization. Nixon believed that allies of the United States should be responsible for defending themselves. This policy became known as the Nixon Doctrine.

Nixon was an outspoken opponent of communism. However, he and Kissinger believed that the nation's policy against communism was too rigid. They believed the policy worked against the interests of the United States. Nixon and Kissinger wanted to contain communism, but they believed that negotiation was a better way for the United States to achieve its international goals.

Kissinger and Nixon developed an approach called **détente**. Détente was a relaxation of tensions between the United States and its Communist rivals, China and the Soviet Union. Nixon said that the United States had to build a better relationship with the two countries in the interest of world peace.

In February 1972 Nixon made a historic visit to China. He hoped to improve American-Chinese relations. Leaders of both nations agreed to set up more normal relations between their countries. Nixon believed that relaxing tensions with China would encourage the Soviet Union to pursue diplomacy.

Shortly after negotiations with China took place, the Soviets proposed a **summit** to be held between the United States and the Soviet Union in May 1972. A summit is a high-level diplomatic meeting. During the summit, the two countries signed the first Strategic Arms Limitation Treaty, or SALT I. This was a plan to limit nuclear arms. The two nations also agreed to increase trade and to exchange scientific information.

Section Wrap-up

Answer these questions to check your understanding of the entire section.

1. What was New Federalism?

_____

_____

_____

2. What were Nixon's foreign policy achievements?

_____

_____

_____

Persuasive Writing

In the space provided, write a letter to a newspaper editor in support of or against Nixon's policy of détente with the Soviet Union and China.

_____

_____

_____

_____

_____

_____

_____

_____

_____

_____

_____

_____

The Watergate Scandal

Big Idea

As you read pages 712–717 in your textbook, complete the outline using
the major headings of the section.

The Watergate Scandal

I. The Roots of Watergate
  A. _____
  B. _____
II. _____
  A. _____
  B. _____
  C. _____
  D. _____

 **Notes** | **Read to Learn**

The Roots of Watergate (page 712)

Distinguishing Fact from Opinion

Reread the first paragraph. Underline a sentence that describes an opinion.

Nixon became president when the nation was in turmoil. He viewed protesters as people out to bring down his administration. Nixon was expected to win re-election in 1972. His approval rating was high. However, the Vietnam War continued. Nixon and his advisers also remembered that he won in 1968 by a slim margin. As a result, his team tried to gain an advantage by any method. This included spying on the opposition, spreading rumors, and stealing information from the Democratic Party's headquarters. On June 17, 1972, a security guard at the Watergate complex discovered burglars. The police arrested the men.

One of the burglars, James McCord, was a member of the Committee for the Re-election of the President (CRP). Questions came up about the White House's connection to the burglary. To cover up any involvement, members of Nixon's administration destroyed documents and gave false testimony. The White House denied any involvement in the break-in. Most Americans believed the denial. Nixon was re-elected.

The Cover-Up Unravels (page 714)

Detecting Bias

Give two reasons why Nixon may not have wanted the White House tapes released.

1. _____

_____

_____

_____

2. _____

_____

_____

_____

_____

Formulating Questions

Underline the sentences that can help you answer the following question:

How did Watergate affect the way Americans viewed their government?

The Watergate burglars went on trial in 1973. James McCord agreed to testify before the grand jury and the Senate's Select Committee on Presidential Campaign Activities. Many people testified after McCord. John Dean, the counsel to the president, testified that former Attorney General John Mitchell had ordered the Watergate break-in and that Nixon had helped cover it up. The Nixon administration denied the charges. The committee then tried to find out who was telling the truth. White House aide Alexander Butterfield testified that Nixon had ordered a taping system installed in the White House to record conversations. The committee believed that the tapes would tell them what the president knew and when he knew it.

Everyone wanted the tapes. However, President Nixon refused to give them up, claiming **executive privilege.** This is the principle that White House conversations should remain confidential to protect national security. Nixon appointed Archibald Cox as a **special prosecutor,** or a lawyer from outside the government, to investigate the Watergate cases. Cox took Nixon to court to force him to give up the tapes. Nixon had Cox fired.

In the fall 1973 Vice President Spiro Agnew resigned because it was discovered that he had taken bribes. Gerald Ford, the Republican leader of the House of Representatives, became vice president.

President Nixon appointed a new special prosecutor, Leon Jaworski. He also wanted the president's tapes. In July the Supreme Court ruled that the president had to turn over the tapes. Nixon did so. A few days later the House Judiciary Committee voted to impeach Nixon, or officially charge him with misconduct. The committee charged that Nixon had obstructed justice in the Watergate cover-up. The next step was for the House of Representatives to vote whether or not to impeach the president. Investigators found evidence against the president. One of the tapes showed that Nixon had ordered the CIA to stop the FBI's investigation of the break-in. Nixon's impeachment and conviction now seemed certain. As a result, on August 9, 1974, Nixon resigned. Ford became president.

After Watergate, Congress passed laws to limit the power of the executive branch. The Federal Campaign Act Amendments limited campaign contributions. It also set up an independent agency to administer stricter election laws. The Ethics in Government Act required that high government officials provide financial disclosures. Watergate made many Americans distrust their public officials. Other Americans saw Watergate as proof that no one is above the law.

Answer these questions to check your understanding of the entire section.

1. Describe Richard Nixon's character and the attitude of his administration.

   _____

   _____

   _____

2. After Watergate, what steps did Congress take to limit the power of the executive branch?

   _____

   _____

   _____

In the space provided, write an article explaining the Watergate crisis to someone who has never heard of it. In an objective and unemotional way, describe the time, place, people, and events of Watergate.

_____

_____

_____

_____

_____

_____

_____

_____

_____

_____

_____

Ford and Carter

Big Idea

As you read pages 718–723 in your textbook, complete the graphic organizer by listing the causes of economic problems in the 1970s.

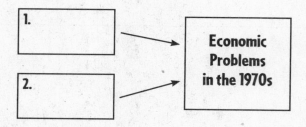

1.

2.

Economic
Problems
in the 1970s

Notes | Read to Learn

The Economic Crisis of the 1970s (page 718)

Drawing Conclusions

Reread the passage and underline two ways Nixon tried to control inflation. Then draw a conclusion about Nixon's ability to help the economy.

_____

_____

_____

_____

_____

_____

Economic problems started in the mid-1960s under President Johnson. During the Vietnam War, he increased government spending. This led to **inflation,** or a rise in the cost of goods. The United States also had become dependent on oil imports. In the early 1970s, the Organization of Petroleum Exporting Countries (OPEC) began using oil as a political weapon. OPEC decided to **embargo,** or stop shipping, oil to countries that supported Israel. OPEC ended the embargo a few months after it began, but oil prices continued to rise. Americans had little money to spend on goods. This caused a recession.

By the 1970s U.S. manufacturers faced international competition. Factories closed and unemployment grew. Nixon faced **stagflation,** a combination of inflation and economic stagnation with high unemployment. He tried to control inflation. The government cut spending and raised taxes. However, people opposed the idea of a tax hike. Nixon then tried to get the Federal Reserve to raise interest rates. He hoped this would reduce consumer spending. This plan failed. Nixon then placed a freeze on all wages and prices. This plan also failed.

Ford and Carter Battle the Economic Crisis (page 720)

Analyzing Information

How would deregulating the oil industry make the nation less dependent on foreign oil?

_____

_____

_____

_____

_____

_____

_____

_____

_____

_____

Inflation remained high after Nixon resigned. Ford began a plan called WIN—Whip Inflation Now. He urged Americans to use less oil and conserve energy. Ford then tried cutting government spending and raising interest rates. Both plans failed.

Ford continued Nixon's foreign policy. In 1975 Ford and the leaders of NATO and the Warsaw Pact signed the Helsinki Accords. They agreed to recognize the borders of Eastern Europe set up at the end of World War II. The Soviets promised to uphold basic human rights.

The 1976 presidential election pitted Ford against Democrat Jimmy Carter, who won. Carter dealt with the economy by increasing government spending and cutting taxes. When inflation rose in 1978, he tried reducing the money supply and raising interest rates. This was unsuccessful. To curb the nation's dependence on foreign oil, he proposed a program to conserve oil and to push for the use of coal and renewable energy sources. He also convinced Congress to create a Department of Energy. Many business leaders wanted Carter to end regulations on the oil industry that made it difficult for oil companies to make a profit, which they could use to invest in new oil wells at home. Carter agreed to deregulate, but he created a profit tax so that oil companies would not overcharge consumers. Because of this tax, however, oil companies did not have money for new wells.

Carter's Foreign Policy (page 722)

Making Generalizations

Reread the passage. Circle two examples that support the generalization that Carter had mixed success in his dealings with the Middle East.

Carter believed the United States should deal honestly with other nations. He agreed to turn over control of the Panama Canal to the Panamanians. He pointed to the Soviet Union as a violator of human rights. When the Soviet Union invaded Afghanistan in 1979, Carter placed an embargo on the Soviet Union and boycotted the Olympic Games in Moscow.

In 1978 Carter helped set up the Camp David Accords, a peace treaty between Israel and Egypt. A few months later, Carter faced conflict in Iran. The United States had supported Iran's ruler, the Shah, but he was unpopular with Iranians. In 1979 Iranian protesters forced the Shah to leave. The new government distrusted the United States. In November 1979 revolutionaries took 52 hostages at the American embassy in Tehran. Carter tried unsuccessfully to negotiate for their release. A rescue mission failed and resulted in the death of eight American servicemen. The hostages were released the day Carter left office.

Answer these questions to check your understanding of the entire section.

1. Why did the United States face economic troubles in the 1970s?

_____

_____

_____

2. How did Carter try to combat the nation's dependence on foreign oil?

_____

_____

_____

In the space provided, write a journal entry as if you were Jimmy Carter on the last day of your presidency. Cite at least one of your successes and one of your failures.

_____

_____

_____

_____

_____

_____

_____

_____

_____

_____

_____

New Approaches to Civil Rights

Big Idea

As you read pages 724–729 in your textbook, complete the time line to record groups in the civil rights movement and their actions.

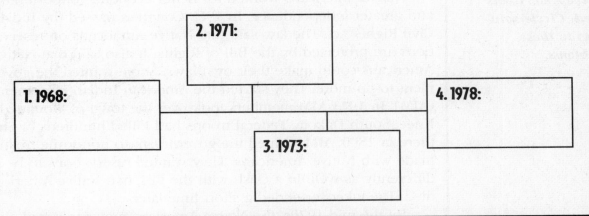

2. 1971:

1. 1968:

4. 1978:

3. 1973:

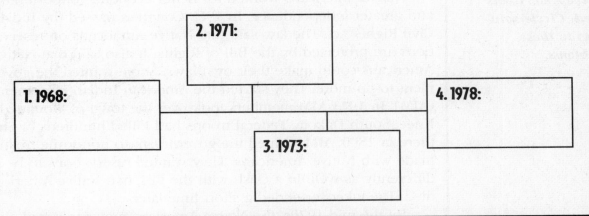

Notes

Read to Learn

African Americans Seek Greater Opportunity (page 724)

Determining Cause and Effect

Write the cause.

Cause:

_____

_____

_____

_____

_____

Effect: Local governments began busing.

In the 1970s, African Americans began to push for equal access to education. Many schools were segregated because children went to neighborhood schools. A segregated neighborhood had segregated schools. Local governments started **busing.** They transported children to schools outside their neighborhoods to gain racial balance. Many whites opposed busing.

Civil rights leaders advocated **affirmative action.** It called for companies, schools, and institutions to recruit African Americans. Supporters hoped this would give African Americans new opportunities. Critics called it "reverse discrimination." In 1974 a white man named Allan Bakke was denied admission to the University of California medical school, which had set aside slots for minorities. Bakke sued. The Supreme Court ruled in favor of Bakke, but said that schools could use racial criteria for admission as long as they did not use quotas.

African Americans found new political leaders. One leader was Jesse Jackson. He started People United to Save Humanity (PUSH). In 1984 and 1988, Jackson ran for president.

 **Notes**

Read to Learn

Native Americans Raise Their Voices *(page 727)*

Problems and Solutions

Reread the passage and underline examples of problems the Native Americans faced. Circle solutions to these problems.

Native Americans faced many problems. Their unemployment rate was 10 times the national rate. Unemployment was especially high on reservations, where more than half of Native Americans lived. Life expectancy for Native Americans was almost seven years below the national average. In the 1960s and 1970s, many Native Americans began trying to improve these conditions.

Native Americans worked for better economic opportunities and greater independence. In 1968 Congress passed the Indian Civil Rights Act. The law said that Native Americans on reservations are protected by the Bill of Rights. It also said that Native Americans could make their own laws. Some wanted the government to do more. They started the American Indian Movement (AIM). In 1973 AIM members took over the town of Wounded Knee, South Dakota. Federal troops had killed hundreds of Sioux there in 1890. AIM wanted the government to honor the treaties it made with Native Americans. They wanted reservations to be run differently as well. In a clash with the FBI, two Native Americans died. The takeover ended a short time later.

By the mid-1970s, the Native American movement had made some progress. In 1975 Congress passed the Indian Self-Determination and Educational Assistance Act. The law increased funds for Native American education. Native Americans also won land and water rights.

The Disability Rights Movement *(page 729)*

Comparing and Contrasting

Compare and contrast two laws discussed in this passage.

1. _____

_____

_____

2. _____

_____

_____

During the 1960s and 1970s, many persons with disabilities looked to the federal government to protect their civil rights. They wanted the same access to buildings and jobs as others had. One victory was the 1968 passage of the Architectural Barriers Act. It required that persons with disabilities be able to access all new buildings built with federal money. The Rehabilitation Act of 1973 went further to protect the rights of persons with disabilities but wasn't enforced at first. In 1977 one group staged protests across the nation to force authorities to enforce the act.

In 1966 Congress started an agency to give money to help educate children with disabilities. A 1975 law made sure that all students with disabilities received a free, appropriate education. One trend in schools at this time was to mainstream students with disabilities. This meant bringing them into the regular classroom. In 1990 Congress enacted the Americans with Disabilities Act. It banned discrimination in many areas.

Answer these questions to check your understanding of the entire section.

1. What was the goal of affirmative action policies?

_____

_____

_____

2. How did Congress help Native Americans meet some of their goals?

_____

_____

_____

Suppose you are a Native American living in the 1970s. Write an article for your local newspaper describing how your struggle for better opportunities is similar to and different from the struggle of African Americans in the same time period.

_____

_____

_____

_____

_____

_____

_____

_____

_____

_____

_____

Environmentalism

Big Idea

As you read pages 730–733 in your textbook, complete the graphic organizer by including some of the actions taken to combat environmental problems in the 1960s and 1970s.

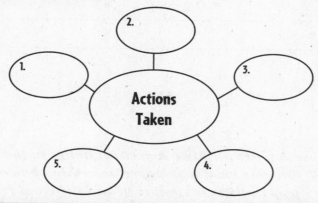

 **Read to Learn**

The Origins of Environmentalism *(page 730)*

Determining Cause and Effect

What effect did Rachel Carson's book Silent Spring *have on many Americans?*

_____

_____

_____

_____

_____

_____

_____

In 1966 a Long Island family discovered that the pesticide DDT was being used to control mosquitoes at a lake near their home. They feared that the pesticide might poison the lake and sued to stop its use. Scientists involved in the case established the Environmental Defense Fund to help stop the use of DDT throughout the country.

Rachel Carson helped start the new environmental movement. In her book *Silent Spring*, Carson wrote of the danger of the increasing use of pesticides. Many Americans took Carson's warnings seriously. They also saw that **smog,** or fog made heavier and darker by smoke and chemical fumes, covered many cities. Acres of forests were being cut down in the Northwest. Pollution and garbage had caused the death of nearly all the fish in Lake Erie. Many people believed it was time to take action.

In April 1970 the nation held the first Earth Day, a day devoted to environmental issues. Soon many people formed local environmental groups, such as the Sierra Club and the Wilderness Society. The Natural Resources Defense Council was made up of scientists, lawyers, and activists working on environmental issues.

The Environmental Movement Blossoms *(page 732)*

Making Generalizations

Reread the passage. Underline examples that support this generalization.

In the 1970s, the U.S. government actively established laws to protect the environment.

Predicting

Make a prediction about the United States's use of nuclear energy after the Three Mile Island accident.

_____

_____

_____

_____

_____

_____

_____

_____

_____

_____

_____

With the environmental movement gaining support, the federal government became involved with environmental issues. In 1970 the Environmental Protection Agency (EPA) was established. Its job was to set and enforce pollution standards. The agency also coordinated antipollution activities with state and local governments. The Clean Air Act set up air emissions standards for factories and automobiles. The Clean Water Act limited the amount of pollutants that could be released into the nation's lakes and rivers. The Endangered Species Act set up measures for saving threatened animal species. These laws eventually helped improve the nation's environment.

In the 1970s, people living in a housing development called Love Canal near Niagara Falls, New York, noticed a high rate of health problems in their community. The problems included nerve damage, blood diseases, and cancer. The people learned that their community was located on top of an old toxic waste dump. The hazardous materials in the dump had leaked into the ground. The people of Love Canal demanded that the government address the problem. After they made the problem known to the entire nation, the state relocated about 200 families. In 1980 President Carter declared Love Canal a federal disaster area. He moved the 600 remaining families to new locations. The Love Canal residents sued the company that created the dumpsite. They settled the case for $20 million. The site was cleaned up and homes above the dumping ground were burned.

During the 1970s, many Americans were concerned about the growth of nuclear power. Those who supported the use of nuclear power claimed it was a cleaner and less expensive alternative to **fossil fuels,** such as coal, oil, or natural gas. Those who opposed the use of nuclear power warned of the risks that nuclear energy posed, particularly if radiation was accidentally released into the air. On March 28, 1979, one of the reactors at the Three Mile Island nuclear facility outside Harrisburg, Pennsylvania, overheated. Two days later, low levels of radiation escaped from the reactor. Nearby residents were evacuated. Others left on their own. Citizens staged protests. The reactor was closed down and the leak was sealed. The Three Mile Island accident left many people doubtful about the safety of nuclear energy. The doubts continue today.

Section Wrap-up

Answer these questions to check your understanding of the entire section.

1. What were the origins of the environmental movement?

_____

_____

_____

2. How did citizens outside of the government combat environmental problems?

_____

_____

_____

Descriptive Writing

In the space provided, write a newspaper article describing what you have done, or would like to do, to help preserve the environment.

_____

_____

_____

_____

_____

_____

_____

_____

_____

_____

_____

_____

The New Conservatism

Big Idea

As you read pages 740–745 in your textbook, complete the outline using the major headings of the section.

The New Conservatism

I. Conservatism and Liberalism

A. _____

B. _____

II. _____

A. _____

B. _____

C. _____

D. _____

E. _____

F. _____

G. _____

Notes | Read to Learn

Liberalism and Conservatism *(page 740)*

Drawing Conclusions

Underline the statement in the passage that supports the following conclusion:

Liberals would not favor federal funding of religious schools.

Liberal politics dominated the United States for much of the 1960s. **Conservative** ideas gained strength during the 1970s. People who call themselves liberals believe that the government should regulate the economy. They also think it should help disadvantaged people. Liberals do not believe the government should try to control social behavior. They also oppose the government's support of religious beliefs in any way. Liberals believe that economic inequality is the cause of most social problems. They argue that high taxes on the wealthy makes society more equal.

Conservatives distrust the power of government. They believe that government control of the economy weakens the economy. Conservatives believe in free enterprise. They argue that when people are able to make their own economic decisions, there is more wealth for everyone. As a result, they oppose high taxes, believing they discourage people from working hard. Conservatives think that most social problems result from issues of morality. They believe that these issues are best solved through commitment to a religious faith.

Notes | Read to Learn

Conservatism Revives *(page 742)*

Determining Cause and Effect

List two causes of the shift to conservatism after World War II.

1. _____

_____

_____

_____

2. _____

_____

_____

_____

Evaluating Information

Why is the information about the population growth in the Sunbelt useful? Put an X next to the answer.

____ **It helps to explain a change in voting patterns in the country.**

____ **It helps to explain the problems in the Northeast.**

Conservative ideas gained support after World War II for two main reasons, both related to communism. One was that some Americans believed liberal economic ideas were leading the country toward communism. Secondly, Americans of deep religious faith embraced the struggle against communism. They saw it as a battle between good and evil. Communism rejected religion and stressed material things. Thus, many Americans turned away from liberalism, which focused on economic welfare. They turned toward conservatism.

In 1955 William Buckley founded a new magazine, the *National Review*. It helped to revive conservative ideas in the United States. In 1964 conservatives in the Republican Party displayed their power. They got Barry Goldwater, a conservative, nominated for president. Lyndon Johnson, however, defeated Goldwater in the election.

During and after World War II, many Americans moved to the South and West to get jobs in factories. This area was known as the Sunbelt. Its population began to view government differently than others did. Americans in the Northeast were battling high unemployment and pollution in cities. They looked to the government for help. People living in the Sunbelt were experiencing economic growth. They feared increased taxes and federal controls would stop growth in the region. For the first time since Reconstruction, many Southerners voted Republican. By 1980 the population of the Sunbelt was greater than the Northeast. This gave conservative regions of the country more electoral votes.

During the 1960s and 1970s, many Americans moved to the suburbs. They hoped to escape problems in the cities. However, rising inflation threatened their middle-class lifestyles. Many resented paying high taxes for social programs while their situations worsened. Antitax programs sprang up all over the country. Many middle-class Americans began to believe the conservatives were right—government had become too big.

Some Americans thought the country had abandoned its traditional values. They became conservatives for this reason. Religious conservatives included people from many faiths. The largest group were evangelical Protestants. Ministers known as **"televangelists"** reached large audiences through television. A new group called the "Moral Majority" backed conservative candidates. By 1980 the movement had formed a conservative bloc of voters.

Conservative voters were concerned about many issues, but they were united by a common belief. They thought American society had lost its way. Their spokesperson, Ronald Reagan, offered hope to a nation in distress.

Section Wrap-up

Answer these questions to check your understanding of the entire section.

1. How do liberal and conservative views differ regarding the government's role in the economy?

_____

_____

_____

2. How did some Americans' views about communism influence them to become conservatives?

_____

_____

_____

Suppose you are working for a conservative politician's campaign in the 1970s. Write a profile of a typical conservative voter that your candidate might want to reach. Include data such as where the voter lives and what his or her values are.

_____

_____

_____

_____

_____

_____

_____

_____

_____

_____

The Reagan Years

Big Idea

As you read pages 746–753 in your textbook, complete the graphic organizer by filling in the major points of the supply-side theory of economics.

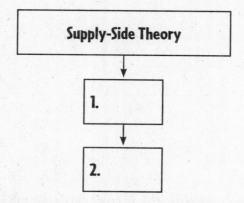

Supply-Side Theory

1.

2.

Notes

Read to Learn

The Road to the White House (page 746)

Identifying the Main Idea

What is the main idea of the passage?

_____

_____

_____

_____

_____

_____

_____

_____

Ronald Reagan started out as an actor. Over 25 years, he made more than 50 movies. In 1947 Reagan became president of the Screen Actors Guild, an actors' union. As the head of the union, he testified about communism in Hollywood before the House Un-American Activities Committee. In 1954 Reagan became the host of a television program called *General Electric Theater*. He was also a motivational speaker for the company. As he traveled across the country speaking to people, he became more politically conservative. He heard stories from Americans about high taxes. They described how government regulations made it impossible for them to get ahead in life.

In 1964 Barry Goldwater asked Reagan to speak on behalf of his presidential campaign. Reagan's speech impressed several wealthy people from California. They convinced Reagan to run for governor of California in 1966, and he won. In 1980 he was the Republican candidate for president. Reagan promised to cut taxes and increase defense spending. He called for a constitutional amendment banning abortion. His positions on issues won him the support of conservatives. Reagan won the election.

 **Notes** | **Read to Learn**

Domestic Policies (page 748)

Copyright © Glencoe/McGraw-Hill, a division of The McGraw-Hill Companies, Inc.

Problems and Solutions

Identify Reagan's solution.

Problem: The country was suffering from economic problems.

Solution:

_____

_____

_____

_____

_____

_____

Reagan's first priority was the nation's economy. One group of economists believed inflation was the biggest problem and raising interest rates was the solution. Another group supported **supply-side economics.** They believed high taxes weakened the economy and cutting taxes would allow businesses to grow and create more jobs. Reagan combined the two ideas. He urged the Federal Reserve to raise interest rates and asked Congress to cut taxes. Critics called this Reaganomics, or "trickle-down economics." Cutting tax rates would increase the government's **budget deficit,** the amount by which spending exceeds income. To control the deficit, Reagan proposed cuts for social programs such as welfare.

Reagan applied his conservative ideas to the judicial branch. He elevated a conservative Supreme Court justice to chief justice. Reagan also nominated Sandra Day O'Connor to be the first woman on the Court.

Reagan believed that government regulations also caused economic problems. He got rid of price controls for oil and gasoline, and energy prices fell. Other deregulations followed. The economy began to recover in 1983. This made Reagan very popular. He was reelected in 1984 in a landslide.

Reagan Oversees a Military Buildup (page 751)

Making Inferences

Write two inferences you can make based on the passage.

1. _____

_____

_____

_____

2. _____

_____

_____

_____

Reagan believed the United States had to show strength in dealing with the Soviet Union. He started a huge military buildup, which created new defense jobs. It pushed the annual budget deficit to $200 billion. Reagan also thought the United States should support guerrilla groups who fought to overthrow Communist or pro-Soviet governments. This policy became known as the Reagan Doctrine. In Nicaragua, the Reagan administration secretly armed guerrilla forces known as "contras." U.S. officials also secretly sold weapons to Iran and sent profits to the contras. This became known as the Iran-Contra affair.

Reagan disagreed with the military strategy known as nuclear deterrence, or **"mutual assured destruction."** It assumed that as long as both the United States and the Soviet Union could destroy each other with nuclear weapons, they would be afraid to use them. In 1983 Reagan proposed the Strategic Defense Initiative, nicknamed "Star Wars." It called for the development of weapons that could destroy incoming missiles. In 1985 Mikhail Gorbachev became the leader of the Soviet Union. The two leaders signed the Intermediate-Range Nuclear Forces (INF) Treaty. The treaty marked the beginning of the end of the Cold War.

Answer these questions to check your understanding of the entire section.

1. What was "Reaganomics"?

_____

_____

_____

2. Why did Reagan propose the Strategic Defense Initiative, or "Star Wars"?

_____

_____

_____

In the space provided, write a short speech Reagan might have given in his campaign for reelection to the presidency.

_____

_____

_____

_____

_____

_____

_____

_____

_____

_____

_____

Life in the 1980s

Big Idea

As you read pages 754–759 in your textbook, complete the graphic organizer by listing kinds of the social issues that Americans faced in the 1980s.

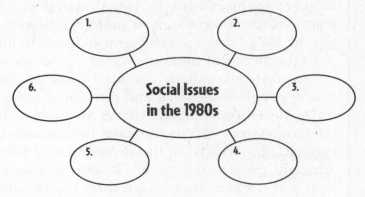

 **Notes**

Read to Learn

A Booming Economy (page 754)

Synthesizing Information

Circle the statement the author would most likely agree with.

Yuppies both fed and benefited from the country's economic growth.

Technological innovation was stagnant during the 1980s.

The American economy had revived by 1983. Many young brokers, speculators, and investors made multimillion-dollar deals buying and selling companies. The value of real estate and stocks soared. Journalists referred to these young moneymakers as **yuppies,** short for "young urban professionals."

By the 1980s, many baby boomers were focused on getting ahead in their jobs and acquiring goods. Due to their numbers, their concerns helped to shape the culture. The strong economic growth, however, mostly benefited middle- and upper-class Americans. Businesses also found a new way to sell goods to customers. It was called **discount retailing.** Discount retailers sell large quantities of goods at very low prices. They created millions of new jobs in the 1980s.

Technology changed news and entertainment. Cable television became available in homes across the country. In 1981 music and technology came together when Music Television (MTV) went on the air. A new style of music, called rap, became popular. Cassette tapes and the Sony Walkman made music portable. VCRs allowed people to watch movies at home.

Notes | Read to Learn

New Social Activism *(page 758)*

Making Generalizations

Write an X by the generalization supported by the passage.

_____ *Activism in the 1980s addressed many different social issues.*

_____ *AIDS awareness was the biggest social issue of the 1980s.*

Predicting

Place an X next to the sentence in the passage that supports the following prediction.

Budget pressures on the federal government will continue to increase.

The United States dealt with many social problems during the 1980s. Drug abuse made many city neighborhoods violent and dangerous. Drug use also spread from cities to small towns and rural areas. Some schools even began searching student lockers and bags for hidden drugs. Alcohol abuse, particularly by teenagers, was another serious problem. Young people were involved in thousands of alcohol-related accidents. In 1980 Mothers Against Drunk Driving (MADD) was founded to find solutions to the problems of underage drinking and drunk driving. In 1984 Congress cut highway funds to any state that did not raise the legal drinking age to 21. All states complied.

In 1981 researchers identified a disease that caused healthy young people to get sick and die. The disease was called AIDS, or "Acquired Immune Deficiency Syndrome." It weakens the immune system. HIV is the virus that causes AIDS. It is spread through body fluids. In the United States, AIDS was first seen among homosexual men, but it soon was seen in heterosexual men and women. Some got it from blood transfusions. Some were drug users who shared needles with infected blood. Others were infected by sexual partners.

AIDS increased awareness of the gay and lesbian community in the United States. Some homosexuals had been involved in defending their civil rights since the 1960s. On June 27, 1969, New York City police raided the Stonewall Inn, a nightclub. The police had often raided the club because of its clients' sexuality. On this night, gays' and lesbians' frustration with the police actions peaked. They rioted. The Stonewall riot was the beginning of the Gay Liberation Movement. The movement tried to increase acceptance of homosexuality.

In the 1980s, many singers and other entertainers took up social causes. In 1984 Irish musician Bob Geldof organized musicians in England to put on benefit concerts to help starving people in Ethiopia. Country singer Willie Nelson organized benefit concerts to help American farmers going through hard times.

Senior citizens became activists in the 1980s. With new medical technology, more Americans were living to an older age. The birthrate had also declined. That meant younger people made up a smaller proportion of the population. More Americans were receiving Social Security payments, which created budget pressures for the government. Older Americans became more active in politics. They opposed cuts in Social Security or Medicare. Because they voted in large numbers, they were an influential group. Their major organization was the American Association of Retired Persons (AARP), which was founded in 1958.

Section Wrap-up

Answer these questions to check your understanding of the entire section.

1. How were yuppies and baby boomers influential economically during the 1980s?

_____

_____

_____

2. In what ways did social activism in the 1980s grow as a response to social issues?

_____

_____

_____

***In the space provided, write a news bulletin designed to increase
awareness of one of the social problems mentioned in this section.
Tell what the problem is, who it affects, how it can be addressed,
and who can help.***

_____

_____

_____

_____

_____

_____

_____

_____

_____

_____

_____

The End of the Cold War

Big Idea

As you read pages 762–767 in your textbook, complete the chart by describing U.S. foreign policy in each of the places listed.

Place	Foreign Policy
Soviet Union	1.
China	2.
Panama	3.
Middle East	4.

Notes

Read to Learn

The Soviet Union Collapses (page 762)

Formulating Questions

Place an X next to the question that is answered in this passage.

____ **What changes did Gorbachev make to try to save the Soviet Union?**

____ **What were Reagan's policies with the Soviet Union?**

President Reagan left office in 1988, but most Americans wanted his domestic policies to continue. George H.W. Bush promised not to impose new taxes. Democrat Michael Dukakis promised to help working-class Americans, minorities, and the poor. Bush won.

President Bush continued Reagan's policies with the Soviets. Their leader Gorbachev instituted **perestroika,** or restructuring, to save the Soviet economy. He allowed some private businesses and profit-making. Gorbachev also encouraged **glasnost,** or openness. It allowed more freedom of speech and religion. Glasnost spread to Eastern Europe. Revolutions overthrew Communist leaders in Poland, Hungary, Romania, Czechoslovakia, and Bulgaria. In November 1989 the gates at the Berlin Wall were opened. Bulldozers leveled the wall, and East and West Germany reunited.

In August 1991 some Communist leaders tried to take over the Soviet government. Russian president Boris Yeltsin defied the attempt. Soon, all fifteen Soviet republics declared their independence. In December 1991 Gorbachev announced the end of the Soviet Union. The Cold War was over.

A New World Order (page 764)

Comparing and Contrasting

Compare the United States's dealings with the two dictators.

Noriega:

_____

_____

_____

_____

Hussein:

_____

_____

_____

_____

After the Cold War, President Bush noted the arrival of a "new world order." His first crisis occurred in China. In May 1989 Chinese students and workers demonstrated for democracy. At protests in Beijing's Tiananmen Square, government forces killed many demonstrators. They arrested thousands more. Some received death sentences. The United States and other countries reduced their contacts with China.

A crisis also developed in Panama. The United States had agreed to hand over control of the Panama Canal, so it wanted to be sure Panama's government was stable and pro-American. The dictator, Manuel Noriega, would not cooperate with the United States. In late 1989, U.S. troops invaded Panama and arrested Noriega. He stood trial on drug charges in the United States. U.S. troops helped the Panamanians hold elections.

In August 1990 Iraq's dictator Saddam Hussein had troops invade Kuwait. President Bush persuaded other nations to join in a coalition to stop Hussein. On January 16, 1991, coalition forces launched Operation Desert Storm. After about six weeks of bombing and a brief ground attack, President Bush declared that Kuwait was liberated. Iraq accepted the coalition's cease-fire terms.

Domestic Challenges (page 767)

Analyzing Information

Place an X by the statement best supported by the passage.

____ President Bush's plan to cut the capital gains tax was misguided.

____ Not all of the nation's problems were President Bush's fault.

In addition to focusing on foreign affairs, President Bush had to address domestic issues. He faced a growing deficit and a recession. The recession was partly caused by an end to the Cold War. The United States began canceling orders for military equipment, resulting in the layoffs of thousands of defense workers. Many companies began **downsizing,** or laying off workers and managers to become more efficient. The federal government also faced a deficit, and had to pay interest on its debt.

Bush tried to improve the economy by suggesting a cut in the **capital gains tax.** This is a tax paid by businesses and investors when they sell stocks or real estate for a profit. He thought it would help businesses. Democrats defeated the idea. Bush finally had to break his campaign promise of "no new taxes." Many voters blamed him for increasing taxes.

Bush was the Republican nominee in the 1992 presidential election. The Democrats nominated Arkansas governor Bill Clinton, who promised to cut taxes and spending. H. Ross Perot ran as an independent candidate. A **grassroots movement,** in which groups of people organize at the local level, placed Perot on the ballot in all 50 states. Clinton won the election.

Answer these questions to check your understanding of the entire section.

1. What events brought an end to the Cold War?

_____

_____

_____

2. What domestic challenges did President George H.W. Bush's administration face?

_____

_____

_____

Write a diary entry describing your experience as a German citizen when the gates to the Berlin Wall were opened in November 1989. Your loved ones have lived on the other side of the wall for many years. What did you see, hear, smell, touch, and feel?

_____

_____

_____

_____

_____

_____

_____

_____

_____

_____

The Technological Revolution

Big Idea

As you read pages 774–777 in your textbook, complete the chart to describe products that revolutionized the computer industry.

	How It Revolutionized Computer Industry
Microprocessors	1.
Apple II	2.
Macintosh	3.
Windows	4.

Notes   Read to Learn

The Computer Changes Society *(page 774)*

Analyzing Information

Complete the sentence.

Microprocessors making computers smaller and faster was important because

_____

_____

_____

_____

_____

_____

The first computer debuted in 1946 and weighed more than 30 tons. In 1959 Robert Noyce made the **integrated circuit**—a whole electronic circuit on a single silicon chip. In 1968 Noyce's company, Intel, put several integrated circuits on a single chip. These **microprocessors** made computers even smaller and faster. Stephan Wozniak and Steven Jobs founded Apple Computer in 1976, and they built the Apple II in 1977. In 1981 International Business Machines (IBM) introduced the "Personal Computer," or PC. Then Apple put out the Macintosh, which used on-screen symbols called icons.

Around the same time, IBM hired Microsoft, cofounded by Bill Gates, to make an operating system for its new PC. The system was called MS-DOS. Microsoft came out with the "Windows" operating system in 1985. Computers became essential in business. By the late 1990s, many workers were able to **telecommute,** or do their jobs from a computer at home.

In the 1970s, the government began to deregulate telecommunications. The Telecommunications Act of 1996 led to the development of new technologies, such as cellular phones. Wireless digital technology also led to new products.

Notes

Read to Learn

The Rise of the Internet *(page 776)*

Determining Cause and Effect

Reread the passage. Circle three sentences describing events that led to the development of the Internet.

Comparing and Contrasting

List one trait of the Internet and one of the World Wide Web.

Internet:

_____

_____

_____

_____

_____

World Wide Web:

_____

_____

_____

_____

_____

The U.S. Defense Department's Advanced Research Project Agency set up a computer networking system called ARPANET in 1969. This system linked computers at government agencies, defense contractors, and several universities. Doing so allowed them to communicate with one another. In 1986 the National Science Foundation built a network called NSFNet, which connected several supercomputer centers across the country. NSFNet was soon linked to ARPANET. As other computer networks were added, the system became known as the Internet. Computers on the Internet are physically connected by phone lines, cable lines, and wireless communications. As personal computers became cheaper, more people began connecting to the Internet.

In 1990 researchers at a physics laboratory in Switzerland developed the World Wide Web. It was a new way for computers on the Internet to present information. It used hypertext, or "links," and could be accessed with a Web browser. It allowed users to post information in the form of Web pages with links that enabled users to jump from Web site to Web site.

The World Wide Web started a "dot-com" economy. This name comes from the practice of using ".com" as part of the address of a business Web site. Many companies made millions of dollars for stock investors. Internet-related stocks helped fuel the economy of the 1990s, but the stocks of these companies fell in 2000. A few Web-based companies became major successes, including the bookseller Amazon.com and the search engine Google. Other companies made money using the World Wide Web by charging fees for advertising on their sites.

The World Wide Web has become more than a source of information. It has become a way to build communities. Many people have public diaries called **blogs,** short for Web logs. Web sites such as MySpace also allow users to share stories, comment on events, and post photos.

Section Wrap-up

Answer these questions to check your understanding of the entire section.

1. How did the computer evolve from a scientific tool to a household appliance?

_____

_____

_____

2. How did the Internet change the way businesses operate?

_____

_____

_____

In the space provided, write a diary entry that describes what a typical day would be like if there were no computers anywhere, including in your school and home.

_____

_____

_____

_____

_____

_____

_____

_____

_____

_____

_____

The Clinton Years

Big Idea

As you read pages 780–787 in your textbook, complete the outline using the major headings of the section.

The Clinton Years

I. Clinton's Agenda
  A. _____
  B. _____
  C. _____
  D. _____
II. _____
  A. _____
  B. _____
  C. _____

III. _____
  A. _____
  B. _____
IV. _____
  A. _____
  B. _____
  C. _____

Notes

Read to Learn

Clinton's Agenda (page 780)

Comparing and Contrasting

List one success and one failure of Clinton's domestic agenda.

Success:

_____

_____

_____

Failure:

_____

_____

_____

President Clinton believed the huge federal deficit was a problem. It forced the government to borrow money and drove up interest rates. Clinton wanted to lower interest rates to help businesses and consumers borrow money and spur economic growth. However, reducing government spending would involve cutting programs such as Social Security and Medicare. Clinton decided to raise taxes instead. This unpopular plan narrowly passed Congress.

Clinton created a task force led by his wife, Hillary Rodham Clinton, to create a plan that guaranteed health care to all Americans. The plan put too much of the burden of payment on employers. Small businesses, the insurance industry, and many members of Congress opposed it. It never came to a vote in Congress.

Clinton succeeded in having the Family Medical Leave Act passed. It gave workers time off for some family issues. Clinton also created the AmeriCorps program. It put students to work improving low-income housing, teaching children, and cleaning up the environment. Clinton also got Congress to pass a gun-control law and a bill that gave states money to build new prisons and hire more police officers.

 **Notes** |

Republicans Gain Control of Congress (page 782)

Problems and Solutions

Write the solution.

Problem: Congress and President Clinton clashed over the federal budget.

Solution:

_____

_____

_____

_____

_____

_____

_____

_____

Despite his successes, Clinton was unpopular by 1994. He had raised taxes and did not fix health care. Republicans in Congress created the Contract with America. It called for lower taxes, welfare reform, and a balanced budget. The Republicans won a majority in both houses in the 1994 elections. The House passed most of the Contract with America, but the Senate defeated parts of the contract, and Clinton vetoed others.

In 1995 Republicans in Congress clashed with Clinton over the new federal budget. Clinton vetoed several Republican budget proposals, claiming that they cut into social programs too much. The Republicans thought that if they stood firm, the president would finally approve the budget. Clinton did not budge, and the government shut down for lack of funds. Clinton regained much of the support he had lost. The Republicans realized they would have to work with the president. They eventually passed a budget as well as the Health Insurance Portability Act and the Welfare Reform Act.

In the 1996 presidential election, Clinton was very popular. The economy was good and crime rates and unemployment were down. Clinton won the election. Republicans kept control of Congress.

Clinton's Second Term (page 784)

Identifying the Main Idea

Why was Clinton impeached?

_____

_____

_____

_____

_____

_____

_____

_____

During Clinton's second term, he and Congress continued to shrink the deficit. In 1997 Clinton presented a balanced budget to Congress. By 1998 the government collected more money than it spent. Clinton focused on the nation's children. He asked Congress to pass a $500 per child tax credit. He also signed the Children's Health Insurance Program, which provided health insurance to children whose parents could not afford it. Clinton also increased aid to students.

By 1998 Clinton became involved in a scandal. He was accused of setting up illegal loans for an Arkansas real estate company while he was governor of Arkansas. Kenneth Starr, a former federal judge, was appointed to investigate. A new scandal emerged involving a personal relationship between Clinton and a White House intern. Some evidence showed that Clinton had committed **perjury**, or lied under oath, about the relationship. Starr determined that Clinton had obstructed justice and committed perjury. The House began impeachment hearings and passed two articles of impeachment in December. The Senate voted that Clinton was not guilty, but Clinton's reputation had suffered.

Clinton Foreign Policy (page 785)

Predicting

Based on the passage, make a prediction about future U.S. relations with the Middle East.

_____

_____

_____

_____

_____

Clinton faced many foreign policy challenges. In 1991 military leaders in Haiti overthrew the elected president. To restore democracy, Clinton urged the United Nations to set a trade embargo on Haiti and ordered an invasion of the country. Former president Jimmy Carter, however, convinced Haiti's rulers to step down. A civil war between Serbs, Croatians, and Bosnians began in Bosnia. Serbs began **ethnic cleansing**, the brutal removal of an ethnic group from an area. The United States convinced NATO to attack the Serbs and force them to negotiate. When another war broke out in Serbian Kosovo, NATO again used force to end it. In 1996 Iraq attacked the Kurds, an ethnic group in Iraq. The United States attacked Iraqi military posts. Clinton repeatedly failed to broker peace in the Middle East between Israel and the Palestinians.

Section Wrap-up

Answer these questions to check your understanding of the entire section.

1. Why was Clinton able to achieve reelection in 1996?

_____

_____

2. How was the nation involved in world affairs during the Clinton presidency?

_____

_____

_____

Persuasive Writing

In the space provided, write a newspaper editorial that presents your opinion on whether a president's personal life should be exposed to the American public.

_____

_____

_____

_____

_____

_____

A New Wave of Immigration

Big Idea

As you read pages 788–791 in your textbook, complete the graphic organizer by listing the effects of the Immigration Act of 1965.

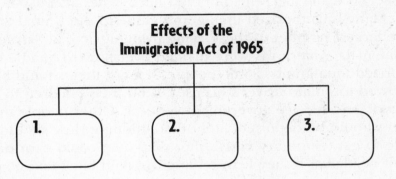

Effects of the Immigration Act of 1965

1.

2.

3.

 **Notes** | **Read to Learn**

Changes in Immigration Law *(page 788)*

Making Inferences

Put an X by the inference supported by the passage.

____ *The 1986 Immigration Reform and Control Act was mostly successful.*

____ *The 1986 Immigration Reform and Control Act did not stop illegal immigration.*

The Immigration Act of 1965 got rid of the national origins quota system and gave preference to people with close relatives who were U.S. citizens. This caused **migration chains.** As immigrants became citizens, they sent for relatives in their home countries. Immigration from non-European countries grew. Some newcomers were **refugees**—people who flee their country due to persecution based on race, religion, or political beliefs.

Congress passed the Immigration Reform and Control Act of 1986 to stop illegal immigration. It punished employers who hired illegal immigrants. It made border controls stronger. The law also gave **amnesty**—or a pardon—to people who had entered the country illegally before January 1, 1982. But illegal immigration was still a problem. In 1996 Congress passed a law that required families sponsoring an immigrant to have an income above the poverty level. It also strengthened border control and toughened laws against smuggling people into the country. The terrorist attacks of September 11, 2001, also led to changes in immigration laws. The USA Patriot Act made border control and customs inspections even stronger.

Recent Immigration (page 790)

Detecting Bias

Why would Latinos protest a bill allowing criminal prosecution of unauthorized aliens?

_____

_____

_____

_____

_____

_____

_____

Formulating Questions

Write two questions you have after reading the passage.

1. _____

_____

_____

_____

2. _____

_____

_____

_____

More immigrants moved to some states than other states. In 1990 California, Texas, New York, Illinois, and Florida had the most immigrants. More than half of immigrants who arrived in the 1990s came from Latin America. Approximately one-fourth came from Asia. Many immigrants were refugees. These included Cubans coming to the United States after the 1959 Cuban Revolution. The Vietnam War also created refugees. Many people from Vietnam, Laos, and Cambodia settled in the United States after 1974.

Many unauthorized immigrants came to the United States. The largest number of these came from Mexico, El Salvador, and Guatemala. Americans were divided over how to handle unauthorized immigrants. Some people thought they should be allowed to obtain driver's licenses, send their children to public school, and receive government services. Other people thought they should be deported. Still others thought they should be able to get temporary visas. After that, they could earn permanent residence if they learned English, paid back taxes, and had no criminal record.

In 2006 President George W. Bush focused on immigration reform. Congress was split on how to solve the problem of undocumented aliens. Most senators wanted tougher enforcement of immigration laws. They also wanted some kind of earned citizenship for undocumented immigrants, or aliens. The House wanted to build a wall along the U.S.-Mexican border. Congress debated a bill that would allow criminal prosecution of unauthorized aliens. Latinos throughout the country protested this.

Other options were suggested. Some wanted to start a guest-worker program and find a way to legalize unauthorized immigrants that were already in the country. Many undocumented immigrants had lived in the United States for years. Many had raised families. Their children born in the United States were citizens and could not be deported. Deporting undocumented aliens would mean separating family members.

Section Wrap-up

Answer these questions to check your understanding of the entire section.

1. How did patterns of immigration into the United States change after 1965?

_____

_____

_____

2. What was one way Congress tried to address the problem of unauthorized immigration?

_____

_____

_____

In the space provided, write a short newspaper article that compares and contrasts two approaches to immigration reform.

_____

_____

_____

_____

_____

_____

_____

_____

_____

_____

_____

_____

An Interdependent World

Big Idea

As you read pages 794–797 in your textbook, complete the graphic organizer to chart the major political and economic problems facing the world at the turn of the century.

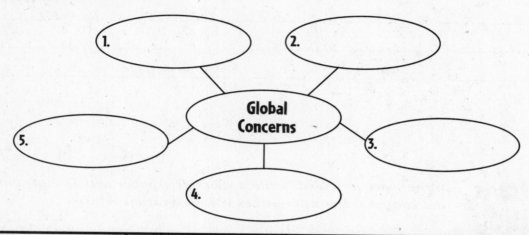

1.

2.

3.

4.

5.

Global Concerns

Notes | Read to Learn

The New Global Economy (page 794)

Identifying the Main Idea

Why were regional trade pacts, such as NAFTA, created?

_____

_____

_____

_____

_____

_____

_____

_____

The idea that the world is becoming more linked and interdependent is called **globalism.** Americans who support international trade believe it helps U.S. businesses sell goods abroad. They also think importing low-cost goods keeps inflation and interest rates low. Others think the global economy causes manufacturing jobs to move to nations where wages are low.

In the 1990s, trade pacts increased international trade. The North American Free Trade Agreement (NAFTA) joined Canada, the United States, and Mexico in a free-trade zone. The European Union (EU) joined many European nations. It promoted economic and political cooperation. The EU set up the **euro,** common money used by member nations. The Asia Pacific Economic Cooperation (APEC) set up a Pacific trade community.

The World Trade Organization (WTO) promoted world trade. It helped form trade agreements and settled trade disputes. China played a big part in world trade. It was a huge market for American goods. In 2000 a U.S. bill gave China permanent normal trade relation status, despite concerns that inexpensive Chinese goods would flood the U.S. market.

Notes | Read to Learn

Global Environmentalism *(page 797)*

Synthesizing Information

What two discoveries increased awareness of environmental issues?

1. _____

_____

_____

_____

2. _____

_____

_____

_____

Drawing Conclusions

Circle two sentences that support the following conclusion:

The Kyoto Protocol was not entirely successful.

With the rise of globalism, people realized that the environment is also a global system. In the 1980s, scientists found out that chemicals called chlorofluorocarbons (CFCs) could break down ozone in Earth's atmosphere. Ozone is a gas that protects life on Earth from the ultraviolet rays of the sun. CFCs were used in air conditioners and refrigerators. In the late 1980s, scientists found a large hole in the ozone layer above Antarctica. Many people wanted to stop the manufacture of CFCs. In 1987, the United States and other nations agreed to phase out the manufacture of CFCs and other chemicals that might be weakening the ozone layer.

In the early 1990s, scientists found evidence of **global warming.** This is an increase in average world temperatures over time. This rise in temperature could lead to more droughts and other types of extreme weather. Many experts believe that carbon dioxide emissions from factories and power plants cause global warming. Others disagree. The global warming issue is controversial because the cost of controlling emissions would fall on industries. These costs would eventually be passed on to consumers. Developing nations that are beginning to industrialize would be hurt the most.

In 1997 thirty-eight nations and the EU signed the Kyoto Protocol. The nations promised to reduce emissions, though very few nations put this into effect. President Clinton did not present the Kyoto Protocol to the Senate because most senators opposed it. In 2001 President George W. Bush withdrew the United States from the treaty. He believed that it had flaws.

Section Wrap-up

Answer these questions to check your understanding of the entire section.

1. Why do many people support international trade?

_____

_____

_____

2. What environmental issues have become important internationally?

_____

_____

_____

In the space provided, write a short magazine article about the ban on CFCs. Present facts in an objective way, explaining why CFCs were banned and who banned them.

_____

_____

_____

_____

_____

_____

_____

_____

_____

_____

_____

_____

America Enters a New Century

Big Idea

As you read pages 804–807 in your textbook, complete the graphic organizer by charting the key post-election events culminating in George W. Bush's victory.

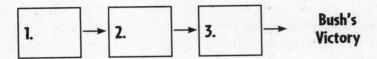

| 1. | → | 2. | → | 3. | → | Bush's Victory |

 **Notes**　　　　**Read to Learn**

The Election of 2000 *(page 804)*

Drawing Conclusions

Underline statements in the passage that support this conclusion:

The U.S. president is not always elected by a majority of voters.

In the 2000 presidential election, Democrat Al Gore ran against Republican George W. Bush. The election was one of the closest in American history. Gore won the popular vote. However, to win the presidency, candidates have to win a majority of the electoral votes. Both candidates needed Florida's 25 electoral votes to win. The vote in Florida was so close that state law required a recount using vote-counting machines. Thousands of ballots were tossed out, however, because the machines could not read the voting cards. Gore asked for a hand recount in strongly Democratic counties. A battle began over how to count a ballot when the **chad** was still attached. A chad is the piece of cardboard punched out on a voting card.

Florida law required election results be certified by a certain date. The Florida Supreme Court postponed the date, but some counties still could not meet the new deadline. On December 12, 2000, the United States Supreme Court ruled that there was not enough time for a manual recount before the electoral votes had to be cast. The ruling left Bush the winner.

Bush Becomes President (page 807)

Making Inferences

Write an X by the inference that can be made based on the last paragraph.

_____ *The United States was unprepared for an attack on its own soil.*

_____ *The United States was entering a war against terrorism.*

Predicting

Make a prediction about educational reforms based on the No Child Left Behind Act.

_____

_____

_____

_____

_____

_____

_____

_____

Bush became the forty-third president of the United States. His first priority was to cut taxes to boost the economy. During the campaign, the economy began to slow. The stock market dropped sharply, some companies went out of business, and unemployment began to rise. Congress passed a $1.35 trillion tax cut. Bush's plan introduced tax cuts over a 10-year period. However, it also gave taxpayers an immediate rebate. By mid-2001 Americans began receiving tax rebate checks. Bush hoped the rebates would put about $40 billion into the economy to prevent a recession.

Bush proposed two major educational reforms. He wanted public schools to give annual standardized tests. He also wanted to allow parents to use federal funds for private schools if their public schools were performing poorly. Congress did not support the idea of using federal funds for private schools. It did support the idea of states being required to annually test students' reading and math skills. This law became known as the No Child Left Behind Act.

Bush also focused on a Medicare reform bill that added prescription drug benefits to Medicare. The bill was controversial. Some opponents argued it would be too costly. Others believed the law did not go far enough. However, the bill was passed in November 2003.

Congress reacted to a number of corporate scandals. The most famous took place at a large energy trading company called Enron. The company's leaders cost investors and employees billions of dollars. The company eventually went bankrupt. Congress passed a new law—the Sarbanes-Oxley Act—that tightened accounting rules and created tougher penalties for dishonest executives.

Bush called for new military programs that would meet the needs of the post-Cold War era. He favored a program known as **strategic defense.** Its purpose was to develop missiles and other devices that can shoot down nuclear missiles. Bush argued that missile defense was needed because hostile nations were developing long-range missiles.

Debate about the nation's military programs continued during the summer of 2001. Then, a disastrous event changed everything. On September 11, 2001, terrorists attacked the World Trade Center in New York City and the Pentagon in Washington, D.C. A new war had begun.

Answer these questions to check your understanding of the entire section.

1. What unusual circumstances surrounded the outcome of the 2000 presidential election?

_____

_____

_____

2. Summarize the proposals Bush made early in his presidency.

_____

_____

_____

In the space provided, write a letter to your representative in Congress voicing your support or opposition to a proposed constitutional amendment abolishing the electoral vote in presidential elections.

_____

_____

_____

_____

_____

_____

_____

_____

_____

_____

_____

_____

The War on Terrorism Begins

Big Idea

As you read pages 808–813 in your textbook, complete the graphic organizer to show causes of terrorism.

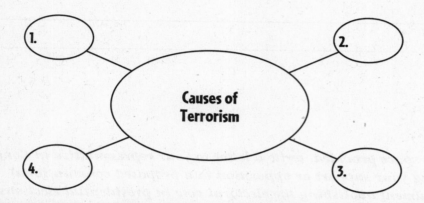

1.

2.

Causes of Terrorism

4.

3.

 **Notes**　　　**Read to Learn**

September 11, 2001 *(page 808)*

Formulating Questions

Write one question you have after reading the passage.

_____

_____

_____

_____

_____

_____

_____

_____

_____

_____

On September 11, 2001, hijackers crashed two passenger jets into the World Trade Center in New York City. Hijackers crashed a third jet into the Pentagon in Washington, D.C. A fourth plane crashed in Pennsylvania. Thousands of people were killed. President Bush declared a national emergency and put the armed forces on high alert. Intelligence sources and the FBI determined that the attacks were the work of Osama bin Laden and his group, al-Qaeda. The attacks were acts of **terrorism**—the use of violence by nongovernmental groups against civilians to achieve a political goal.

Fundamentalist militants wanted to topple pro-Western governments in the Middle East. They used terrorism to reach their goals. In the 1970s, several Middle Eastern nations began providing terrorist groups with money and weapons to fight the United States and Israel. When a government secretly supports terrorism, it is called **state-sponsored terrorism.** Bin Laden operated al-Qaeda from Afghanistan. Al-Qaeda attacked American embassies in Tanzania and Kenya and the USS *Cole* in 2000.

Notes | Read to Learn

A New War Begins (page 811)

Copyright © Glencoe/McGraw-Hill, a division of The McGraw-Hill Companies, Inc.

Identifying the Main Idea

Read the second paragraph. Write the main idea. Write one detail that supports it.

Main Idea:

_____

_____

_____

Detail:

_____

_____

_____

Distinguishing Fact from Opinion

Read the statements. Write F next to one that tells a fact. Write O next to the one that includes an opinion.

____ *He warned that the war on terrorism would be a war like none other.*

____ *Several occurrences of anthrax were found, but no suspects were arrested.*

President Bush demanded the Taliban—the rulers in Afghanistan—turn over bin Laden and his followers and close all terrorist camps. He declared that the war on terrorism would not end until every terrorist group had been defeated. Secretary of State Colin Powell worked to form an international coalition to support the United States. Secretary of Defense Donald Rumsfeld began sending American troops, aircraft, and warships to the Middle East. He warned that the war on terrorism would be a war like none other. President Bush announced that the United States would not tolerate countries that helped or harbored terrorists. He also warned Americans that the war would not end quickly.

There are several ways to fight terrorism. One major way is to cut off terrorists' funds. President Bush issued an order to hold the money of several individuals and organizations suspected of terrorism. He also asked other nations to help. Within weeks, about 80 other nations also held the money of individuals and groups suspected of terrorism. The president also created a new federal agency—the Office of Homeland Security. Its purpose is to coordinate the dozens of federal agencies and departments working to prevent terrorism.

Bush asked Congress to create a law to help agencies track down terrorist suspects. This took time. Congress had to make sure the law would protect Americans' Fourth Amendment rights. In October 2001 Bush signed a new antiterrorist law—the USA Patriot Act. The law permitted secret searches and allowed authorities to use a single nationwide search warrant. The law also made it easier to wiretap suspects.

The Office of Homeland Security struggled to manage all of the federal agencies now fighting terrorism. President Bush asked Congress to combine all of the agencies into the Department of Homeland Security.

Terrorists posed a new threat in October 2001 when they began to use the mail to spread anthrax. **Anthrax** is a type of bacteria that can become lethal if left untreated. The United States, Russia, and Iraq are among the nations that have used anthrax to create biological weapons. Several occurrences of anthrax were found, but no suspects were arrested.

On October 7, 2001, the United States began bombing al-Qaeda's camps and the Taliban's forces in Afghanistan. President Bush explained to the nation that Islam and the Afghan people were not the enemy. He said that the United States would send food, medicine, and other supplies to Afghan refugees. The attack on the Taliban was only the beginning of the war on terrorism.

Section Wrap-up

Answer these questions to check your understanding of the entire section.

1. What was the political goal of Middle East terrorists and how did they try to achieve it?

_____

_____

_____

2. How did the United States respond to the terrorist attacks on the World Trade Center and the Pentagon?

_____

_____

_____

Write a front-page newspaper article covering the events of September 11, 2001. Tell the who, what, where, when, and how of the events. Include at least one quote from an "eyewitness," as well as a headline.

_____

_____

_____

_____

_____

_____

_____

_____

_____

_____

The Invasion of Iraq

Big Idea

As you read pages 814–819 in your textbook, complete the graphic organizer to show the different groups in Iraq.

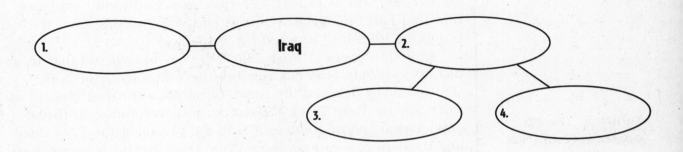

1. Iraq 2.

3. 4.

Notes

Read to Learn

The War on Terror Continues *(page 814)*

Analyzing Information

Write an X by the statement the author would most likely agree with.

____ *Afghanistan is on a slow road to recovery.*

____ *Democracy probably will not work in Afghanistan.*

In October 2001 the United States launched a war in Afghanistan. The goal was to bring down the Taliban regime and capture Osama bin Laden. The United States also began sending military aid to the Northern Alliance, an Afghan group who had fought the Taliban for many years. In December 2001 the Taliban government collapsed. Afghanistan slowly began to recover from decades of war, but its people are still poor. In 2004 Afghanistan elected a president in its first national democratic election, but the country still suffers from violence.

American intelligence agencies believe Osama bin Laden entered Pakistan to hide out in its mountains. Pakistan has not officially allowed American troops to enter its country to search for bin Laden. Some news reports, however, suggest that U.S. Special Forces may be operating in the region. Pakistan also has been searching for al-Qaeda and Taliban forces. However, Osama bin Laden has not been captured. The United States continues its worldwide hunt for al-Qaeda members. In 2003 Pakistan and the United States captured Khalid Shaikh Mohammed. He was suspected of planning the September 11 attacks.

 **Notes** | **Read to Learn**

Iraq and Weapons of Mass Destruction *(page 816)*

Problems and Solutions

Write the problem.

Problem:

_____

_____

_____

_____

_____

_____

Solution: The UN passed a resolution threatening serious consequences.

President Bush worried terrorists might acquire **weapons of mass destruction** (WMD), which can kill many people at once. Nuclear, chemical, and biological weapons are examples of weapons of mass destruction. The United States' old policy of deterrence would not work against state-sponsored terrorism.

In 2002 President Bush warned the nation about an "axis of evil" made up of Iraq, Iran, and North Korea. He considered Iraq an immediate threat because it had used chemical weapons before. After the Gulf War, UN inspectors had found evidence that Iraq had biological weapons and was working on a nuclear bomb. In 1998 Iraq ordered the inspectors to leave.

In 2002 President Bush asked the UN to demand that Iraq's dictator, Saddam Hussein, readmit the weapons inspectors. While the UN debated the issue, Congress approved the use of force against Iraq. The UN passed a new resolution. It threatened serious consequences if Iraq did not meet the UN's deadline to readmit weapons inspectors. The UN also required Iraq to declare its weapons of mass destruction.

Confronting Iraq *(page 818)*

Formulating Questions

Place an X by the question answered in the passage.

_____ *How and why would the new Iraqi government train its own forces?*

_____ *In what ways did fighting continue after Bush declared an end to major combat in Iraq?*

Iraq agreed to readmit weapons inspectors, but denied it had weapons of mass destruction. The Bush administration thought Iraq was lying and pushed for a war resolution in the UN Security Council. Although France and Russia refused to back it, the United States and Britain prepared for war. World opinion divided between those supporting the United States and those against the attack. Antiwar protests erupted around the world.

On March 20, 2003, U.S.-led coalition forces attacked Iraq and quickly seized control. On May 1, President Bush declared that major combat was over, but bombings, sniper attacks, and battles continued to plague American troops. Some groups carrying out attacks were linked to al-Qaeda. Other attacks were by ethnic or religious militias. Between 2003 and 2006, insurgents killed more than 3,000 American soldiers.

The United States was now trying to prevent a civil war while setting up a new Iraqi government. As the fighting dragged on, and no weapons of mass destruction were found, domestic support for the war began to decline. The Bush administration believed the best solution would be to set up a democratic Iraqi government that could train its own forces. Iraqi's first free elections were held in 2005. Voters also approved a new constitution.

Section Wrap-up

Answer these questions to check your understanding of the entire section.

1. Why did the United States launch a war in Afghanistan?

_____

_____

_____

2. Who were the supporters of the Iraq War? Who opposed it?

_____

_____

_____

In the space provided, write a brief speech explaining the important connection between weapons of mass destruction and Middle East terrorism today. Assume you will give the speech at your school's Current Events Club's monthly meeting.

_____

_____

_____

_____

_____

_____

_____

_____

_____

_____

_____

_____

A Time of Challenges

Big Idea

As you read pages 820–827 in your textbook, complete the outline using major headings from the section.

A Time of Challenges

I.   The Election of 2004

II. Security vs. Liberty

   A. _____

   B. _____

   C. _____

III. _____

   A. _____

   B. _____

   C. _____

   D. _____

   E. _____

 **Notes** | **Read to Learn**

The Election of 2004 (page 820)

Evaluating Information

Why is it important to know about high voter turnout in the 2004 election?

_____

_____

_____

_____

_____

_____

_____

As the war in Iraq dragged on, President Bush's popularity with Americans sank. Osama bin Laden had not been captured. Inspectors had not found weapons of mass destruction in Iraq. Many Americans were also upset by the abuse of Iraqi prisoners by American guards at Abu Ghraib prison. The war on terror and the war in Iraq took over the 2004 presidential election. Republicans renominated President Bush. Democrats nominated John Kerry, a Vietnam veteran who turned against the war after his return. His opponents used his actions from the 1970s against him in the 2004 election.

The candidates offered the country two distinct choices. President Bush promised to continue cutting taxes while building a strong national defense. Kerry pledged to focus on domestic issues such as health care and Social Security. He also promised to continue the war on terror. The candidates took opposite stands on most social issues. Nearly 61% of eligible voters went to the polls on Election Day—the highest turnout since 1968. The election was decided in Ohio in a very close vote. Despite the war in Iraq, voters felt it was safer to reelect President Bush.

Read to Learn

Security vs. Liberty *(page 822)*

Comparing and Contrasting

List two ways the courts and the Bush administration differed in their views about civil liberties.

1. _____

_____

_____

2. _____

_____

_____

_____

The war on terror increased tension in the United States between national security and civil liberties. Questions arose about what to do with al-Qaeda prisoners. President Bush decided to hold them indefinitely at Guantanamo Bay, an American military base in Cuba. Some people questioned this. They argued that the prisoners should have the same rights as Americans in custody. The administration claimed the prisoners were illegal enemy combatants—not suspects charged with crimes.

The Supreme Court disagreed. It ruled that prisoners should have their cases heard in court. The Bush administration reacted by creating military tribunals to hear the cases. The Court ruled against that too. The president then asked Congress to pass laws setting up tribunals that were acceptable to the Court. In doing this, Congress gave the prisoners some rights. However, it allowed tribunals to hold prisoners indefinitely without trial.

The National Security Agency expanded its use of wiretapping to include calls made to suspected terrorists overseas. Civil rights groups feared this violated Americans' free speech and privacy rights. A federal judge declared the practice unconstitutional.

A Stormy Second Term *(page 823)*

Making Generalizations

Circle the generalization that can be made based on the passage.

Many Americans lost confidence in Bush during his second term.

Bush was responsible for the Gulf Coast damage in 2005.

President Bush began his second term with an effort to reform the Social Security system. The plan failed, but Congress did enact Bush's prescription drug program.

President Bush was able to move the Supreme Court in a more conservative direction. He nominated federal judge John G. Roberts, Jr., to replace Chief Justice William Rehnquist, who had died. He also nominated Samuel Alito, Jr., to replace Justice Sandra Day O'Connor, who had retired.

On August 29, 2005, Hurricane Katrina smashed into the Gulf Coast. Thousands of people became homeless. At least 1,200 died. Floodwaters breached the levees around low-lying areas in New Orleans, Louisiana. Many people were forced onto roofs to await rescue. Thousands more found shelter in the convention center and Superdome, where there was little food or water. The government was unprepared in its response.

Confidence in the Bush administration dropped sharply. Congress suffered several scandals. Federal spending rose rapidly, partly because of earmarks added to spending bills. **Earmarks** specify money for particular projects, such as building a bridge, usually in a Congressperson's own state. In the 2006 election, Democrats gained control of the House and the Senate.

Section Wrap-up   *Answer these questions to check your understanding of the entire section.*

1. How did the war on terror also threaten Americans' civil liberties?

_____

_____

_____

2. What challenges did President Bush face in his second term?

_____

_____

_____

In the space provided, write three entries in your diary for August 29–31, 2005. You live in New Orleans. Describe the events of those days as you experience them. Be as vivid as possible in your description, using all five senses in your writing.

_____

_____

_____

_____

_____

_____

_____

_____

_____

_____

_____